STRANGE
CURES

Published by
ROTHCO PRESS
8033 West Sunset Blvd.
Suite 1022
Los Angeles, CA 90046

Cover Design: Bobby Microwave
Technical Assistance: Jeff Marc Grossman
Back Cover Design: Will Staehle, Unusualco

Author's note: some names of the persons in this memoir have been purposely changed with respect to friends and family.

Rothco Press is a division of Over Easy Media Inc.

ISBN: 978-1-945436-23-9

STRANGE CURES

A MEMOIR

Rob Zabrecky

ROTHCO PRESS • LOS ANGELES, CALIFORNIA

For Little Foot

Life is the living you do. Death is the living you don't do.
—Joseph Pintauro

CONTENTS

PART THREE

EPILOGUE

PART ONE

BULLET FOR THE BOY

"YOUR UNCLE ED will be staying with us for a little while," says my good mother before scooting me out the door for school. It's just after Christmas and Uncle Ed's set up camp in our den, again. His trusty sleeping bag is unrolled right next to the fake Christmas tree that's still over in the corner, and his suitcase is sandwiched between the bar and the barstools. Based on his other visits, he'll be here anywhere from a few days to a few weeks. Uncle Ed is my idol. When I grow up I'm going to be like him.

If you don't know Uncle Ed, you might think he's one of those cool undercover cops, like the kind you see on TV. If you do know him, you'd be certain of it. His job title, as he often likes to remind me, is a high-ranking Secret Service Agent for the Federal Bureau of Investigation. It's like having Columbo, Baretta, or Barnaby Jones as our very own special houseguest. It's never boring when he comes to stay.

It's Saturday afternoon and just the two of us are home. I'm bored flipping through the latest issue of *MAD magazine* in my room and join him in the den. He's in one of his typical work outfits; a solid-colored turtleneck shirt under a cardigan that looks good on his skinny body, and pants that are the right kind of tight. Under the cardigan I notice his black leather gun holster, which holds a loaded .38-caliber revolver he needs to wear for his job. At his feet is his black-leather briefcase. It has important paperwork for his job and he guards it with his life. It is never opened in front of my older brother Gordy, my older sister Laura, or me. I get the feeling that whatever's in there can change the universe. His clothes and briefcase give him an air of importance — much more so than the weathered toolbox, lunch pail, worn-out work clothes, and dusty boots my father wears to the construction site five days a week.

He's sipping vodka and orange juice from a coffee mug and studying the 1979 *Farmer's Almanac*. Behind his thick, black-framed glasses, his eyes twitch and blink at weird times.

"What are you reading about?"

"The weather forecast. The *real* weather forecast. Not this bullshit they're telling you about on TV. It'll be a nice one tomorrow. Says it right here," he says, pointing a lit cigarette at the open page. The fact that he uses the *Farmer's Almanac* to find out the weather puts him in this super-smart category above everyone I know, who just learn about it from TV. Plus, he curses all the time like it's no big deal. I join him on the couch and pretend to understand the weather chart he's studying. I could care less about any of it. I just want him to think I'm smart like him.

"Oh yeah, I see. Uh huh."

Uncle Ed smells funny. The combined scent of his burning Marlboro, this grooming liquid he wears called Vitalis, and the Smirnoff vodka oozing from his pores smells flammable, but it overpowers my father's nasty cigar smoke that otherwise dominates our house.

"I need to make a run to the store. Anyone calls, I'm not here."

He tosses the *Farmer's Almanac* on my lap, stabs out his cig in one of the three ashtrays going in our den, and leaves. That's when I notice the chrome latches on his briefcase are accidentally left open.

I get a sudden urge to check out the cool stuff that must be in there, and even though I know I shouldn't, I know this is my only chance. I go outside and see him disappearing into the alley at the end of California Street and Burbank Boulevard. The coast is clear, I say to myself, carefully placing the briefcase on my lap like a set mousetrap. My heart's racing all over the place. I'm about to find out what all the fuss of being an FBI agent is all about. Suspect profiles. Typewritten letters and documents. Fingerprint kits. A magnifying glass. A disguise or two. Maybe some of that yellow tape you see at crime scenes that says, "CRIME SCENE, DO NOT CROSS," and things like that. I'm certain it's all inside, and I don't have much time.

With both hands, I open the top to reveal its contents: two shiny gold "Special Forces" badges, a nearly empty bottle of Smirnoff vodka, two plastic prescription pill bottles, and the latest issues of *Playboy* and *Hustler* magazines. That's it. I close the top and add up what I've just seen. I open it again and take another look. Something's a little messed up. Where's all the stuff I'd imagined? The porno mags must be part of a bigger picture; maybe they're pieces of evidence for some sting operation and contain fingerprints of criminals or something.

The babe with her legs sprawled out on the *Hustler* cover reminds me of something that happened after he dropped me off one Saturday last year at Golfland, the Valley's gift to miniature golf and arcade games, to meet some friends. Through the chain-link fence from inside, I saw him in the parking lot and figured I'd see him drive off, but instead, saw him walk right up to these two teenage foxes with long feathered hair, tube tops, and colored Dittos. He held his badge up near their faces and started talking to them. At first they looked tense but then started giggling and had big smiles. Before I knew it the three of them squeezed into the back seat of his freshly waxed metallic-blue Chevy Chevelle and shut the doors. All I could think was Uncle Ed had the best job of any adult I ever knew.

While blowing my paper route money on putting colored golf balls through mini windmills and hobbit houses with my buds, I wondered what those girls must've done, and why Uncle Ed was investigating them. As we moved from hole to hole, I couldn't stop wondering what was happening inside his car, which put me in last place at each hole. I could've cared less about losing at piddly golf, because I was daydreaming of day I'd be a secret agent man like my real life hero, Uncle Ed.

I froze at the sight of him when later, he exited the backseat. He popped out, looked around, tucked his turtle neck back into his tight pants, tightened his belt, and zipped up his fly. Then came those two babes adjusting their tube-tops with their hair all messed up. Both of them had this freaked out look in their eyes.

As my favorite song — the theme song from *Grease* — pumped through a loudspeaker, I bopped along thinking how damn exciting his job was. While other adults work as teachers, bankers, or building makers, Uncle Ed's questioning *and* messing around with sex-dream worthy chicks at Golfland to solve mysterious sex crimes.

But then another memory came back from when he was staying with us last Halloween. I was making a peanut butter and marshmallow crème sandwich before suiting up in my home-made Dracula costume and heading out for a round of trick-or-treating. Uncle Ed was pouring vodka and orange juice in his mug, and telling me about his latest mission.

"Next week I'll pick up the documents at a secret location, and head over to Lockheed Airport. From there, I'll take a private jet to Hawaii. I stay there undercover there until..."

"Don't believe him ma' boy, he's lying to you. Uncle Ed's full of shit. He doesn't work for the F.B.I., and he's not getting on any private jet!" My father abruptly barks in from the den. Even though my father says things I don't always understand — like how eating bacon makes him walk sideways — he's making his point loud and clear.

"You don't know shit, Ralph. Shut up and stay out of my fucking business," Uncle Ed quickly responds.

"What business? You don't have any business, you Godamned drunken mooch!"

Trying to process what my father said, I take a huge bite of my gooey afterschool treat, and look over at our little brown mutt, Rusty, who's crashed out on the linoleum floor. Although it sounds like my father's being a real dickhead to Uncle Ed, he must just be protecting his little brother's important government job. Uncle Ed must be telling me too much, and my father's just keeping him in check. His job *is* top-secret and all.

"It's nobody's business but mine anyway. Ah, fuck all. Fuck you, Ralph," Uncle Ed says to him, and disappears out the front door with his coffee mug.

I close the briefcase and replace it where I'd found it, trying to forget what I'd just seen and thought about.

The front door opens and closes. I hear a paper bag crunch to death and a bottle set on the kitchen counter. He's back.

"Anyone call for me, Robbie?"

"No," I say, in my best trying-not-to-sound-guilty voice.

As I hear the familiar sound of vodka and orange juice pouring into his mug, I can also barely hear him whisper, "Good. Fuck all anyway."

A week later Uncle Ed, his briefcase, and his sleeping bag are gone.

***

Six months later, on my twelfth birthday, I wake to a quiet house on a Sunday morning. I roll out of bed, pull on a T-shirt and corduroy shorts, and head into the kitchen to make a bowl of cereal. The house is void of the usual TV noise or family chatter, which means I'm home alone. I somehow feel a little older, because for a change, nobody's making a big deal it's my birthday. My days of party hats, noisemakers, and Pin the Tail on the Donkey must be things of the past, thank God.

Then I notice a note placed on a long, unwrapped, cardboard box on the kitchen counter: "Happy Birthday Robbie, Uncle Ed." Since the box isn't wrapped and nobody's home, I peek at its contents. Inside is the ultimate gift, unlike any I've received before — a .22-caliber Winchester sporting rifle. It's more than a gift I think, it's a damn rite of passage from my idol, who also happens to be my uncle, who also happens to do secret work for the government. Yes!

More importantly, it means I've got something I've been wishing for a long time: Uncle Ed's approval. Surely he's got to see some of me in him, otherwise there's no way he'd present me with such an awesome gift. I marvel at it for the longest time before lifting it from the box, examining it from barrel to butt. I hope he asks me to join him on his next shooting mission so I can try this thing out.

After pounding a quick bowl of Lucky Charms and zipping through my paper route, I carry the rifle into my room and spend the next couple hours becoming accustomed to its weight and balance. With one eye cocked, I zoom in on the scope and take fake shots at the KISS, Cheap Trick, and Van Halen posters that wallpaper my room. I lean my shiny new rifle in the corner and can't wait to fire it.

Like I'd hoped, Uncle Ed invited me to join him next Saturday for a shooting outing. They're kind of like school field trips, only with just two people; Uncle Ed and me. My good mother says they're important because they help me get out of the house, where I've been staying inside too much lately, listening to the same 10 records over and over. She says I'm not cut out for the Boy Scouts like Gordy, and too old to tag along with Laura and her friends, who don't want me around anyway. These short getaways are the funnest weekend thing I'm allowed to do, but lately, there are times when we're out there that get intense.

We leave before sunrise and drive away from Burbank for what seems like an eternity, to a place where there are no people — just desert bushes, streams, and hills — called Canyon Country, and find a place off the main sand road to set up our day camp. Before the first shot is fired, Uncle Ed opens his briefcase and pours himself a mug full of vodka and orange juice. He sips at it while carefully laying out his collection of weapons and ammunition on a clean beach towel, on the hood of his spotless Chevelle. Uncle Ed likes everything clean — it's one of the things I like about him. Like a doctor, he examines the tools of his trade: a single-barrel shotgun, a .45 Magnum pistol, two

.38-caliber pistols, and a few hunting knives. With great authority, he holds them up to the sun that's just starting to come up, and polishes them until they look brand new.

Over the past 10 or so trips, he's shown me how to load, aim, and fire all kinds of guns. I've been pretty good at following his instructions and have become a decent shooter. It's been about a year since the first time I pulled the trigger of his single-barrel shotgun, annihilating one of his empty vodka bottles on rock from about 20 feet away. I remember the massive jolt that nearly forced me on my ass after shooting it, and the high-pitched ringing in both my ears I thought would never stop. Part of the thrill after the ringing finally faded was that I didn't feel like a kid anymore.

This time, after we're set up with all the regular stuff, he reaches for my birthday rifle.

"They call this the rifleman's rifle. It's got bolt action," he says, effortlessly loading a bullet into the chamber.

"Load, aim, and fire the fucker. That's all there is to it. It'll shoot by itself," he laughs, firing a fresh bullet into the morning sky. It soared off with the same echoing boom as a sole firework.

He puts the rifle in my hands along with a handful of warm bullets, stands back, crosses his wiry arms, and waits for me to follow suit. I carefully insert a bullet into the chamber, awkwardly cock it into position like he showed me, point it up in the sky, and shoot. The kick to my shoulder and the sound of a shell landing on the nearby sand prove it fired. It's not even half as intense as the blast from his shotgun.

"You got it," he says, slapping me on the back.

Throughout the morning, we annihilate a collection of empty vodka bottles he'd brought along and destroy a few found, empty, beer cans. I take a break from my rifle and wander up the ankle-deep stream to explore the bushy desert terrain on my own. He's over by his car, refilling his coffee cup in the morning sun, carrying on a quiet conversation with himself.

If today is anything like our last few shooting outings, sooner or later he's going to start a little game that could be called Bullet Dodge. Here's how it goes; when I'm least expecting it, he starts firing bullets around my feet. It's up to me to do three things very fast; hear where they're coming from, see where they land, and swiftly move to dodge the next one. The game scares me out of my mind, but I know I'm helping him and the government.

This game — though now that I think of it, it's not *exactly* a game because no one wins or gets a prize or anything — is part of the deal under Uncle Ed's supervision. I idolize him and all, but this part sucks. I forget how much I hate it until he starts shooting around my feet and my heart starts racing like mad.

Up the narrow and shallow stream, I see him kneeling in a nearby bush. There he is, in his bright-colored turtleneck and cardigan, pointing my rifle at me. He fires. Game on.

Bang! Bang! Bang!

The echoing shots land near my feet, sending me into high-alert mode. For some reason I forget to move this time. I'm just standing there, worrying about where the next shot will land.

"What'd I tell you? When someone points a loaded gun at you, fucking *move*, kid!" he hollers from the bush. My eyes follow his voice, and I can see him crouched down in the bushes. He's still pointing the rifle in my direction. I move upstream as fast as my body allows me to, away from the sound of his voice.

My heartbeat slows down a little. I look back at the bush. He's not there anymore. Except for the stream running below my feet, everything is quiet and back to normal. I'm safe again. This round of Bullet Dodge must be over, I think.

Bang! Another gunshot echoes off the mountains as a sharp pull tugs my arm back, and a little trickle of smoke rises through a fresh hole in the left arm of my black T-shirt. I pull up the sleeve, and discover a deep hole about the size of a dime. The sound of the gunfire fades. I realize I've been shot. I don't want to believe it, but when I do, I nearly collapse right there in the stream. Every muscle is clenched. My breath is held, my body and mind paralyzed.

I'm trying to ignore this numbing pain that's spreading through my arm, but I can't. If I can keep my body parts in place, everything'll be back to normal when I let my breath out. Holding in as much air as my lungs can hold, I look around the desert forest in every direction. The bushes, trees, and rolling hills that surround me look just like they did before. Everthing's still and quiet until a lizard zips across the nearby sand and a screaming crow flies overhead, squawking in a language that sounds like German. The only sound and motion come from the running stream I'm standing ankle deep in. I'm still here, but wish I wasn't. I just want to go home and start the day over.

The air I'm holding in finally bursts and my body feels like it does after I hyperventilate; my vision softens and I'm so dizzy I feel like I do right before I fall asleep. As I draw in my next breath, smelling the hot sand and baking desert bushes, I pull up my sleeve again and focus on the hole in my arm in near disbelief, fearing the worst. Nobody told me about the rules of getting shot. As far as I know, you get shot, you die.

Then everything makes sense: Uncle Ed hunted me.

He appears out of nowhere like a stage magician. His face is inches before mine and he's holding half a bottle of vodka. With one hand gripping the bottle, he grabs my shoulders and shakes me back to reality. The sun's nearly overhead, illuminating his slicked-back, raven-black hair, and beady blue eyes, which are twitching and blinking like crazy behind his glasses. He pulls up my sleeve and splashes vodka inside the wound. It burns like a mean bee sting. I want to scream, but the pain is overpowered by a new kind of fear I've never had before — a fear of dying. Even though I'll be dead soon, I can't show Uncle Ed my pain. I need to keep cool till the end.

"Keep this between us," he says, looking in my eyes, and then somewhere into my soul.

"You tell anyone about this and I'll kill you. Anybody asks about the hole, you tell 'em a tree branch cut you. Hear me?"

I'm far too freaked out to answer.

"Hear me?" He's not *asking* a question; he's *giving* orders. Firm ones. I still can't answer, though. He shakes me again, this time a little harder. "Robbie! You hear me?"

I'm still in trying-to-understand-what-just-happened mode, but Uncle Ed needs to know I agree to our deal before releasing me from his grip.

"Yeah. Yes. Okay."

In one swift motion, he releases me, sparks a cigarette, and heads back to his Chevelle that's parked in the sand about 100 feet away, glowing in the sunlight. Uncle Ed remains cool no matter what. The stream water is still running beneath me at a steady pace. My mind is stuck and I can't think about what to do next. All I know is Uncle Ed just shot me, the sun is starting to burn the top of my head, and my mouth is becoming more dry with each breath. The last thing I had to drink was a cherry Slurpee from 7-Eleven last night and I could really go for some Gatorade.

The burning sun forces me to step out of the steam. I sit down in a nearby patch of shade, trying not to bail and find help. Then it occurs to me; there's no place to run, and nobody who'd hear my voice if I did scream. The last car I remember seeing was a couple of hours ago, just after before we pulled off the main road — and that's miles from here. I'm freaking *trapped* here.

***

I've heard somewhere that before you die, your life flashes before you. Knowing this, my eyes catch a few puffy white clouds passing by. Focusing on them helps me from completely losing it. While taking a panic break while gazing into them, I feel myself drifting into one of my deep fogs. Since I can remember, when something goes terribly I detach from the real world and drift off to some a faraway place. Out of nowhere I enter this unknown dreamlike dimension. Sometimes I'm on a merry-go-round at some carnival I've never been to before. I'm strapped into one of those carousel horses, being slowly lifted up and down and round and round. Other times I'm peacefully drifting alone through outer space, while random memories flash by like shooting stars. Then right in the middle of it, just when it's like I'm really there, something always brings me back, and I snap out of it like a dream.

As I'm wondering if I'm transitioning from this world into the next, I feel myself getting sucked into what must be my last great deep fog. As I start drifting off, a bunch of random life events in quick succession play for the last time: looking into the eyes of my dog, Rusty, and wondering why he got to be a dog and I got to be a boy, that curious feeling I'd get from listening to records over and over again, the confusion and excitement of my first boner, the anticipation and excitement of Christmas Eve when I still believed in Santa, walking barefoot on the train tracks until the bottoms of my feet turned black and calloused, smiling for school pictures, and lying in the backyard after school and letting my mind drift into familiar shapes in clouds, kind of like what I'm doing right now. That's what I remember about my twelve years on Earth.

CAW! The sound of another gawking bird brings me back to my uncertain reality. Crap. I'm back.

I shade my eyes to see the clouds roll over the hills, and start wondering what happens to people after they die. The idea that I'm going to heaven or hell today is just too much to take in. As of now, I can't think of anything I've done that's too *good* or too *bad* that'll send me to either place.

I keep pulling up my shirt to examine my wound, and every time I do, it's still there. The pain is fading, or I'm getting used to it — I'm not sure about too much right now — my thoughts are still racing all over the place and I can barely keep up with them. I start thinking that I might be dreaming, so I do the dream-pinch test that's worked before. Yep, I'm awake and alive, and all this is real. I can't stand it anymore, and my body just gets up and starts moving towards Uncle Ed, over by his damn Chevelle. His back is turned to the sun and he's polishing a pistol. I look up at him, push my bangs away from my face, and squint my eyes up in his direction. I finally get the courage to say what I'm thinking.

"We heading back soon?"

"Fuck all, we got all the time in the world, there's no rush to get home," he replies in a confident slur. There's no point in asking if we can leave now. Uncle Ed's *not* the kind of person you can haggle with. No way. Never.

I shuffle back over to my little patch of shade, which is getting smaller and smaller with the rising sun. An eyeshot away is Uncle Ed, popping a pill and washing it down with the vodka/orange juice combo. He's keeping his cool, puffing his cig, fussing over his weapon collection, and having another quiet conversation with himself. It's like nothing happened.

I'm dying, but also dying to know what he's thinking. He shot me, and he knows it, but it doesn't seem to be any big deal to him at all. He must see people get shot all the time. Maybe if I end up living I'll get older and experience more stuff like this and look back on it like its no big deal.

Then it occurs to me there's *no way* he could've shot at me all those times not thinking he might hit me — even though I haven't done anything to deserve it. All those empowering feelings I felt from idolizing Uncle Ed are melting away. What a real creep he is for shooting me, and then telling me not to tell anyone.

After the longest chunk of time goes by, and I've swatted a hundred bugs that've been crawling on me, he starts putting the weapons in the trunk and neatly rolls up the towel over the hood on which they were placed.

"Okay, let's get the fuck out of here," he says.

Not a word is said on the car ride home. "Heart of Glass" by Blondie plays over the engine as I sit there, wondering if I'm going to drop dead at any moment. With each freeway exit we pass under, I'm still here, keeping it together and kind of proud of myself for not completely freaking out. We exit Interstate 5 at Hollywood Way, head down to Burbank Boulevard, and make the trusty right turn onto California Street. I've never been so happy to see my house. He parks and throws me one his blinky, firm looks.

"Remember what we talked about?"

"Yes," I say, exiting as fast as I can, trying not to slam the door or appear paranoid, and start heading for the front door.

"Wait. Don't forget this." He opens the trunk and puts my rifle in my hands. With the coolness of one of those TV detectives, he grabs my arm and studies the hole one last time.

"You'll be fine, kid."

I give him a phony look, one that tries to say I'm not scared of dying or anything, but he doesn't notice. Instead he fires up another cig, hops back into his Chevelle, and zooms off. I make a beeline for my bedroom with the biggest secret I've ever had in my life.

***

I place the rifle back in the corner of my room and lay on my bed to look at the wound for the millionth time. The pain is reduced to a mild sting and I'm practically sure I'm not going to die. I'm staring at my rock posters, and convincing myself I'll be okay. Each time I tell myself I'm fine I know it's a lie, and the incident replays: hearing the shot, feeling the tug, and seeing smoke come from the hole in my arm. Out of nowhere, my body pulls itself off my bed and I run out of the house. I gotta tell someone what happened — it's the only way I can believe it's *real*.

Sprinting up to the other end of California Street to my friend Jason's house, my body is throbbing head to toe and I've never been so happy that I'm not dead. I stop on his lawn, catch my breath, and bang three times on his window like I always do. He bangs back once, which is our code that means he's opening the front door to let me in. When he does, the look in his eyes detects I have news. I can hardly wait to tell him. We bolt to his room and shut the door. I take a big breath and whisper with excitement, "Look." I pull up my shirt sleeve and show him my wound.

"What happened?"

"You aren't going to believe this. Uncle Ed shot me."

His eyes grow big and his mouth slowly opens. In some messed-up way, I felt like I'm making it up. "You can't tell *anyone*. I swore to him I wouldn't tell anybody. It's a secret." But by the time the word "secret" leaves my mouth, it's too late. His eyes bug out and, at the top of his voice, yells, "Mommy!"

His mother's footsteps head toward us.

"Shhh. Dammit, Jason. I'm not supposed to tell anyone!"

The door opens and there's Jason's mom in the doorway, looking at us like we've done something wrong. Without skipping a beat, Jason blabs, "Uncle Ed shot Robbie, right in his arm. Look!"

She looks at me for some sort of confirmation, but my mind goes blank and I just stare at her. She grabs my arm, nearly breaking the skin around the bullet wound with her manicured claws.

"Oh my God! What? Have you told your parents?" she shrieks, before releasing her grip and rushing for the phone. Jason and I just stand there looking at each other. Whatever's happening next is out of my control. Somehow, all this sudden commotion is almost as bad as getting shot.

A minute later our beat-up, bronze, Chevy Impala pulls up in front of Jason's with my good mother behind the wheel. She's sitting very still as Jason's mother is leaning in, explaining what happened. We dash off to St. Joseph's Hospital emergency room, where I was born twelve years earlier. On the short ride, my good mother is quiet. She gets quiet when something's really wrong. Maybe she's in a fog of her own. I'm still dazed while we check into the emergency room, where she quietly tells the staff I *might* have been shot. X-rays are taken, and reveal a bullet next to my left humerus.

"There's a bullet lodged in your arm. Right here," the doctor says matter-of-factly, pointing to the bullet. It's right there next to my arm bone, clear as day.

"If it landed a few inches over, you wouldn't be here right now. You're very fortunate. You need to tell us what happened." This man's a real doctor, and this is serious stuff. Uncle Ed's "Tell 'em you got poked with a branch" story isn't going to fly.

"Well. I got shot. But it was an accident. He didn't mean to *actually* shoot me." That's what I said anyway.

"By who? Who shot you?"

The game is over. All I can do is tell the truth.

"My Uncle. Uncle Ed. Am I going to be okay?"

"Yes, you'll be fine," the doctor reassures me. I get this great sigh of relief as I catch my good mother's bright blue eyes sweeping back and forth across the freshly polished hospital floor, still in disbelief.

"He shot you? Did he really do that?" she asks in a whisper, like it's still some secret, in her sweetest Scottish accent.

"Yes. But he didn't mean to," I whisper back. She hugs me and kisses the top of my head. "Everything's going to be okay, little fellow."

I'm still stunned. I want to believe her, but I'm not sure of anything anymore.

"The bullet is embedded in the muscle tissue near the bone. It needs to stay in for at least a month so the surrounding muscle can heal properly. We can remove it after that," the doctor tells us, while wrapping some white gauze around my arm, and then placing it in a temporary sling and sending us on our way. After getting the news that I'll be fine, I start feeling almost normal again.

The sun's going down as we pull up to our house. There's Uncle Ed and my father on our half-dead front lawn. The vodka and pills have really affected Uncle Ed by now. I've never seen him like this. He can barely stand. He's waving his boney arms all over the place and slurring his words. From what I gather, he's making a crap attempt to get off the hook for the whole thing. My father's shirtless and barefoot, in his blue jean cut-offs, looking at him like he's gonna deck him at any second.

As they move like two dogs getting ready to fight, something clicks. Maybe my father doesn't have an exciting job, drive a neato car, wear nice clothes, carry a briefcase, or have a secret job for the government like Uncle Ed does, but he's not afraid of anything, especially setting things straight. He works long, hard hours every week, and year after year, makes sure my good mother and us kids have what we need. Uncle Ed's world is shady. Strange. Uncertain. I can't make sense what's real in his world and what isn't. All I know is it's a dangerous place. My father's been the hero the whole time, not Uncle Ed. I just didn't realize it till now.

My good mother puts her arm around me and ushers me past them. The commotion is so intense they don't even notice us.

"You go to your room, little fellow," she says quietly, under their voices. I look down, shuffle past them, and head for the front door. I go inside and watch the three of them attempt to sort things out through our smoke-stained living room curtains. I can't hear what they're saying, but can guess she's telling them what the doctor told us at the hospital.

I'm trying to read their lips, and the part of the Styx song, "Renegade," where he says, *"The jig is up, the news is out, they've finally found me,"* starts playing repeatedly in my head, and I wish it would stop.

While they're trying to settle this mess, I've calmed down about 80 percent and tune out to see it's a normal early summer evening for the rest of the kids, passing up and down our street in shorts and tank tops on glittered Schwinn bikes, bomber skateboards, and roller skates. I can hardly wait for this day to be over.

I pop a few aspirin and head down the creaky hallway to my room. I put the rifle in the back of my closet, lay back on my bed, and stare into my rock posters. The next week, Uncle Ed left on a top-secret "special government mission" and we don't see him for a long time.

***

Uncle Ed's drinking problem worsened. He eventually lost all his material things — except his sleeping bag. He showed up at our door on a couple more occasions, each time sicker and less composed than before.

As a last-ditch effort, my father put him on a train to Flagstaff, Arizona, to stay with my aunt Agnes, where he eventually died at forty-three from cirrhosis of the liver. His passing was a relief for the world, which had no use for him. Seeing him disintegrate like that, I knew I was assured a life lesson. I regularly swore to myself that I'd never ever drink alcohol or let any kind of drugs have control over my life.

ROBBIE'S STRANGE CURE

IT'S THE FIRST DAY of first grade and my teacher, Mrs. Evans, who looks like a lot like a man, but in a woman's, plaid pantsuit, is assigning us new students to tables with different colored table cloths inside the brightly lit classroom at Bret Harte Elementary. With my last name beginning with the letter Z, I'm the last kid assigned to a table. She looks down at a piece of paper and reads:

"And last is Robbie Zabrecky. Robbie, you will join the others at the red table." I march to the red table. The table is void of any vacant seats, so I drag over an empty chair and squeeze in with the others. The other kids are all looking at me like I've done something wrong. Some of them start whispering and giggling. Mrs. Evans looks up from behind her tortoise-shell glasses and beehive hairdo.

"No, Robbie, I said the red table." I shoot back the biggest smile I can give and nod. I know there's some mistake, but she is teacher after all, and I'm not about to correct her — especially not on the first day of school. She blurts in a clear voice that's on the verge of sounding aggravated.

"The red table, Robbie. The *red* table." The room goes quiet.

"Yes, I know. The red table. I'm right here." I reply in a low self-conscious tone, moving my eyes around the table, noticing the other kids, who are still staring at me. I keep my face in the smile position, but inside I'm not smiling. I don't like any of this.

"Robbie, you are sitting at the *green* table. Now please do as I said and sit with the others at the *red* table!"

Now every single kid in this classroom is looking at me. Then I notice an empty seat at another table on the other side of the room.

"That's the red table," she exclaims, pointing to the table with the open seat. To avoid further embarrassment, I shuffle over and look down at the tablecloth, which looks red, wondering what's wrong. For the next hour, I feel stupid and confused — like I've done something wrong that I can't fix —struggling to keep focused. Then out of nowhere my good mother is looking inside my classroom trying to spot me. My eyes swell at the sight of her. Mrs. Evans acknowledges her and walks over to the table and says:

"Robbie, your mother is here. You may go with her now." As we shuffle off to our Chevy Impala, she tells me we are going to have a little visit with our family eye doctor, Dr. Kurtowsky. I don't know what this means, but it can't be good.

Inside Kurtowsky's wood paneled office, I sit in a big chair in a small, dark room and look at a series of designs and color charts. He asks me about the names of colors I'm seeing and after what feels like an endless number of tests asks me to take a seat.

"You don't see colors the way most people see colors. You have a something called color vision deficiency. You're color-blind." he says.

Even though he says it like it's no big deal, the news is frightening. My little-kid mind tells me I'll need some type of gimmicked spectacles to wear for the rest of my life or attend a special needs school for colorblind kids and end up working in a factory with other colorblind people.

"One in every 12 men is colorblind, you'll be fine," he says, trying to relieve me. That night I go to sleep thinking about how embarrassed and stupid I felt about sitting at the wrong table when I thought it was the right one, and about how this discovery of seeing things different will be an ongoing reminder that I'm not like the other kids.

***

My early childhood can be summed up by the message that was printed on a pair of canvas sneakers from J.C. Penney. The ones I had were all worn out, and I needed a new pair before heading back to school to start second grade that fall. While browsing the kid's shoe section with my good mother, a certain pair caught my eye. They were different from the other boring ones on display. On these, in big letters, the word RUN was printed over the rubber toe of one, while the other read HOME. The sides had cartoony baseball players all over them.

"Can I get these?"

"Why certainly, little fellow. But they'll have to last you all year," says my good mother, with a look that says, "Get them and you're stuck with them." The Zabreckys were a "one pair of shoes per school year" kind of family.

"I like'em a lot." I say, trying them on real quick before dropping them in the shopping cart. Although they aren't too comfortable, they have a message I can understand and follow: "RUN HOME."

And that's what I do. Each day, after the last bell rings at my school, Bret Harte Elementary, I tear down the sunny sidewalks, under the trees and past the houses, as fast as my feet can go, until I get to my front door on California Street. After catching my breath, I set my hand-me-down metal Peanuts lunch pail onto the kitchen counter and retire to the backyard. I stretch out on a patch of grass and lie flat on my back, next to my faithful brown mutt, Rusty, to watch the shapes of clouds turn from one object to another. It's my favorite part of the day.

The next week, I'm sitting in class one morning, minding my own business and waiting for school to start when I feel someone nudging me with their foot. It's freckle-faced Andrew Anderson, and he's looking at me the way everyone looked at Jonathan Fisk in preschool the day he pooped his brand-new Toughskins. "Hey Robbie, do you know you're wearing your shoes on the wrong feet?" Andrew thinks he knows everything. I'm not sure what he means until I look down and see he's got the *same* shoes as me, with the baseball players and everything, but for some reason he's wearing his on the opposite feet.

"They're supposed to say 'home run,' not 'run home,' Robbie. Doy!" he says in his stupid snitchy voice. I take a second to think. Baseball players on the shoes. Home run. I don't know what a home run is exactly, but start wondering if it has something to do with baseball, and the message I think the shoes mean is wrong.

By the time I'm sure Andrew is right, and that I'm wearing my shoes on the wrong feet, he and some other kids are pointing at them and having a good laugh. I freeze and my mouth goes dry. Then I do what I always do when I get embarrassed: Go into a trance-like silence and don't say anything. It's not because I don't want to, I just can't. I watch the second hand go around the clock, looking down and comparing the message on my shoes versus the message on Andrew's shoes until the school day is over. With zero desire to run, I walk home, feeling more like Charlie Brown than I ever did.

The next morning, I try on the shoes so they say "HOME RUN." They fit much better, but I like my message way better than "HOME RUN." Andrew and the other kids are going to laugh at me again no matter how I wear them, so I drag out the boring pair with worn-out bottoms and a small hole breaking through one of the toes I had from first grade, and never put on the "RUN HOME" shoes again. My shoe trouble no longer makes me want to run home—instead it makes me want to stay home. And as time's moving on, I'm learning about more things that are setting me apart from the other kids at school.

I'm a little kid of average weight and size, gifted with a general knowledge that I have a pretty good start in life. My school report cards remind me that I'm shy and terrible at sports. Even though I feel "different," I think I'm in the perfect time and place to be alive. Whenever I'm called on for anything, my shyness gets the best of me and I feel out of step with the other kids. Every time the recess bell rings and it's time to participate in group sports I get queasy and lopsided. The sound of the bell brings on these awful flutters of pain and embarrassment because I know I'll have to face the playground facts: I'm not naturally athletic like most of the other boys. These feelings are confirmed by mean comments from other kids, which end in even more embarrassment.

"Robbie, you run funny. Why do you run so funny?" "You kick the ball like a weirdo." "How come you swing the bat like a girl?" ask other kids whenever my turn comes around. I spend most of my class time wondering why these normal physical activities feel unnatural but am too embarrassed to ask someone who's good at them to teach me how to do them right.

***

That winter I'm sitting in our kitchen stuck in the middle of dreaded math homework, and notice a wart on my left thumb. It's a nice distraction from trying to get division right, and feels good to rub my other fingers over it. By Christmas there is a whole bunch all over my hands. Like 15. I keep them to myself until my good mother catches sight of them one night while we're playing backgammon.

"Those warts can't be good, son. You must have caught an awful infection. Let's have the doctor take a look at them."

A few days later we're in the waiting room of our family doctor, Dr. Mathias. I've only been here to see him for check-ups, so coming in with all these warts is a big deal. My good mother and I are brought into a small room that's bright and clean and smells like floor cleaner. He comes in studying a clipboard and wearing the long, white coat he always wears. I wonder if he wears it at home? Every time I see him I think he could be Mr. Rogers' twin brother. He looks and acts *just* like him. Today I wonder if he is him. I can tell right away it's not a dilly dally kind of visit where he's going to take my temperature and check my heartbeat and stuff.

"What's bothering you today, Robbie?" he asks in his Mr. Rogers' voice.

He's so calm and nice that for a second I forget why I'm here. I start telling him my problems. "Um, I sleepwalk. I can't tell green from brown and blue from purple. I get shy around people I don't know. Other kids tell me I run like a girl on the playground."

I look down at my hands, see a bunch of warts and remember why we're here.

"Oh, Plus, I have all these warts." I tell him, putting my hands out.

He chuckles and says, "Let's focus on the warts today."

He takes one of my hands and examines the warts with a magnifying glass. He's poking away at them with a metal stick, and I can hardly wait to see what's going to happen next. My good mother is sitting in a chair in the corner with her purse in her lap, working on her checkbook. She looks up and reassures me like she always does.

"Don't worry little fellow, you'll be just fine." Dr. Mathias takes a syringe and injects a numbing liquid into my hands.

"This shouldn't hurt too much," he whispers, producing a medical tool that looks just like a soldering iron. He takes one of my sweaty hands and with the tip of his device, starts zapping off mounds of warty skin. Each time he touches wart zapper to wart, it makes this terrible noise and smoke shoots up. The smell of the burning warts makes me want to puke, but I don't want to embarrass my good mother, so I do all I can to hide the pain and hold back the tears that are building up. After he zaps the last wart away, he wraps my fingers in thick white gauze and sends us on our way.

As my fingers start healing, more warts start popping up. In no time, I've got around two dozen warts all over my hands. Back to Dr. Mathias, and he burns the warts off like he did before. It's just as awful as the first time, but worse because this time there are so many more. "If they keep coming back, I'd like you to try a wart-removing liquid called Compound W. You can pick it up from Thrifty Drugstore on the way home." I like the way he calls it Thrifty Drugstore. It makes it sound like some important place. We just call it Thriftys.

When more warts start popping up, I bust out the Compound W. It's this awful stuff that that's clear and gooey, and smells like burning Styrofoam and paint thinner. I hate the way it smells and feels, but it burns off the warts, and the skin around them. Every night I lie in bed after gooping it on, and I fuss and yank at my warts until they bleed. After I can't stand the pain, I carefully wrap them in toilet paper and wish them away while falling asleep as *Love, American Style* and *The Dating Game* play from the den TV. It's comforting hearing all the laughs from the TV, especially knowing they aren't making fun of my warty hands.

After a few weeks, I see the Compound W isn't working and my warts aren't going away. Instead, more are sprouting up until I can count about fifty that are spread all over my hands. Kids at school are starting to notice them, and the things they are saying aren't very nice.

"What are those things?"

"What happened to you?"

The less polite kids react like I'm a monster or something.

"Ewww! What's wrong with your hands, did you touch a frog?"

"What's wrong with you?"

I never know what to say because I don't know where they came from and why I have them in the first place. I just freeze, get tongue-tied, and stuff my hands deep in my pockets to keep them hidden. Five days each week, school has become an awful place where most of the time I'm worried about other kids making fun of me because of my stupid warts. It's the worst on the playground. Since I already run like a girl and keep my hands in my pockets, when teams are picked for kickball, I can bet my life I'll be last or, on a good day, second to last to Clouse Jensen, who wears a leg brace. Me and the playground hate each other.

Somewhere amidst my daydreams and seeing ventriloquists on TV lead to visions of becoming a ventriloquist. During a Christmas morning in the mid 1970s, I was the happiest kid on California Street when I received my high ticket present that year — my very own Simon Sez vent puppet.

It caught my eye in the J.C. Penny Christmas Catalog. For months, all I could dream about was becoming a great ventriloquist. Having my own puppet, a best friend and sidekick who'd say hilarious things would *for sure* be my passport to fitting in, I thought. After I became good, I'd put on skits for neighborhood kids, concealing my wart hands inside the doll, and be accepted by everyone.

After Simon arrived under the tree, I learned ventriloquism was harder than it looked. With no one around to show me the ropes of operating the puppet, writing jokes, and putting together an act, my attempts to entertain others didn't go as planned. My one and only show for Gordy and Laura was a pathetic disaster. At the end Laura yawned and said, "Are you done. Can we leave now?"

They despised the doll and took great joy in using Simon to antagonize me. I'd come home to find my siblings had Simon in compromised positions in my room, sometimes reading books or looking at record covers, but usually with his hands stuffed in his pants. Within a year, Simon made his way to the back of my closet and later sold at a family yard sale for a whopping five dollars.

***

One afternoon at a school assembly in the auditorium, the students at Bret Harte are visited by none other than Ronald McDonald. I can hardly believe he's here — but somehow he's able to take a break from being on TV to tell us about eating right, getting lots of sleep, and staying clear of trouble. McDonald's must be good for you, I thought.

"Now I'll need the assistance of one of you fine children!" he says like it's someone's lucky day.

My eyes look straight into my lap and I slide myself down my auditorium chair. I'm wishing I'm invisible, when he announces, "You, right there! Come on stage and join me!" I look up and see he's pointing directly at me. All I want to do is curl myself into a ball and disappear, but now everyone is waiting for me to get on stage. I stuff my warty hands into my pockets and head up while all I can feel is my heart beating fast and hard. I get up there and he places me next to him under the bright auditorium lights. It's like staring into the sun, and I can't see much of anything, but at least I can hear okay.

"What's your name, young man?" he asks in a squeaky cartoon voice through a microphone. "Robbie," I barely grunt out, ready to pee my pants from the nerves rushing through my body.

"I can barely hear you, son."

"Robbie," I say, trying again at a not-much-better volume. "Well, Ronnie, you just stand right here and everything will be fine." The last thing I can think to do was tell him he called me Ronnie instead of Robbie. No one noticed or cared anyway.

I look up at his painted face and big hair and things get a little clearer. He's making this large cone from a piece of newspaper. He holds it just above my head and says, "Now Ronnie, it's important that every boy and every girl drink plenty of milk every day. Today I'd like to give you a special glass of milk — the Ronald McDonald way!" He takes this clear pitcher filled with milk and says, "Watch everyone, I'm going to pour this evaporated milk right into Ronnie's head."

Even though I'm still more nervous than I've ever been, I'm starting to get sick of him calling me Ronnie. I can't see what he's was doing with the paper cone and milk, but whatever it is, it's some big thing and everyone is laughing and saying, "Whoa!" He places the pitcher aside. It's empty. The milk must have gone into my head somehow. He crumples the cone into a ball, smacks me on my butt, and sends me back to my seat. "Everyone cheer for Ronnie, for helping me out today!" As the students clap and cheer, with my hands still in my pockets, I tiptoe back to my seat and sink back with huge relief. My first time onstage before an audience is over, and I hated every second of it.

***

"What's a Freemason?" I ask grandpa, interrupting him whistling away. He's up on a ladder in his dark blue coveralls, fiddling with a ceiling light fixture in the Lodge. There's a long pause. I can't tell if he doesn't hear me, or did and just doesn't feel like answering. After what seems like an hour, he responds.

"Freemasons are an organized group of men who work to better ourselves and better the world," he replies.

I'm pretty sure that's what he said, but can't quite get my head around it. Grandpa's Scottish accent is thick and tricky to understand. Like when he says "better," it sounds like "bayder," but I think he means "better."

"If you're just trying to do good and help people, why does everything have to be a secret? Why do you need such a big old building?"

"A didnee mayk the rules, son. Just hay it werks." I translate that to, "I didn't make the rules, son. That's just how it works."

"Oh." I say, knowing that's the end of that.

Grandpa's the live-in groundskeeper and member at the Scottish Rite Cathedral Freemason Temple in Pasadena. My family calls it "the Lodge." It's this ginormous four story cement building that takes up half the block, where outside, a pair of fantastical, larger than life, stone statues of men with lion's bodies guard the inside. No building in Burbank looks like it, except maybe a couple of churches I've visited once or twice. But inside the Lodge, they're no signs of Jesus, and everything's a big secret. For the past hour I've been following him around the shadowy interior while he's cleaning and fixing everything.

On weekends while Gordy and Laura are off doing Boy Scout and Girl Scout stuff, I come here with my good mother to spend time with my grandparents. They have a small but comfy apartment on the third floor. I tag along with grandpa while he performs maintenance duties around the building. Unlike my father, whom I never get to visit at the construction site, grandpa welcomes my company while he's working. He's kind and patient and likes having me around.

Inside the Lodge are endless wood-paneled meeting rooms and nice offices with all kinds of old furniture. In every room, big old wooden tables and altars surrounded by heavy carved wood chairs are carefully placed on black and white checkerboard floors. The tables are decorated with all sorts of curious images of compasses, suns, moons, and things that seem important. These guys must have a million secrets, because the rest of world doesn't have any of this stuff. I wish I knew every one. The walls are packed with framed portraits of grey-haired freemasons who look as important as US presidents, some of them draped in witchy looking robes. The entire Lodge smells like old people and there's never a thing out of place. I love it here.

Being here takes my mind from feeling like a failure on the playground. Today before my good mother and I arrived, I got up early and went to the schoolyard to practice outdoor activities, again. On the deserted asphalt at Bret Harte Elementary, I pretended to play dodge ball, kickball, and softball. There were imaginary balls, bats, and schoolmates everywhere, and there I was, fitting in perfectly as one of the swift kids. I did the same thing last weekend, but when recess on Monday morning came, nothing changed. I was still as rotten as I was the week before. I'm starting to feel like I'll never fit in in that sort of way.

I'm deep in the Lodge, trailing after grandpa as he pushes the widest broom I've ever seen up one of the Lodge hallways. He's whistling away — he's always whistling away — just like my neighbor Stuart's cockatiel. The sounds echo all over the place. I wonder if someday I'll be a good whistler like him, or be good at anything.

"Stay close or you'll get lost. Nobody'll ever find ya in here, laddie," he says unpacking his maintenance cart. Sometimes when he gets focused on his work and forgets I'm tagging along, I wander off to explore the building's massive interior. I find my way to the room I'm drawn to most: the Lodge's magnificent auditorium theater. It's a special place.

I'm standing alone on the big empty theater stage. Next to me is a single light bulb that's mounted on a metal stand that grandpa calls the "ghost light" for some reason. It's easy to imagine a ghost light being a light that keeps away ghosts, but I'm not sure. It looks like any other lightbulb, casting a soft glow, barely illuminating the first few rows of empty velvet-cushioned seats. Something about the way the light fills the surrounding space—those seats, the hardwood stage under my feet, the high ceiling, the ropes and pulleys that move the curtains on the sides of the stage, and the big velvet curtain behind me—creates a certain magic that makes me feel empowered. Even though nobody's here but me, the room is alive.

I head into the dressing room, which has similar magic powers. It's packed with a long rack of costumes, wigs, make-up tables, lecterns, stools, and pieces of painted scenery. It smells of dirty cigarettes and paint thinner. The costumes are all adult-sized, not the kinds used for trick or treating. I rummage through them, imagining how they look like on the actors. It must be a lot of work to put a play on.

I've picked out a thick plastic helmet that's supposed to be made of metal or bronze, a robe that's three times too big for my little kid body, and a big plastic sword and shield. After suiting up I head back to the stage and take in the quiet atmosphere in, feeling the great weight of the room. Looking out in the big quiet space, my mind drifts. All of a sudden I'm an ancient warrior in the middle of some war, effortlessly moving through the chaos of men stabbing each other as horses charge and make terrible noises at each other on their hind legs. In my mind, I can see all these well-dressed Freemasons in those seats, cheering on my every move, applauding my greatness. As my thoughts trail off, I'm overcome with the idea that I'm the most important living person alive.

Bouncing around on that hardwood floor, I feel waves of invincible elation. My warts are gone. I'm not the awkward kid on the playground — I'm the king of the universe. It's the opposite of what I feel when I'm on the schoolyard. I take the biggest leap I ever have and thrust my sword into some bad guy's guts. I draw out my bloodied sword, knowing I've done a brilliant and noble deed, but nearly jump out of my skin when grandpa chimes in for a reality check.

"What are you doing up there son? Put those things away, lad. There not for you. Those belong the Lodge actors, son. You'd bayder put them back," he yells from the darkness in the back of the auditorium.

My nerves calm and I settle back to dull reality. I look around and see the ghost light and the empty seats before me. I nod to grandpa, confirming I'll return the costume where I found it. There goes the best part of the day, when nobody — not one boy or girl from school — was around to tell me I was swinging the sword wrong or jumping like a girl.

***

A few months after Uncle Ed shot me, my warts and I graduate from Bret Harte Elementary School and the Zabrecky family is taking a vacation to Europe. We don't take too many vacations, and when we do it's by car and only for a night or two, so going to Europe is a big deal. It's my first time on a plane and a break from boring Burbank. We are joined by my good mother's younger sister, my best Aunt whom I call Auntie, her husband, Uncle Jim; and my little cousin Jamie. After looking at the Eiffel Tower and the Roman Coliseum, we have a long visit planned to spend time with relatives who live in a quiet Scottish village called Patna.

Patna is this little village near a place called East Ayrshire. It's about an hour away from a big city in Scotland called Glasgow, not too far from where my good mother and Auntie grew up. We are staying at my Aunt May and Uncle Davey's place, who own the village's only grocery store. They are very nice, but like my grandpa, I can barely understand what they are saying half the time. They sound like they have socks stuffed in their mouths. There isn't much in cloudy and rainy Patna for a 12-year-old like me to do. For the next couple of weeks I'm on my own to amuse myself.

Wandering past rows of two-story brick houses that zig-zag over rolling hills looking for something to do, I can barely tell one house from another. They look like they've been there forever. Behind them are these rolling grassy hills that fade into each other as far as I can see. The streets all seem to end up at Uncle Davey's grocery store. Next door is a place where they sell fish and chips, a bar which they call "the pub," and this big freestanding phone booth — the kind you have to stand inside to make a call. Dreary Patna makes Burbank seem like New York City, even though I've never been to New York City.

I'm standing there looking at the phone booth, thinking I don't have anyone I want to talk to, when I hear this group of kids chanting a chorus to a song I've never heard before. It goes, "No future, no future, no future, for you," over and over. They come bouncing around the corner like a pack of wild dogs from Uncle Davey's grocery store, and I see who they are. I duck in the phone booth, where I'm unnoticed, and spy on them. There are about six of them, about my age, and they all have a similar look.

It's the Little Rascals dressed like members of the Clash, but in real life.

They have short jagged hair that looks like it's been cut by someone who doesn't know how to cut hair, ripped-up jean jackets with band names written all over them, safety-pinned zippers going in crazy directions over their dirty pants, and army boots. I recognize their look from the pages of my collection of *Creem* music magazines at home. The must be punk rockers, but really young ones. What else could they be? They look poor, but happy, having a fine time just goofing off, jumping around and shoving each other. Then they disappear up one of the streets like a passing tornado.

Uncle Davey comes out of his store holding a broom and shaking his head. He discovers me inside the phone booth. "Ya stay away from them, laddie. They're no good, the lot of them. They're trooble!" he says at the top of his voice so I can hear him, pointing to the side of his store, where there are three spray-painted big letters in white on a brick wall that read "PPA." "That's the lot of them there, the Patna Punk Army. They come in my shoppe n'take things that no belong tae them, they do. Goddamned hooligan kids!"

The next day I'm wandering around boring Patna, and around the corner from Uncle Davey's shop, I come face to face with the PPA. They surround and study me like I'm a zoo animal. With my hands stuffed in the pockets of my worn corduroy pants, I look down waiting for something bad to happen. "You're one of dos American laddies, aren't ya?" I think one of them says, but I'm not sure because he too sounds like he's got a sock in his mouth. "Yeah," I reply in a tone that says please don't kick my ass.

"C'mon with us, mate. We're jest goofin aboot, havin' a laugh," says one of them. "What's yer name?"

"I'm Robbie," I tell them.

"Raw-bee from Am-air-ika," one of them says, mocking the way I say my name, like I'm from Texas or something. I get it though; they think I sound funny and I think they sound funny, so we're even. They smoke lots of cigarettes and carry on in street-smart Scottish accents I pretend to understand, but they don't seem like bad kids at all. In fact, they're friendly and welcoming, so that afternoon I join their punk parade, playing hide-and-seek in the back streets and alleys of Patna. Even though Uncle Davey warned me to stay away from them and they stole from his store and graffitied his walls, I can tell they're okay. All of a sudden, Patna is the greatest place I've ever been.

The PPA has only one female member, Mad Margaret. Her short, jagged haircut outlines her pretty face of milky white skin that looks like it's never once seen the sun. Her big dark eyes are outlined with smeared makeup and her torn jean jacket, that has a bunch of band badges pinned to the pockets, says she can kick your butt if you so much as look at her the wrong way. She starts giving me these twinkly looks that make me think she doesn't want to kick my ass, but that she likes me. I can't begin to understand how my longish, feathered hair and surfer clothes can be attractive to her, let alone my bumpy hands that have been kept inside my pockets at all costs.

After running around cloudy Patna with the PPA the next afternoon, she waits till the other kids disbanded and out of nowhere, pulls me behind Uncle Davey's shoppe. Before I can think, she has me pinned me against the wall. She shoots me this crazy look I've never seen from a girl before. She grabs the collar of my shirt, stares at my mouth, and giggles. Other than a few failed attempts at 7 Minutes in Heaven at house parties just before sixth grade let out, no girl has ever been this close to me or made me so nervous.

"C'mon...give us a kiss," she whispers in this sweet and sexy way.

My mind spins out like when Ronald McDonald called me on stage but this time is different because my nuts tingle.

She says it again, this time a little more demanding. "C'mon now, give us a kiss!"

I'm too scared and confused for my first make-out session. I want to, and it's not because she's not pretty, she is — even though her teeth are crooked and yellow and she smells a little funny—but because I can't understand who she means when she says "us" when it's just the two of us. But the idea of touching another person with my disease-ridden hands, especially in that way, is just too much, so I just stand there frozen and stare at her, trying to be cool. My hands are in my pockets and I'm running my warty fingers over each to help calm my nerves. It probably looks like I'm jerking myself off, but I'm not.

"I gotta go," I say, pushing past her and racing off, leaving Mad Margaret in the Scottish dust. Later that night I fall asleep back at Aunt May and Uncle Davey's, wondering what Mad Margaret looks like in the nude, and if I'd blown my only chance of getting to first base.

***

It's late one afternoon and my good mother and I are visiting her Aunt Nan when my warts become the subject of conversation.

"It's the strangest thing, we keep going back to the doctor to get them removed and they keep coming back. Each time they come back, there's more and more," says my good mother over tea, cigarettes, and mounds of shortbread.

"Let me get a good look at them," I think she says, though I'm not sure because of the accent. She takes my hands and pulls me to a nearby reading lamp. I look up at her and see her raising her eyebrows and dragging off a filterless cigarette, smelling of talcum powder and nasty smoke. Almost everything about it is different than being in Dr. Mathias' office but she carefully examines them, completely unfazed, like he did. She has a different idea to get rid of them.

"Emmm, it's quite simple, really. Just head down the wee road tae the New Bridge at River Doon n'wait for one of them cows to relieve itself. Then, you just dip your hands deep into the cow dung and let them soak them for a few moments. Let that dung set for twenty or so minutes and rinse it away. You'll need to do this each day for a fortnight and those warts will vanish. I promise you, laddie."

The way she says it is so matter-of-fact I can't tell at first if she was putting me on. After a long talcum-ciggy-scented silence, I know she isn't.

"Um, what's a fortnight?" I ask.

"Two weeks, love. Two weeks."

I'm sitting there thinking, rubbing my bumpy fingers against one another, as this crazy sounding idea of dipping my hands in cow poop for fourteen days in a row sinks in. Then the words just pop out of my mouth.

"Which way to the River Doon?"

She draws a simple map on a paper napkin leading to New Bridge and the River Doon, or the *River Doom,* as I'm imagining it. Following her map down Patna's main road feels like a lifetime, but it's probably more like ten minutes. Down the wet and windy sidewalks, I pass the cloned, dull, brick homes with a new hopeful excitement. My mind is racing like it always does before some big thing is about to happen. Caught in my thoughts, I've arrived.

Running beneath this moss-covered brick bridge that's anything but new, is the River Doon. It's barely a river, it's more like a wide stream, and there's nothing special about it. A group of ten or so sleepy cows look bored out of their minds and stand like statues among tall grass next to the almost still water. It looks more like a boring painting than the real thing. I'm thinking about her remedy and now that I'm actually here it seems like a dumb idea.

Wondering what to do next, one of the larger black-and-white cows which looks lost in some deep thought, slowly turns its head and acknowledges me, knowing in some way why I'm here. Our eyes lock, my heart rate slows down, and everything feels right. A burst of sound from the cow's rear breaks off our stare. I jump out of the way just in time so that I don't get sprayed by this stream of shit shooting from the cow's back side. It runs like water from a garden hose on full throttle for a few good seconds and turns off in a snap. And there, deep in the grass a few feet away, lies the possible solution for my wart troubles. My palms and forehead are sweaty and my insides are overwhelmed with the same kind of charge I felt just after Uncle Ed shot me.

I approach the steaming poo, and as I do it's transforming into something I've never seen before. It's steaming like a boiling pot of soup and developing a thick outer crust, morphing from liquid to solid. I gawk at its mystical transformation, telling myself I can't back out. I want my warts gone and can't let this chance get away. There, just under New Bridge, I look down at my pathetic hands knowing I have nothing to lose. There's no time to think, only do. Taking in the biggest breath I can hold, I close my eyes and plunge my hands deep into cow pie. It's hot and thick, with the consistency of mud, and the fumes are making me choke. I have to look away, keeping my hands submerged for as long as I can before releasing them.

With every muscle clenched, I slowly bring them before my eyes. I'm standing in mild shock, knowing my hands are underneath the mushy, steamy dung. Using all the strength I have, I do everything I can not to puke. As my hands cool off and the dung starts to harden, I surrender them above my head and in the cold Patna air, figuring it's time to start the shameful jaunt back to Uncle Davey and Aunt May's place, displaying my shit mittens for the world to see. Thank God I made it back without seeing a soul.

I find a hose near the back door to rinse my fecal-frosted hands. It's caked on so thick it takes lots of pressure before it starts coming off in clod-like clumps. After I get most of it off, I sneak in the back door and nearly scrub them to death with a bar of horrible-smelling Scottish soap. Over the next hour, I check them ten or twenty times to see if my warts are still there, and they are. The next day takes every bit of belief that Aunt Nan's remedy might work to repeat the task. There's more to gain than lose, so I head down to meet the cows and do it again. And like the day before, I gag and plunge my hands into another steaming pool of excrement until I can no longer stand it, head back the relatives' house, and rinse them off again. For the next week, I've made the mission at New Bridge my secret crusade, and I'm halfway through the treatments.

The next week, on this particularly windy day, while returning from my daily ritual, a gust of wind blows a wad of cow crap directly into my right eye and instantly blinds me. The initial sting in my eyeball morphs into a fire-like burn that hurts so bad it makes me dizzy. I panic and rub it deeper into my eye socket with my shoulder, increasing the pain until it makes me want to throw up. That's it. I give up. I'm this helpless, half-blind fool, certain the universe is playing an evil joke on me. Fighting back the tears, my emotions turn to fear and panic, making me certain I'll never see again out of my right eye again and my evil and humiliating warts are spreading throughout my body. Tears are rushing down my face, flushing out little pieces of poo. The vision in my right eye starts coming back, and my panic cools down as I make my way back to the relatives.

There's no chance I'm telling the PPA about my visits to the River Doon. I'm doing everything I can to keep my daily field trip a secret, but start noticing nosey onlookers peeking from behind their windows, seeing me pass by their houses with my shit mitts shamefully held above my head. Every few houses, there's someone watching me head to and from the River Doon, and before I know it, everyone in Patna is going on and on about it. Even the PPA, who I was sure would think I was fool for trying such a thing, surprised me by applauding my efforts, awarding me punk points and rooting me on. To them, dipping one's hands in cow dung was the hippest thing happening in Patna.

Each excursion to the River Doon becomes a little easier. I get used to dunking and lathering my hands in the excrement and enduring the walk of shame back to my relatives for the rinse and wash. As the routine of it all becomes a little more tolerable, and the weight of the dung becomes lighter and lighter, I start feeling like I'm in a movie — kind of like Sylvester Stallone in the training scenes in *Rocky*.

On the last afternoon while rinsing off the poo and humming the main riff from "Gonna Fly Now," I'm examining my hands and noticing the warts reducing in size. The noticeable difference makes me feel jazzed, and that I wasn't doing it all for nothing. I say goodbye to our kind relatives, the PPA, and the cows of River Doon, and we head back over the Atlantic on a 747 to sunny Los Angeles.

Back home at the end of the summer something changed. My dreaded warts, all of them, disappeared. Each day they became smaller and smaller until they vanished into my hands. I couldn't believe my eyes. Within a week before starting junior high school, they were all gone. Aunt Nan's witchy remedy worked. For the first time since I can remember, I don't need to stuff my hands into my pockets all the time. My good mother reported the news to our Scottish relatives. In late September, the first piece of mail ever addressed to me arrived in our mailbox. It was from our relatives in Patna, and contained an article about my wart victory in the *Ayr Advertiser* on September 11, 1980. It read:

ROBBIE'S STRANGE CURE

Young American holiday-maker, Robbie Zabrecky, got an unexpected bonus when he spent a fortnight with his Aunt and Uncle, Jim and Patricia Cran, in Patna.

Robbie (12), who was in Scotland with his parents, brother, sister, and cousin, arrived with 47 warts on his hands. The family had spent 800 dollars the previous year having them removed, but the cure was only temporary.

While in Patna, Robbie heard that cow manure helped erase the ugly and uncomfortable warts. So, every morning for a fortnight, Robbie paid a special visit to a field at New Bridge, Patna.

Some folk felt he was daft—but Robbie had the last laugh. When he left for America the warts were dead and his hands were almost smooth again.

***

It's the first week of junior high and my wart-free hands are turning the combination I'm trying to remember to open my locker inside the busy halls at Luther Burbank Junior High School. Kids around me are doing the same thing, shuffling around books, and passing off to their next class. I recognize some from Bret Harte Elementary, but mostly, it's a sea of new faces. I finally get the lock to click and I exchange my history book for my math one, shut the locker, and head down the hall. This pretty girl I've never seen before is heading towards me, and I have no idea why. Her hair is feathered like one of Charlie's Angels and her clothes are shiny and tight. She gets closer, and I notice her lips slathered in lip gloss. She's smiling right at me, revealing a full set of nearly blinding braces, and all I can think is that there's a lot going on with her mouth. She puts this folded up piece of notebook paper along with a fresh pack of Bubble Yum into my wart-free hand, and walks off. I get settled in math class and open the note. In big bubbly writing, it says:

DEAR ROBBIE!!!
I JUST WANTED TO LET YOU KNOW MY NAME IS CHRISTINE AND I KEEP SEEING YOU PASSING IN THE HALLS AND WANT TO SAY "HI." THERE'S NO TIME TO TALK AND MEET YOU IN PERSON, SO I'M GIVING YOU THIS NOTE SO YOU DON'T THINK I'M A TOTAL SPACE CADET OR ANYTHING! ISN'T JUNIOR HIGH CRAZY? WHEN I SEE YOU IN THE HALLS I CAN'T STOP LOOKING AT YOU. YOU LOOK LIKE YOU COULD BE ROBBIE BENSON'S LITTLE BROTHER. :) ARE YOU? JUST KIDDING! BUT REALLY, DO PEOPLE TELL YOU THAT ALL THE TIME?

SOOOO, DO YOU LIKE ME? IF YOU DO, CHECK THE BOX, YES OR NO, AND GIVE IT BACK TO ME TOMORROW. OK?

BYE!
CHRISTINE
P.S. I HOPE YOU LIKE WATERMELON BUBBLEYUM!
IT STICKS TO MY STUPID BRACES, (GROADY!) BUT I
STILL LOVE IT!!!
P.S.S. DO YOU HAVE MRS. CARTER FOR SCIENCE?
SHE'S SUCH A TOTAL BITCH!!!!!

I fold up the note and shove it into my pocket, trying to figure out if it's a joke or not. The next day I get another note and
pack of gum from another girl, and then another. By the end of
the week, I've got this pocket full of notes from other girls and
more gum than I'll ever chew. I'm starting to wonder if Aunt
Nan is a witch and cast a spell on me, turning me into a popular
seventh grader, because out of nowhere it seems like everyone
wants me to be their boyfriend or something. It's happening so
fast I can barely keep up with myself. No longer are my hands
shoved in my pockets in class and on the schoolyard. Now, I
place my new, smooth hands on each desk I sit at and then lean
back and marvel. My wart war is over, and all the crummy years
of having them now seems like a bad dream.

It's like I was one person with the warts, and another person without them. Now I've got problems of a whole different kind: trying to understand why this flood of dick-harden-
ing, gum-chomping, twelve- and thirteen-year-old girls want me
to be their *boyfriend,* and that's something I don't know how to
do. Heading from one class to the next I'm fired up and terri-
fied while getting bombarded with these secret notes and packs
of gum from my new admirers, inviting me to weekend house
parties. And, after school my phone at home is ringing off the
hook, which is annoying my brother and sister to no end. Every
morning I wake up, feeling like I'm in some other kid's world, but
whose exactly, I don't know.

ARCADE DAZE

THE MAGNOLIA PARK part of Burbank, where I live and do my paper route six days a week looks tired and set in its ways. Pedaling along faded storefronts, chucking papers at empty dress boutiques, desolate corner markets, and dusty antique shops on Magnolia Boulevard between Hollywood Way and Buena Vista Street, it feels lost somewhere in time. These quiet little businesses could be anywhere in America, like a dead set from TV's *Twilight Zone* —waiting for a Martian attack that isn't coming.

Besides Johnny Carson's cheeky references to "Beautiful Downtown Burbank," Magnolia Park shows zero signs of Tinsel Town's glitz. All that jazz is happening on the other side of the goliath mountain that separates Burbank from Hollywood, called Mt. Lee. If you've never heard of Mt. Lee, you've probably seen it on TV or in the movies. It's that mountain that holds up the Hollywood sign. The problem is that that big white sign is mounted on the other side of Mt. Lee with its back turned to Burbank. But Burbank's a safe place, most people are nice, and we don't have much crime.

On most days, the worst thing about living here is the air. Burbank is a pollution magnet, and sucks in the dirty air that lurks in the Valley. Several days each year at school, we're advised to stay inside classrooms during these intense Stage One smog-alerts. On smog-alert days, the thick air is considered so poisonous, some people say it can give any kid who dares to run on the playground an instant case of lung cancer. On TV, the outside world is troubled with stuff like the oil crisis, high inflation, and starvation in third world countries, but Burbank seems to exist in its own safety net, giving you this sense that nothing too bad will ever happen. Under our sun-drenched skies, there are no traces of bubonic plagues, world wars, icy winters, or starving kids like there are in Africa.

I'm a thirteen-year-old trying to figure a lot of things out, but I'm not doing it alone. I've become nearly attached at the hip to my two best friends, Mike Keys; who I always call by his first and last name because it sounds cool, and Richard—two confident and smart kids from single-parent homes. I knew them both from school, but after a few chance meetings at a nearby 7-Eleven at the end of seventh grade, we've been spending most of our time together, bonding over BMX bikes, skateboards, music, and a shared sick sense of humor. When I'm with them, I feel indestructible — a radical 180-degree turn from my wart years. Transitioning from boys to teens, we rely on our power of three, seeking reinvention of ourselves in our town that seems like any town.

I was the last one in. Mike Keys and Richard were already buddies and had already gotten into trouble together. Just before meeting them, they'd been busted at 7-Eleven during a failed beef jerky heist. They have the kind of risky fun I used to only dare of having. When we're together, we challenge and bring out the best, and worst, in each other. Exploring every street and alley in Magnolia Park on our skateboards and bikes, Mike Keys and Richard are showing me that being a kid can be a blast, as long as there were no adults around. Sometimes that means throwing eggs at passing cars on Hollywood Way, other times it's ding-dong-ditch at some girl's house we think is cute, and other times it's standing around and maybe dancing at house parties thrown by other kids on weekends. We're sharing our final moments of innocence together, and we kind of know it.

Mike Keys is the only kid I know who's connected with show business. He used to model clothes for Gemco department stores. After appearing in their catalogs, which happened to be delivered to every doorstep in Burbank, he became sort of famous at our school, especially among the girls. Looking like he'd just strolled off the pages of the latest Gemco catalogue, this best-dressed and well-groomed kid was impressive, and definitely going places.

I met Mike Keys sometime in third grade. He caught my attention during an altercation with our school's most militant teacher, Ms. Dawson. She's this angry and mean woman, known for her drill-sergeant-like teaching tactics. Most kids simply did as she said because she frightened them, but Mike Keys wasn't scared of anyone. The kid was a fearless wonder.

I couldn't have dreamed that a nice-looking kid like Mike Keys would provide one of the most indelible moments of grade school: the day he threw a full-blown punch into Ms. Dawson's muffin-topped midsection after a playground dispute. Seeing his fist jam her belly resulted in a victory for the rest of us. That kind of courage could only come from some super kid-genius, I thought. How else could he carry himself with that kind of confidence? At that moment, I learned that Mike Keys did what Mike Keys wanted to do. Nothing could stop him. It was that simple. I privately appointed him as my kid idol and wanted to be his friend. I invited him over to my house a few times and we hung out in my den, listening to records and talking about girls. One day he invited me over to his place, a duplex on Hollywood Way.

"My mom's a Buddhist. She's also a lesbian," he says casually as we we're about to enter the front door. Not entirely sure what either of those things are, I can't wait to find out. This kid is becoming cooler by the second. "Take your shoes off before coming in. House rules," he informs me. The inside of their duplex is spotless and there's hardly any furniture or stuff. She meets us at the door with this great big smile, and she's holding a large bottle of prune juice. She's not like other mothers I've met. "Hi, Mrs. Keys," I say, introducing myself, wanting her to like me. "Oh, call me Bev, please," she replies in a soft and velvety voice. Over her shoulder, I see into their small kitchen where on the frig is a bumper sticker that reads, "QUESTION AUTHORITY." I'm not sure what it means, but I like the idea of it. Unlike most other parents I've met, Bev treats Mike Keys, and now me, like we are real people, not dumb kids. Bev doesn't even dress like an adult. She's sporting a black T-shirt, cut-off shorts, and Birkenstock sandals. The fearless kid with a modeling career and a cool mom—I'm convinced Mike Keys has it all.

Richard's the red-headed son of our trusted and chipper mailman, Mr. Williams. Like Mike Keys, he's also fearless and has this knowledge of things that aren't found by listening to records or watching TV. He's a total prankster and loves playing jokes on other kids. The other week he cut the loudest fart in class and looked over at poor Nick Peters, who was sitting right next to him, and said, "Geez Nick, your mom serving meatloaf again last night?" He's always doing funny stuff like that. Plus, he can talk to anyone about anything, even adults. He'll just go up to them and start talking. I instantly admired his natural self-confidence—something I wasn't finding on my own. His folks are divorced, and his dad didn't mind him being away from home, spending hours, sometimes days, at the Zabrecky house.

Then there's me. In a slightly weathered three-bedroom house on California Street, just north of dormant railroad tracks on Chandler Boulevard, live my father, my good mother, my brother Gordy, who's five years older than me, my sister Laura, who's four years older than me, our spoiled mutt Rusty, and me.

My father's a construction worker. He's a meat-and-potatoes, manly man with a strong build and hair like Elvis. He smokes Roi-Tan cigars all the time, and even when he's not smoking them, their awful smell lingers in our house. Most of the time people that don't know him think he's in show business, because he's always going for laughs at the weirdest times. He entertains most everyone he meets by speaking his mind and sharing his views on the world. Three of those views were repeated and instilled in me at a young age.

"Ma boy, there's three things you need to know about life. The first is that it isn't fair. The second is that not everyone is going to like you, no matter how bad you might want someone to, they won't, so don't count on it. The third is that when someone is coming to attack you, all you need to do is reach down, scoop up a handful of dirt, throw it in their eyes, punch them in the balls, and run. You got me?"

He works hard to provide for us, with his workdays starting and ending early. He's gone by the time I'm up and home when I return from school, sitting in front of the TV, drinking Coors beer from a glass mug, and puffing one of those nasty Roi-Tan cigars.

My good mother was gifted with a heart of gold. She's the sweetest, kindest person there ever was. Her shoulder-length raven-colored hair and sharp widow's peak complement the brightest and caring blue eyes that have this magic of only seeing the good in things. A day hasn't passed when I haven't felt lucky about being her son.

Neither of my parents are nostalgic or show interest in the past, and don't seem to really like talking about it much. We're here on California Street and that's that. At some point I learned that my father was from a large working-class Pennsylvania family. After deciding he didn't want to retire to an early grave from working in the coal mines like his father, he joined the Navy and served in the Korean War before settling in Burbank and taking up construction work. I also learned, from eavesdropping here and there, that my good mother was from a small town called Clydebank, in Scotland, where my grandparents met and married as teenage sweethearts. She was born in Stirling Castle, near Glasgow, amidst the chaos of World War II, while my grandfather was serving in the Navy, dropping bombs on enemy countries, and aiding in the construction of the Queen Mary ocean liner. But anytime I ask what things were like when she was my age, she'll say stuff like, "Oh things were just different back then. It doesn't really matter, does it? What's important is now, little fellow."

She still loves calling me little fellow, even though I'm thirteen.

Most of the time my brother, Gordy, and sister, Laura, share an indifference to my existence. Older than me by four and five years, respectively, they're from a different father than mine, but like the rest of our family history, he's never talked about. By the time I arrived, they'd already developed a tight brother-sister bond, and three was a crowd. I used to desperately want affection they couldn't give. They had each other, and nothing I seemed to do could gain their admiration.

My desire for their love and acceptance sometimes led to extreme measures. On countless occasions, I'd quietly wait until they were watching cartoons in the living room side by side, sneak up behind them, spread my arms out as far as I could and, with all my might, bang their heads together and take off running. It was the same thing every time: When they'd recover from the shock of their skull collision, they'd chase me around and things got crazy until one of my parents would break us up and send us to different rooms. After too many of these episodes, I start realizing that my "Look at me! Over here!" approach to finding sibling love is having the opposite desired effect I'd wished for and they started hating me. I was too young to appreciate them for being good kids and didn't understand that I was putting them through misery most of the time. Gordy *did* give me his paper route last year, so at least he thinks I can do something right.

***

It's the summer of 1981 and only three things matter: punk rock, video games, and junk food. Nothing else. Earlier this year, Mike Keys, Richard, and I saw our first live punk-rock show inside Hollywood's Whisky a Go Go on the Sunset Strip.

After being dropped off by Bev, we nervously filed inside the packed nightclub and found ourselves squished among a crowd of angry teenage punk rockers booing a band called Flipper. They were in the middle of a song, but their songs barely sounded like songs — they could barely play their instruments, and the singer, who looked much older than us, was yelling what sounded like random stuff into the mic, as if he was making up the lyrics as they were going along. If they were making awful noise just to upset the audience, they did great. Every couple of minutes a punker in the crowd threw up a middle finger or yelled something mean, but the band seemed to like not being liked. When someone in front spit a huge loogie that landed on the singer's ratty button-down shirt, he rubbed it into a big wet splotch, unfazed, and just kept ranting and moaning. He was in his own world and could care less.

As Flipper blared away we stuck close to each other, pushing ourselves through the crowd, and heading upstairs to the balcony to see everything better. We wanted good spots for the band we came to see, the Dead Kennedys. Flipper finished their last song and the crowd booed one last time. After a short break, the Dead Kennedys came on and the room exploded with energy. They sounded just like they did on their album, *Fresh Fruit for Rotting Vegetables*, a record Mike Keys, Richard, and I nearly worn out from playing so much. Their songs are short and speedy, fueled by raw, physical energy, and the audience is reacting to it accordingly. All of a sudden, fearless and radical teenagers with short dyed hair, wearing torn jeans, black leather biker boots, thrift-shop button-down shirts adorned with arm bands and band logos, are flinging themselves on and off the stage, into combative slam dancers who are crashing into each other as fast and as hard as they can.

It was the most exhilarating and frightening thing I'd ever seen.

Throughout their performance, the band's singer, Jello Biafra, gyrated his shirtless body like some uncaged, rabid animal and leaping off the stage while somehow managing to sing every word totally perfect. He threw himself on top of the crowd and got passed around the club on his sweaty back by encouraging audience members. He was the show's ringleader, reminding me of the Joker from *Batman*, if he'd escaped from TV land to have a nervous breakdown before a few hundred of his illegitimate children — most of whom looked like they're headed to juvenile hall. The intimate and intense energy between the Dead Kennedys and the audience is fueling and uniting one another, giving us this feeling that being in the audience is just as exciting as being onstage. It's a world far away from Burbank and unlike anything we've experienced before.

The three of us stood and watched in speechless amazement. For the first time ever, I felt like was in the most important place in the world, and know Mike Keys and Richard felt the same. The swirling energy of the music and the spirit of the crowded room was almost too much to take in. Under a homemade Black Flag shirt I made just for the show, my heart pumped, keeping up with the racing beat of the music. Every few minutes, Mike Keys, Richard and I exchanged jaw-dropping looks at each other, knowing was the single greatest night in each of our lives. As the band blazed through their show, the impact of the whole experience is collectively blowing our thirteen-year-old minds.

The best part of the night was watching them play our favorite song, "Holiday in Cambodia," which we listened to a hundred times, and sang along to every word. It has the same infectious verse, chorus, verse format as my beloved tunes by Cheap Trick and KISS—but faster and way better. We don't know what the song is about, and we don't care; we just like the way the music makes us feel. After that night, we got hooked on punk rock.

***

The streets of Burbank offer little diversion to our hyper teenage world. When Ray & Stevie's Pinball Palace opens its doors out of nowhere in the middle of sleepy Magnolia Park, the three of us found a new home away from home. After finishing my paper route every day, I meet Mike Keys and Richard inside the dark, air-conditioned shoebox of a room lined with rows of our favorite games. Futuristic noises, blips, and beeps emerge from the latest video games, challenging us to beat them for the price of a token, which is the same as a quarter. A jukebox in the corner plays songs of the day by big rock groups like Rush and REO Speedwagon. If a song isn't selected, it somehow defaults to Rush's hit "Tom Sawyer," a song for some reason I hate so much that unless I'm in the middle of a game, I'll go wait outside until it's over. There's a small upper-level perch with a row of old pinball machines that's reserved for the pinball purists — usually older dudes with long hair and mustaches who wear T-shrits that say "I'm With Stupid" and junk like that. There's a mutual respect between the two levels: we don't bother them and they don't bother us.

No matter what, a regular cast of zit-faced stoners and nebbish adolescents is there every day. Some kids just come to watch, or maybe they don't have money to spend on the games — I'm not sure — but they help make the place feel alive. We call them video-game groupies, and they somehow belong there just as much as the kids who are always playing games. Us Pinball Palace locals have one thing in common: None of us are off in Boy Scouts, Eagle Scouts, playing organized group sports, or sitting at home watching reruns of *The Brady Bunch*.

I'm drawn to this new game called Pac Man. It's the first real thing I'm good at. After playing it a few dozen times, I'm addicted to it. I guess I have what some people are calling "Pac Man Fever." Whatever. It's my game, and on a good day, get small audiences of curious onlookers to witness my high scores. Meanwhile Richard holds court over at the Asteroids machine, and nobody — and I mean nobody — can beat Mike Keys at Missile Command, which makes sense, because he's the best at whatever he does. So Mike Keys, Richard, and I have become arcade stars, taking the high scores on the most coveted machines, never missing an afternoon of video-game action.

I still sleepwalk like crazy, can't tell red from brown, can't swing a bat or throw a ball right, but inside the walls of this dark arcade, I'm somebody. It's good to be good at something for a change.

I take video-game breaks by racing home on my second-hand, black, BMX bike to make my signature snack: two Twinkies soaked in maple syrup and heated in the microwave for ten seconds. After the crazy elation I feel after munching down the hot and sweet delights, I zip back to beat the hell out of Pac Man and ride out the sugar high.

***

Pinball Palace is run by two old guys in their thirties, Ray and Stevie. Both of them seem too old to be called by their first names. I always feel like I should be calling them "mister" something or the other. Ray is the arcade's main guy. He's like Arnold from Arnold's in *Happy Days*, but not Chinese. With his wavy black hair and matching overgrown mustache, wire-rim glasses, gym shorts, and long-sleeved button-down shirts, he's his own kind of weird. Equal parts science teacher, gym teacher, and borderline circus geek, he talks really fast. He's always going on about what new video games he might be ordering next, while his eyes dart all over the arcade — like he's got to take a shit or something. His cohort, Stevie, is the opposite. He wears old T-shirts and filthy jeans that settle too low to expose a foul, hairy butt crack that we make jokes about. He putters around at a slow pace, rarely uttering a word to anyone. He mostly tinkers with haywire machines in the arcade's tiny repair shop and office in the back — an area strictly off limits to its customers.

A month or so after opening, we learn Ray and Stevie are promoting more than their video arcade. They're big-time Christians, using Pinball Palace to bring God into the video zone. They just started offering this new deal: for five bucks a month, anyone can join the "Christian Club" and receive two silver tokens per day. Here's the catch: card-carrying members must wear a silver chain necklace with a medallion engraved with a Christian fish symbol to help spread the name of Jesus among video-game enthusiasts. Although it's a good deal, I'm not a Christian and don't feel like promoting Jesus while playing Pac Man or anything.

***

Mike Keys, Richard, and I show up at the arcade just after cutting our surfer hair into short, spiky, punk cuts. We made a pact to go all out and ditch our surfer hair and clothes in exchange for closely cropped hair, ratty button-down shirts with homemade spray-painted band logos and slogans, torn jeans, and Converse high tops. In Burbank, it's risky to go punk. There's a rivalry between rockers, disco dwellers, and punkers, and it's in full effect. We look like West Coast members of the PPA — it's clear three of us aren't going to a Journey concert or dancing to the Saturday Night Fever record or anything like that.

"Punk sucks! Death to punkers! Punk faggots!" people yell from their cars while staring us down. We kind of like the new attention even though it's sometimes threatening, because now, we're different than they are. "Eat the peanuts out of our shit!" Mike Keys wastes no time to respond anytime we're threatened. He and Richard are both tough, plus, Gordy and his friends have thrown me around in our den so many times I'm not afraid of getting roughed up if something goes down. There's an older bunch of Burbankian punkers, who have their own pack thing going, but we get the feeling we're too young and innocent to be part of their circle. The other day we crossed paths with them at a red light while biking and skateboarding. One of them sarcastically said, "Look at you little punkers! You kids are just too punk. I wonder what your parents must think." That pretty much told us they don't want anything to do with us, so it's just Mike Keys, Richard, and me against everyone, which is fine by us.

One late afternoon at the Palace, Mike Keys and Richard bail, and I'm one of last guys there, kicking major ass on my last game of Pac Man of the day. I see someone I don't want to see coming towards me from the reflection of the screen. It's this guy called Stevo, a sour-faced, long-haired rocker who works there part-time and can't keep his shirt on. He thinks he's David Lee Roth from Van Halen. He totally gets off singing along with "Runnin' With the Devil" at the top of his lungs, performing shirtless karate moves in the cramped arcade anytime he thinks someone is watching him, which, if you're there is impossible to miss. If anyone smaller than him threatens his high scores, he bumps the game so hard it resets to zero and erases their score. As his muscular torso closes in on the reflection of the Pac Man screen, I feel something bad is about to happen.

I've just broken the current high score, and without saying a word he grips me in a chokehold from behind. He drags me outside into the blinding light and steers me to the alley behind the arcade. With bear-like brawn, he lifts me off the ground and slams me and my new punk-rock haircut into the dumpster. A bunch of empty cardboard boxes help pad my landing, but I still have the wind knocked far out of me. He forces the dumpster's lid down on me, holding me inside and saying, "Die punker!" over and over from outside. In the pit of the dumpster, where I can't see anything and it stinks of old cardboard and rotting Pup'N Taco leftovers, I give up on trying to push my way out and wait for whatever's going to happen next to be over. Then all of sudden it's quiet again. Stevo Lee Moron — at least that's what I'm calling him from now on — must've gone back inside to bully some other kid. I catch my breath, hop out, jump on my bike, and ride home. Way more crazy stuff has happened to me to let Stevo's dumpster dilemma bother me, I tell myself while riding home.

***

The next few times I show up at the Palace, I notice Ray becoming increasingly friendly with me. Every time I enter the arcade now, he makes this big deal that I'm there. The truth is, I've been there every day and he's hardly acknowledged me, and now all of a sudden I'm someone special. "Ohhhh, Mr. Pac Man has arrived. Don't you have any better place to be? Don't you have a girlfriend? Where's your girlfriend?" he squeals in the world's worst Steve Martin impersonation. I ignore him and wait my turn for Pac Man.

He waits till I'm in full concentration mode in mid-Pac Man drama, sneaks up behind me and slips warm tokens down my back, and steps back while giggling like a girl. I wiggle and let the tokens slide down my back, forging ahead with my game, trying my best to ignore him. Other times, he sneaks up and surprises me by tickling my ribcage while making weird bird noises. Out of nowhere he's distracting and tormenting me, but I can tell he likes having me around.

One day after finishing my paper route a little early, I'm the first kid to arrive at the arcade. Out of the corner of my eye, I notice Ray standing near the jukebox with this concerned look in his eye.

"Something's been bothering me, Robbie. Why haven't you joined the Christian Club?" he asks.

Immediately, I feel something's not right, but I keep my cool.

"Um, well, for one thing, I'm not a Christian. I don't even know what that is," I reply.

"Come with me, please," he says with this slightly deranged look in his eye. I follow him, even though I don't want to. For the first time, I enter the small repair room and office at the rear of the arcade I've peeked into a million times. No sign of Stevie tinkering around. No sign of anyone else. It's just us. There's stuff everywhere—pinball and video-game parts, glass cleaner, piles of bills, tools, a broken clock, a picture of Christopher Atkins from Blue Lagoon that must've been torn from a magazine taped to the wall, and a couple of junky stools. With teacher-like authority, he ushers me in and shuts the door.

The sounds of the arcade become distant and muted. My heart's really starting to race. He guides me to one of the stools.

"Sit down. Relax, it's okay, I'm not going to bite you," he mutters in this intense and shaky voice.

His eyes are darting all over the place. Nothing good is going to come of this meeting. Then, as I'm looking around the room and lock eyes with the picture of Christopher Atkins giving me this dreamy look, everything starts slowing down to a strange unfamiliar rhythm and all I can feel is this numbing panic. He reaches into his shorts pocket and removes something: it's one of those Christian fish pendant necklaces. His hands are shaking and he seems even more nervous than before. He reaches toward me holding the necklace and starts lightly rubbing his hairy body against me.

"I want…I want…I want you to become a member of the Christian Club," he whispers in a quivering tone close to my ear, but murmurs it in a way that informs me he wants more than that. I'm so overwhelmed I'm too frightened to move. I look down and get totally grossed out to see a bulge in his shorts. His hands are shaking even more than before as he moves behind me and slowly places the necklace over my head. He then starts rubbing his hands across my chest and shoulders, making these soft animal like grunts at regular intervals.

I'm in official teenage video-arcade hell and need to do something quick to break him from this messed-up fantasy he's having. But I can't — I feel trapped and defeated. My life's a living game of Pac Man and I need to escape. My father's life rule of throwing sand in the eye of an attacker would come in handy if we were on the beach, but we we're miles away from the Santa Monica shore.

Rather than socking Ray square in the dick and running for the door like Mike Keys or Richard most certainly would have, I remained still. I felt like I was holding my hand over a flame, just to see how long I could keep it there. The dirty little moment became a sick game of chicken. Why I stayed, knowing I was deep in danger's way, I don't know. Maybe I needed the first-hand lesson that certain grown-ups — even ones with dream jobs like Ray and Stevie who appeared to be respectable and responsible adults — were no different than the sick fraud himself, Uncle Ed.

His hands are moving up and down my shoulders when I hear Richard yell from the game room. Thank god, or whatever stroke of luck brought Richard to the Palace that exact moment.

"Hey! Where is everyone? Hello?"

I've never been so happy to hear his voice. I break loose, stand up, and move to the door.

"We'll talk about this later, okay Robbie?" he says, adjusting his groaty dick bulge deep between his legs so it can't be seen.

"I want you to consider accepting Jesus Christ as part of your life. This is for us, and only us, to talk about, okay? Okay?" His words increase in volume, and in that short time, his tone morphs from super-sicko to super-scary substitute teacher. I don't answer. I stand there in a freaked-out befuddlement, watching him transform from one person to another.

"Be right out," he yells out to Richard, rearranging the gross bulge in his shorts. He pushes me aside like nothing happened, and exits.

I reenter the arcade in a daze. Trying to comprehend what just happened, I see Richard, who's just started a game of Asteroids, and a few more kids filtering in. They have no idea what just happened. All I know is that I can't be there anymore. Bolting out the arcade entrance, pinballs smacking against metal targets, an assortment of buzzes, blips, and beeps fade fast as the door closes behind me. For the first time, those sounds I'd grown to love are grating on my ears, and I can't be there for one more second. I hop on my bike and tear down Magnolia as fast as I can pedal. My unsettled mind is racing and I'm not ready to go

home yet. I ride all over Magnolia Park—up and down those faded sidewalks and alleys, zigzagging around the blocks of houses,
pedaling aimlessly until my legs hurt and it's dark.

I never step foot in the Palace again.

BEYOND BURBANK

AFTER THE GLORIOUS echo of the last afternoon bell at Luther Burbank Junior High School fades, Mike Keys, Richard, and I ditch dreaded schoolbooks in our lockers and hightail over to the Hollywood Way bus stop. We anxiously wait for bus number 212 to transport us from Burbank to Hollywood through the bumpy Cahuenga Pass, where everthing starts to get real interesting.

"I can guarantee you guys we learn more in Hollywood than in any Luther classroom," says Mike Keys, stepping up the bus stairs and plopping bus fare into a coin-counting contraption.

"Totally, and way better than watching TV," adds Richard.

And how right they are, I think as we take our seats at the rear of the bus among what seems like a moving fishbowl with all types of weird and exotic fish. The riders are made up of a wide range of characters who seem to live and work outside the conservative walls of Burbank. Men who dress like fancy women, druggies, dropouts, and working-class folks fill the rows of seats, which make the bus ride feel like one from a carnival, and that's only the beginning of these excursions.

Rain or shine, even though it hardly ever rains, the Sheet Lady is always there —that's what we call her, anyway. Appearing like a ghost on the side of the road as our bus descends Barham Boulevard near Universal Studios and the 101 freeway, we can count on her massive glowing eyes; long, flowing, bleach-blonde hair; and dark orange, sunburnt arms waving at us. Unsure if she's a hooker or Greek goddess, she wraps herself tightly in a white toga that reveals a boner-worthy, statuesque, womanly figure. She's become the unofficial patron saint of our Hollywood jaunts, appearing like clockwork, and waving us through from one world into the next.

As the bus heads through the Cahuenga Pass, we crane our necks to check out the cool cars parked at this place called Dean Jeffries Automotive Stylings, an auto garage nestled in the hilly pass, where all sorts of surreal and futuristic sci-fi concept cars and automobiles disguised as robots or animals sit parked next to each other in the world's most surreal parking lot, waiting for their glory in some movie or TV show. If there's a weird car in a TV show, it's parked at this place.

One bus stop that always catches our attention is the one at the mental institution. It looks like a 1950s beach motel that's been built into the mountain, and all kinds of crazy people come and go from there. At this stop, the driver lets on the most strange and deranged people we've ever seen. Usually, at least one of the riders talks to us, or themselves, in some sort of abstract conversation. It's its own weird thrill, sitting face to face with characters that most kids our age probably only read about in books or see on TV, but we're right there with them. One afternoon one of them, who could easily pass as an extra from *One Flew Over the Cuckoo's Nest*, singles me out, and looks through me with a million-mile stare.

"You! Don't look at me as if you don't remember me, mister. We met here exactly one year ago today, remember? Remember?" He's caught me totally off guard and suddenly I'm on the spot. Half the bus riders are watching him interrogate me, and I feel like I should play along. Although I'm totally clueless about what he's talking about, I jump right in the ring with him.

"Oh yeah, I remember you. I remember everything you told me. Don't worry, I haven't told anyone where you buried those treasures, either."

"Good, because when we meet again exactly one year from today, you need to bring the map, and make sure it's in American this time, understand, or I'll cut you!?"

"Yep. Got it. Totally."

We never saw him again, but riffed on the encounter for months afterward like it was our own episode from *The Twilight Zone.*

***

The thing about going to Hollywood, is that you always have this sense of surprise. It's the opposite of predictable Burbank, where we might as well be living on the far side of the Moon. We hop off the bus at the main attraction, Hollywood Boulevard, and wander the bustling streets of Hollywood. We're free to cruise around and absorb the big city — and there's a lot to take in. Walking up and down the Boulevard never lets us down. The Hollywood Walk of Fame, where all the stars are set in the sidewalks, has seen better days, but it's hanging in there. There's always a cast of seedy people weaving in and out of souvenir shops, nearly empty memorabilia stores, dusty bookshops, and grimy pizza places. On street corners, Hare Krishnas with freshly shaved heads, fluorescent robes, and floral necklaces dance and chant to a mysterious God, one beyond Burbank, while evangelists for Jesus and Scientology aggressively promote their churches by handing out pamphlets of hopeful literature to passersby in exchange for cash donations and free personality tests.

Telephone poles are cluttered with exciting flyers for all kinds of upcoming rock shows, while shady characters in dark sunglasses stand beneath them enticing tourists for the chance to win cash by betting on a little game played with walnut shells and a pea, where the person betting always ends up losing. Above old buildings are billboards for new movies like *Arthur, Raiders of the Lost Ark,* and *An American Werewolf in London*, while upcoming celebrities like Angelyne and Dennis Woodruff have themselves plastered all over the place, convincing us they'll be the next Marilyn Monroe and James Dean.

We take a transfer bus down to Melrose Avenue, and wander around between La Brea and Fairfax, in search of records and clothes. There are a few places to get cool stuff, as we brush past other young punky shoppers parading east and west. Inside a record store called Vinyl Fetish, mean employees sport black clothes, eyeliner, teased hair, and blush, pushing the latest New Romantic singles from England. Flip of Hollywood is like the J. C. Penney of new wave, offering long rows of tattered jeans, old button-down shirts, jackets, and dresses from the '50s, while loud new music blares from ceiling speakers; and a little shop called Poseur, which is operated by this friendly English couple who look like lost members of the Sex Pistols, and sell T-shirts featuring band logos, badges, and spiked jewelry.

We started smoking these clove scented cigarettes that come all the way from Indonesia. They smell like Halloween candy and have foreign brand names like Djarum and Jakarta. We bought our first pack from the tobacco shop on Hollywood Boulevard, where the guy working there must have thought we were 18 because he just sold them to us. Since we're only 13 we treat the purchase like it's some heavy drug deal and buy three packs. After finding a shady side street off the boulevard, because we're unsure if we might get arrested for underage smoking, Mike Keys rips open a pack, pops a fresh clove between his lips, sparks it, and puffs it like a pro. He has this gift to do anything for the first time and somehow make it seem like he was born to do it. He hands it off to me. Even though I've never smoked before, I try and make it seem like it's no big deal. I take my first puff and draw in the smoke like Mike Keys did, but cough it out right away and immediately feel like I'm dying.

"You gotta hold it in, and blow it out like a dragon, — like they do in the movies," Mike Keys says, instructing me. I lick my lips and taste the sweet flavor of the clove, and even though I'm a little nauseated, I give it a second try. I take a smaller puff and manage to hold it in for a second before blowing it out. It's a heavy feeling that gives me this crazy head rush and I feel like I've done something right.

"Exactly. Richard's turn," says Mike Keys, who's in charge because he can smoke so well. "Gimmie that thing," says Richard, taking the clove from between my fingers. He's like Mike Keys, and takes a cool drag, looking like he's born to smoke. Even though we're smoking our lungs out and think we're getting away with something, no one could care less.

Later, our bus approaches, and Mike Keys flicks the butt of a lit clove like an expert right onto Hollywood Boulevard, and we take our seats feeling like we've officially achieved cool. From that day forward smoking clove cigs on the walk to and from school has become our thing. Deviant and naïve kids from school are asking where they can get cloves too, so I start buying and re-selling cloves cigarettes while making a nice profit. If I pick up a few packs of cloves at the Hollywood tobacco shop for a $1.50 per pack, I can re-sell them for up to four bucks a pack to kids who don't know any better. The profit not only pays for my bus ride, it also supplies me with my own stash, elevates me to an almost drug pusher status, and allows me to quit my stupid paper route.

***

In Hollywood anything is possible, including meeting television stars. We can barely believe our eyes when actor Sherman Hemsley, whom we immediately recognize as George Jefferson, exits this beat-up white limousine right in front of Licorice Pizza record store on Sunset Boulevard across the street from the Whisky a Go Go one night. We follow him inside, and Mike Keys grabs a copy of Black Flag's latest LP, *Damaged*, and walks right up to him holding the record up.

"Mr. Jefferson, you should totally get this record. It's got this great song called 'TV Party' and they sing about your show. Seriously."

I could hardly believe the way Mike Keys just walked up to a huge star like George Jefferson. The only time I'd ever been in the presence of someone famous was when I saw Alice from *The Brady Bunch* in Alpha Beta supermarket one day buying a huge thing of toilet paper, but that was it.

"Really? Black Flags, huh? They any good?" Hemsley says, taking the record from Mike Keys' hands, examining the back cover.

"You think I'd be wearing this shirt if they weren't?" he shoots back like they're best friends all of a sudden, pointing to the band's logo emblazoned on his shirt that's part of the cover.

"What the hell, I'll give it a shot. Thanks, kid. Hey, here's ten bucks," he says, sliding Mike Keys a bill before heading to the jazz section, with the record under his arm.

***

Our bus jaunts give us something to look forward to after school, but on weekends, we huddle around someone's parent's TV, eat junk food, and watch the latest episodes of this local cable show, *New Wave Theater*. It's the *Saturday Night Live* of punk. It has all these bizarre skits and live music performances, who are introduced by this oddball called Peter Ivers. He brings on the bands, many of whom we've heard from Rodney — the DJ on KROQ — and asks them about the meaning of life. He's like Bob Eubanks from *The Dating Game*, or Richard Dawson from *Family Feud*, but way weirder.

On Sunday nights we gather in the den in my house to listen to Rodney Bingenheimer's radio show, Rodney on the Roq. I stumbled on it, just after we came back from Patna, and my world changed. That sweet spot all the way at the right of the FM dial became my place for finding new music, and for hearing the stuff from bands the Patna Punk Army introduced me to, like the Sex Pistols and the Clash. But mostly, Rodney plays new recordings by bands here in Los Angeles. Unlike the British bands singing about political stuff I don't understand or care much about, Rodney's playlists feature new songs by bands like X, the Go-Go's, and Black Flag. He plays music without making it seem like it's a big show. After spinning cool mixes of all this exciting new music, he tells you all about the bands in this unhurried, high-pitched voice that doesn't sound like any other

DJ. I mean, his voice doesn't even sound like a DJ or anything; it sounds more like the guy from the Carl's Jr. drive-through, which is kinda why it's so cool. Every week I've got a new favorite band. This week it's a band from Long Beach called Suburban Lawns. They're kind of a mix between Devo and the B-52s, and Rodney just announced they're playing at Magic Mountain next month. We're definitely going.

As my obsession with all this new music keeps growing, I've become really fed up with my old records. I just gathered my previously prized and worn out Cheap Trick, KISS, and ELO records, along with my brother's Styx, Kansas, and Ted Nugent LPs, and hid them on a back shelf of our den, where they're starting to collect dust.

***

My good mother, along with Mike Keys' mom, Bev, and few of my other friends' mothers are concerned with punk violence, and have united in this new parental support group called Tough Love. They attend weekly meetings in a local church on Tuesday evenings in efforts to get us kids to behave properly, even though we are mostly behaving well. The thing is, Tough Love is for parents with really screwed-up children, and I personally am not that damaged — not yet anyway. While other kids are getting locked out of their houses for ignoring their curfews and getting wasted, my good mother always welcomes me home with, "I love you, little fellow, but please call me if you're going to stay out late. I love you, son," which is why she's my good mother.

The other week we opted for a parental chauffer over taking the bus, when my good mother drove Mike Keys, Richard, me, and a couple of other punker kids we'd befriended to a live performance in Old Town Pasadena. The show was at this awesome run-down theater called Perkins Palace and featured one of our favorite bands, the Plasmatics.

We got there a couple hours early to wander around before the show, and the band were finishing their sound check. As we're puffing cloves and loitering on the street in front of the theater, a side door flies open and singer Wendy O. Williams, whom I've had more sex dreams about than I can count, along with the band — who we recognize immediately from their record covers — appear before us. Taking in Wendy O. in person, I can hardly believe my eyes. I've never been so close to someone I'd deified *and* had sexual fantasies about. And there she is, right in front of me. I'm so nervous, but not so much I can't blurt something out. "Hey, Wendy O. Can I have your autograph?" Mike Keys and Richard's confidence is finally starting to wear off on me.

She pulls a felt-tip marker from these skin-tight leather pants she's wearing. She looks as good in person as she does from album and 45 record covers.

"Yeah, sure, kid. What do you want me to sign?" she asks, like it's just another day on the job, which it might be — but for me it's a huge deal, because for the first time, I'm face to face with a rock star. I don't know what to do, so I freeze. Then I remember how cool Mike Keys was talking to Mr. Jefferson about the Black Flag record and calm down a little.

"How about this?" I say, pulling my shirt over my face, giving her full access to my hairless torso.

"Bold!" she says, laughing, and scribbling her name in big black letters across my stomach as the band members chuckle.

By show time, the venue is packed. We jam ourselves among this crowd of rowdy, punker teens and root for her as the Plasmatics jet through our favorite songs. She's in full performance mode; sporting cut-off short shorts, black go-go boots, black electrical tape crisscrossed over her nipples, and nothing else. Strutting around the stage with mad energy that's part punk rock concert and part monster truck show, she's smashing television sets with sledgehammers, and chain sawing a guitar into bits. We're having the time of our lives, throwing ourselves around the orchestra pit and off and on the stage, dodging all kinds of stuff being thrown about. All the while, I feel like she and I are almost friends because I've got her autograph right here on my stomach.

In the pit, just over from where we're scrunched in the front, these two shirtless guys start slugging each other out. It's intense. One has blood all over his face and looks hurt, but they just keep going at each other, and it seems like they're enjoying it. Then another fight breaks out and starts overpowering the music. The energy inside the theater is shifting from rock show to dude brawl, and an alarm goes off in my head. While it's a huge thrill being squished among this group of united fans and jumping around to this band I love, the last thing I want to do is see people physically hurting each other. The bombastic nature of this music is one thing, but this jockish behavior, focusing on reckless violence, is another.

Right there, surrounded by all these sweaty teenagers, I'm starting to realize how little I have to rebel against. I'm still a kid who's just starting to feel good about being in the world. I've grown to be this okay-looking kid with wart-free hands, who lives in house with a swimming pool, and has few cares. The more I look around the crowd, the more everyone looks kinda the same, and reminds me that I've been different from most of the other kids, and how horrible at group activities and sports I am. The group mentality of macho single-minded bravado is the opposite of what I thought punk was about: being different and thinking for one's self. I start thinking, "Fuck this." Trying to be punk is a fool's errand, I think, heading for the exit.

I'm standing outside when I see my friend James, who's bending his glasses back into shape after they must have gotten tweaked from getting knocked around in the slam pit.

"Man, it's crazy in there," he says, putting his glasses back on. They don't look right but I don't say anything.

"Yeah, a little too crazy," I respond. Then I notice him looking over my shoulder and onto the street.

"Uh oh. Look who's early to pick us up," he says, nodding towards my good mother's Chevy Impala, which is parked in the loading zone, right in front of the venue. My instructions for her to meet us a few blocks down the street to avoid the embarrassment of being seen getting picked by your mom have been ignored. Bam! Two large bouncers in security jackets toss a shirtless teenager with a Mohawk right onto the windshield of her car. He rolls off the car unfazed, flips them off, and disappears down the street. My good mother looks alarmed behind the wheel of her Impala, and the show lets out. A crowd of punkers spills out onto the Pasadena street like feral cats. I spot the guys and we hop in before there's any trouble by other punkers, or worse: the handful of Pasadena cops accompanied by a group of freakishly alert and straight-laced kids in berets, sporting army pants tucked in shiny boots with clean T-shirts, who call themselves "Guardian Angels." They are ready to get down to business if things get out of hand. She's not going to be thrilled about any of this. It's quiet on the ride home — I'm sure everyone knows their folks will be filled in later. Everyone gets dropped off safely and we're driving home.

"Robbie, those concerts are dangerous. That boy was thrown right on the hood of my car. I don't know why you listen to that music, or be around those people. No more punk-rock concerts!" she firmly says after dropping off Mike Keys, marking her end to concert transportation. She's right, I'm not cut out for this mean-spirited, pointless violence. No more punk rock concerts.

***

As the punk world I thought was so exciting and cool is devolving into something that's losing my interest, I notice a swarm of strange-looking teenagers moving together in a pack zipping past me on vintage Vespa scooters like an army of bees on the streets of Hollywood one afternoon. They look like some weird spy organization, wearing wrap-around sunglasses, old army parkas, and trench coats over tight-fitting suits, knowing something I don't. There's something cool about them; they have short hair and punk attitude — like a new-wave version of the Beatles. Their Vespas are decked out in all sorts of chrome rear-view mirrors and band stickers. I become obsessed with who they were, what kind of music they listen to, and what they stand for. During a visit to the Melrose shop, Poseur, I learn they called themselves "mods," and are reviving a '60s counterculture, British, youth movement. As my obsession is starting to grow, Rodney's been playing records by some of bands who are on the forefront of this small but fanatical mod revival. Bored and ready for something new, going mod seems like the punk thing to do.

Poseur on Melrose not only caters to the punks, but the mods too. I ease in to it, even though Mike Keys and Richard are diving deeper into the hardcore punk stuff, and trade my punker stylings for a messy Beatles cut, immersing myself in all things mod. The mods are amid a new thing happening in Southern California. Like the mods I first saw parading around on Vespas in moth-eaten '60s clothes from Flip with gobbed-on eyeliner, instead of slam dancing and beating each other up, they're reviving the '60s dances at underground nightclubs in Hollywood. It's a different tribe that's creating its own world, with its own bands and revival style. Lucky for me, my good mother's sister, Auntie, was a mod in the '60s and showed me a few of the mod dance moves from its original heyday. Within a couple of months, I've made another teen transformation.

My house chore allowance is spent on mod-infused power-pop records by British groups: the Jam, Buzzcocks, and Secret Affair, as well as first-wave mod groups like the Who, the Kinks, and Small Faces. I've also become obsessed with the movie *Quadrophenia*, which I took the bus to see last week in Westwood.

I'm also completely turned on by this new wave of mid-'60s ska, which has the same spirit as punk, by British bands like the Specials, the Selector, Madness, and local faves, the Untouchables. Their uplifting music electrifies me like punk did, which once again gives me a reason to get out of bed each morning. Each week, Rodney's playing new groups like the Three O'Clock, the Dream Syndicate, the Bangles, Green on Red, and the Rain Parade, and I start catching their shows at the Cathay DeGrande, the Lhasa Club, the Country Club, and the Cavern Club, submerging myself in all of it.

Aside from looks, the mod and punk worlds are two of the same. The biggest difference is the mods don't encourage violence. The mods, like the punks, have a distinct look, support live music, stay out late, and do stupid things to rebel against our smog-drenched suburban communities of LA. Both movements are quickly defining fashion and attitude, and are in unison in taking a stance against the conservative views of president Reagan and the tired, outmoded sensibilities of stoner culture. Melrose is changing, and there are new shops opening all the time, burgeoned by the growth of all this new music. The kids are wearing their fashions like badges of honor; punk, mod, new-romantic, or whatever, all of them saying, without actually saying, "Hey, look at me, I'm different."

Being one of the handful of mods has its setbacks. Three of my new friends—Eric, Chris, and Baba—former punkers who carry themselves with a cocky confidence I admire, have also become weary of the violent direction of punk, and turned mod. All of us had one thing in common: we were street-smart adventure seekers who went to great lengths for fun. Eric, Chris, and Baba were a little more hardcore. Each had been kicked out of one school or another and weren't afraid to fight if they needed to. A few of the kids I'd shared my punk record collection with last year have turned into thuggish punks and have been tormenting me for being different.

Once again, I'm getting harassed and mocked for the kind of music I like, and I'm getting sick of it. I'm being forced into feeling like I've done something wrong by choosing a new path. It hasn't stopped me, though. My mod identity belongs to me, and my independence makes me feel special.

***

Each time I head down Melrose, I notice more mod kids. It's the newest trend. However, Mike Keys and Richard are going deeper down the violent punk rock path. They became friends with the group of older and rougher punk teenagers we'd looked up to from our Pinball Palace days, and are circulating with them in a pack around town. Their look is changing too: they've started fashioning themselves after the Mexican street gangs from the '70s, and formed their own gang, BPO, an abbreviation for Burbank Punk Organization. Mike Keys showed up at my house the other day with coral-red, spiked hair and a cocky, proud grin.

"Hey, check this out," he says, removing a dark plaid Pendleton shirt buttoned up to the top. He pulls up his shirtsleeve to reveal this large mound of freshly burned flesh on his outer bicep.

"Last night a bunch of us burned crosses in our arms. Cool, eh?" I can tell he's proud of his new brand and association with his new friends.

"Yeah. Hurt much?"

"Nope. I was wasted. No one's going to fuck with us now."

"Who's fucking with you?" I ask.

"The world, dude. The world. That is, everyone who's *not* in BPO."

I'm glad he and Richard found a platform to engage his cocky confidence, but can't understand why he's dressed like a cholo.

"Why you wearing that big army coat?" he asks.

"Cause it's cool to me, that's why."

"Dude, how can that thing be cool, it's like 90 degrees today."
He's sort of right, it isn't cool in a practical sense.

I guess I can't understand why he now looks like a low rider, and he can't understand why I look like the guy from *Quadrophenia*. It's fine though, we're still best friends.

Mike Keys and Richard's new gang demands Burbank acknowledge their presence. It's nearly impossible to go more than a mile in any direction and not see those three capitalized letters, BPO, spray-painted across the city's storefronts and alleys. Claiming their stake as Burbank's premier punk gang, they've started rivaling North Hollywood's punker tribe FFF, which stands for "Fight for Freedom." Those guys are led by a nearly mythical figure known as Ranger, who's known to smash teeth or torture anyone in his path whose look he doesn't like. The two gangs are territorial enemies, and spend their days and nights hating and hunting one another. The anger and punk violence is even worse than before. I'm glad I've moved away from it.

Mike Keys and Richard have taken on gang names, and now call themselves Flaco and Otto, and have submerged themselves deeper in this newfound gang life. But no matter what, I'm still calling them Mike Keys and Richard. Last night they came by for a visit.

"Robbie, give up the mod shit. We're having a blast going around fucking shit up. There's a bunch of us now; it's so cool, way cooler than this stuff you're into. We go to shows and take out anyone who thinks they can take us." Mike Keys says, as some sort of half-baked recruitment pitch.

"Yeah, no. Not my thing right now."

Their suburban white combat just isn't appealing, especially while I much prefer spazzing out to the Jam over the latest Discharge album. The violence and chaos they're embracing are no more appealing than two hands full of groaty warts.

"Whatever. We've always got your back, bro. Friends for life?" Mike Keys says, in this almost sad voice he almost never uses.

The writing's on the wall: their lives are going one way and mine another. We stay close buds, but there's no way I'm joining them. Aside from how we look and the records we think are great, we've got our own brotherly bond that's stronger than any piece of clothing or vinyl.

"Yeah, friends for life."

SKIPJACK

" ' I BET YOU'D like to ride the Skipjack, wouldn't you?"
      "Shut up, Gordy. You would! Ya faggot!"
      "No, you would, dickhead! Just you and Mr. R, fagging out, somewhere out at Fag Sea."

My older brother Gordy and his friends Brian and Jeff are goofing around, saying "fag" a lot while wrestling shirtless in the den, listening to a Ted Nugent record. I'm on the couch, reading *MAD Magazine*, thinking they smell like nasty B.O.. Gordy's managed to get them both in a headlock under each of his arms and he's not letting up.

"He'll take you two queer baits up the butt and reward you with extra credit. You'll love every minute of it!" he says, releasing them. After tiring each other out with all the shirtless hugging, they go back to their pre-calculus homework. One thing about Gordy and his friends is that they play hard, but are also straight-A students.

Riding the Skipjack is a roundabout way of saying you are gay, and Mr. R is the captain of the boat. He's also the junior-high metal shop teacher. In-the-know students say he has more than metal on his mind. Over the years he's become known for perving on pet students while taking them out on his fishing boat, the Skipjack. They say he invites favored students to work on metal projects while motoring around the San Pedro harbor on weekends in exchange for extra credit. Once onboard, he gets them drunk and has his way with them. But this is all hearsay, and Gordy and his friends are too smart to take a class like metal shop anyhow. They just want to feel like they're in the know. Actually, nobody we know has proof there's even a Skipjack at all, but the rumors about it, and Mr. R, have become Burbank legend among teenage boys.

***

It's the first day of ninth grade and I see that metal shop is one of the several elective classes offered. I choose it over wood shop for two reasons. The first is because I want to satisfy my morbid curiosity and see the man behind the Skipjack stories in person, and the second is because I've heard that as long as you show up you'll receive a passing grade. The one bummer is that it's in the depressing Industrial Arts building at the farthest end of school, which must be what all of Russia looks like, I think. It's also away from the required math, science, and history classes that I've been struggling with, but where all the hallway action is going down.

I take a seat in the back of the class and am glad to see my good pal from the video arcade, Robert Sullivan, whom I nickenamed Sully, is also in the class. He's also hip to the rumors about Mr. R, who's going on about safety rules or something.

"That old bastard is too old, fat, and normal looking to be a pervert. There's no way he's boinking kids," Sully whispers to me as we're observing the class from its back row of seats. I nod in agreement.

Judging by Mr. R's looks, he doesn't appear to be any kind of weirdo. He's this giant of a man with a big, deep voice. He looks like most of my teachers do, like they're from the 1950s. His salt-and-pepper hair is neatly slicked back above his thick, black-framed, Coke-bottle glasses, which almost help conceal a wonky left eye. He's mastered teaching, and has this calm, but firm, control over his students. He conducts class with a stern authority, barking projects and interacting very little with most of us students—a bunch of burnouts, stoners, and other kids who aren't smart enough to take classes like Journalism or Advanced Math for their electives. The first few weeks of class are uneventful. We work on boring projects and learn basic metal casting, but its actually kind of fun.

Around a month into the semester, I receive a call slip from the administrative office to report to Mr. R during his break period. I have no idea why he wants to see me — no teachers have ever wanted to see me during their break period. So after lunch I head into his empty classroom wondering what's going on. I head in, being reminded that classrooms are the eeriest places when they're not in session. Metal shop is no exception, and it's even more creepy because it's in the Industrial Arts building. The room is still and quiet, reeking of WD-40 and rusted metal. Looking around the empty classroom, I assume the slip must be some sort of mistake and start to leave.

"Up here, kid," comes his deep voice out of nowhere. I'm jumpy when something surprises me, so jump pretty good as I hear something unexpected like that. Then I look up and see him. He's looking down, waving me up to join him.

I climbed each step of the ladder like a moth to a flame. If I could see for my own eyes he was the weirdo everyone said he was, I'd add him to the list of freaky guys like Uncle Ed and Ray from Pinball Palace, as a reminder that not all adults should be trusted.

I follow the voice and nervously climb up the wooden ladder, with the slip gripped in my hand. As I stand to face him, I wonder exactly how his enormous pear-shaped body ever made it up here. He's behind a large metal desk with a cigarette burning in a round, metal ashtray, looking very relaxed.

"Sit down," he says in an unfamiliar friendly voice. It's a different tone than the one he uses during class. I feel chills crawling up my back and my mouth dries up. I don't know where this is going but am certain I'm about to find out.

"I like you, kid," he grumbles with confident conviction, which is followed by a long and uncomfortable pause. "Smoke?" he asks, slowly sliding a pack of Lucky Strikes toward me on the desktop.

"No, thanks," I say, reminded of a fresh pack of sweet cloves I have concealed in my jean jacket. For all I know he's offering me a cig so he can bust me. Then I notice him slowly looking me up and down with his one functioning eye. Perched in his private musty nest, this unknown fear sets in, like the kind I felt right before Uncle Ed shot me, and it sends a shiver down my spine. Then I discover a stack of *Playboy* magazines sitting on a rusty, metal, file cabinet over his shoulder. "You like? Be my guest," he says, gesturing to the mags after seeing I've acknowledged them. I'm a young teenager, and have been experiencing plenty of boner popping, but have no intention of sharing any of that stuff with Mr. R. My heart's racing hard now, and all I want to do is climb down the ladder and bail. The trouble is, I've been taught by my parents to respect adults and elders, especially teachers. My mind is racing like a pinball, wondering what's going on.

"You're doing okay in my class, but I'd like to offer you some extra credit by coming out on my private boat, the Skipjack. You'd like it," he says with this nonchalant coolness. As the words are leaving his mouth, I can barely believe what I'm hearing. Holy smokes, I've been chosen, and the Skipjack is a real thing, I think, sitting frozen and too scared to decline. Then, some unexplainable survival instinct kicks in.

"Okay. But is it okay if I bring along a friend in the class, too? Robert Sullivan?"

He pauses, and looks me up and down again. "I like you, kid. Okay. We sail early next Saturday morning. You'll need a sack lunch, a jacket, and a towel."

"Towel?"

"Yes. We take a mandatory shower at the San Pedro Naval Base at the end of the day. I can't bring you home smelling like a sailor."

"Ha, I guess not," I agreeably force out.

Amidst the strange realization of knowing the Skipjack is legit, I know that soon I'll witness something most kids never will, and somehow it gives me a little rush.

***

The following overcast Saturday morning, Sully and I devour half-a-dozen Winchell's donuts at my house before my father drops us off at Mr. R's place. We pull up to his address, and see that Mr. R's house is the one on the block that doesn't go with the others. The outside gives you the impression it might be abandoned, kind of like Boo Radley's place in *To Kill a Mockingbird* — old paint chipping from walls that look like they hadn't been painted since it was built in the '50s, filthy screens cover some but not all the windows, and a porch with stacks of piled newspapers covered in cobwebs. Plus, there are unidentifiable metal objects in rusty heaps piled on his dead front lawn.

"You say he's a teacher? Somebody better teach him to get all that shit off his lawn. Somebody's gonna trip on something and break their neck. What a shithole," barks my father with a Roi-Tan clenched between his teeth.

We grab our backpacks and head through the cracked cement driveway, to discover some kids in the backyard, which is in the same shape as the front. There's a handful of other boys; a couple of pimple-faced stoners and awkwardly quiet guys we barely recognize from class. Judging from how relaxed they are, they gotta be regular Skipjack crew members. From a barely attached back door strolls Mr. R, and he's already tipsy. Everyone looks at him. He's got a case of Olympia beer under his fat hairy arms.

"What's the difference between a Catholic priest and a zit? At least the zit waits until you're a teenager before it cums on your face! Ha, I love that one," he says, carrying the beer over to a trashed, fifteen-seat, yellow, short bus that's halfway in the garage, looking like it too is ready for the scrap heap.

About ten of us board the bus, which, after several false starts, eventually turns over and starts to move. It somehow maneuvers down the 110 freeway and parks near a dock in San Pedro. We help load a few boxes of metal contraptions and gadgets that look like nothing more than rusted old junk, along with beer, onto the dock. The other kids all seem to know the ropes and assist with various duties.

Sully and I look at one another with raised eyebrows, wondering what's next.

Mr. R establishes his role as Captain. He's wobbling on a nearby jetty, spouting some incomprehensible sea jargon in a bad pirate voice that's too hard to understand. His incantation concludes as he pulls out his privates, and whizzes in the Pedro harbor, humming, "Yo Ho Ho Ho, a pirate's life for me." He's quite a sight; his Santa Claus frame almost overshadows, but doesn't quite hide something I don't want to see: his mutant penis, which looks just like a wilted fig. It's a foul sight but for some reason I can't look away. He sees me, and I wish he didn't.

"Ye want some of this, Robbie matey? Argh! I bet ye do!" he says in that stupid Captain Hook homo-swagger that seems to be setting the tone for the rest of day.

I turn my eyes away and discover the floating legend, The Skipjack. It's this barely floating hunk of junk—an old fifty-foot fishing boat that, like his house and bus, needs major work or a haul to the junkyard. At the front, the ship's name appears crudely in faded lettering. Sully and I give each other that look again and I reluctantly follow the others, being the last one to board. Suddenly, everything about being here seems like a bad idea. We stay close to each other and keep our wits about us. I think I'm an idiot, that seeing the Skipjack in person might be a thrilling adventure, but in real life, it's all just gross. Now, I've gotten myself, and Sully, into this awful thing. And now it's too late—we've left the dock.

The perverse tension brought on by our drunk captain is keeping us alert. We decline an offer from the other kids to chug beers. "It's okay, he won't tell your folks. Mr. R's totally cool," one of them says, offering us each a can of Olympia. "We're cool," I reply with a friendly but cold stare that really says, "Fuck off and leave us alone." This is no time to lose control, and Sully and I both know it. We stay sharp and sober, hanging in the shadows of the frolicking beer cruise that's in full swing. Before long, our group of teenage boys and their drunken leader are in the thick of the harbor amidst the weekend boat traffic, looking out to the murky San Pedro waters. After a while, the morning overcast burns off and soon it's a clear, sunny, picture-perfect, Saturday afternoon in Southern California.

A couple hours into the voyage, Mr. R approaches Sully and me on the deck. By now, he looks more like a hobo than a schoolteacher. His shirt is gone and he's down to a heavily soiled wife-beater tank top, Captain's hat, and sagging, worn-out work pants. He hands the two of us this box of rusty, metal, motor-part contraptions and some screwdrivers. "Here's your extra credit. Take these apart and put them back together. You'll figure it out," he slurs, with a body language that suggests he doesn't give a damn if we complete the task or not. The work doesn't matter, but justifies the academic purpose of our field trip. As he wobbles off, Sully and I look at each other in silent agreement and plop the parts overboard, grinning at each other as they splash and sink into the dirty San Pedro water forever.

In our backpacks, we've packed a couple of borrowed wet-suits along with our sack lunches and towels. We suit up, keeping to ourselves, quietly observing the other kids pounding beers, smoking cigs, and having what appears to be the time of their lives. We climb to the highest point of the Skipjack, a shaky, splintering mast, and jump into the icy San Pedro water. After a few high jumps, we dry off, put on our clothes, and eat our sack lunches and dangle our feet off the side of the barely floating boat, when one of Mr. R's lackeys appears. He's so drunk he can barely stand.

"Robbie. What's up, bro? Mr. R wants you in the Captain's Quarters," he gets out in what sounds like one word. Reluctantly, I leave Sully and duck into the cramped quarters that are the Skipjack's pilothouse. As I step down and look inside the dark quarters — this small musty room with a low ceiling and large steering wheel — I can see Mr. R is more drunk than before. Like my last day in the video arcade, I stepped in knowing in my right mind it was a big mistake, a human error. But some broken part of me craved that first-hand account. And here it was.

"Take the wheel, kid," he mumbles in an assertive tone, nodding to the Skipjack's large and wooden steering device. In my history of doing stupid things, taking the wheel of the Skipjack just took, hands down, first place. Dropping my shooting adventures with Uncle Ed after I knew damn well he was a lunatic down to solid second. I take the wheel and hold on for my life.

Before I have any time to get my balance and get a good grip on the wheel, I feel the strong pressure and demanding physical strength it takes to steer a boat. As the Skipjack gently rocks from side to side, I grip the wheel and try to manage it, feeling these strong pulls from both sides. I think I'm getting a sense of how the Skipjack steers, when Mr. R starts moving towards me from behind. Every muscle in my body cringes while he's positioning himself directly behind me. It's like the first 30 seconds of the Jaws music. You just know something bad's about to happen. And it does, starting with him placing his dirty, bloated hands over mine. His sandpaper-like mitts start massaging my hands that are gripping the ship's wheel. Trapped in the claws of Captain Sicko, some broken part of me was thriving from the surge of energy erupting from the heightening madness.

"Yeah, you're getting it," he whispers in my ear through stenchy beer breath. With my heart racing, blurry vision, and this vertigo that's getting worse by the second, I'm trapped as his prisoner. I look ahead through the filthy window into the dismal harbor, realizing there's nowhere to escape. I'm thinking fast about my options, or lack of them, when I feel Mr. R's crotch grinding on my lower back, followed by these awkward pelvic thrusts. It's as if some farm animal is humping on me — nothing about it feels good and I just want it to stop. I'm horrified, and too scared to let go of the wheel and tear out of there, which might mean capsizing the Skipjack and drowning.

I'm holding the wheel for my life, getting humped by this monster, and all I can think is big deal; now I know for sure Mr. R is a full on perv, but knowing this doesn't mean a damn thing because I'm that teenage boy in the middle of one of his monstrous flare-ups. Among some grunts and incoherent whispers coming from under his beer breath, he says, "I really do like you, kid," like he said back when we were up in his metal shop loft.

I can no longer stand it. I shove my body back and release myself from his grip and squirm out from under him. Then all in one motion, I duck, roll, hit a cabin wall, get up, and head for the door. He's forced to take hold of the wheel as it begins to spin.

"Hey! Where you going? I'm showing you how to steer this boat! Get back here, kid!" I look for Sully, who's on the deck where I last saw him.

"Man, Mr. R was just getting crazy on me. He's drunk and out of his mind, humping me like a hippo," I say, letting out the biggest sigh I ever had. Telling Sully feels like a near déjà vu experience of the day I told Jason that Uncle Ed had shot me. With a dropped jaw, I can see he can barely believes me, but he does.

"Fuck, man, really? That's horrible. Really? Sick creep. Well, now we know he's a sicko. Hope he doesn't call me in next. Swear to God, I'll deck that fat bastard if he lays so much as one finger on me!"

We distance ourselves from the other kids, who are grouped together in the Skipjack's moldy sleeping quarters, drinking beers, smoking cigs, and flipping through girlie mags. Now, in full defense mode, Sully and I look at each other and shake our heads, calling B.S. on this extra-credit misadventure. I don't care what grade I get on my report card now, I just want to go home and forget what just happened.

Shortly after the humping debacle, the Skipjack docks and everyone exits. We stay clear of Mr. R and board his thrashed bus, forgetting we have one dreadful final stop: showering at the Fort MacArthur Naval Base, where we are required to clean up before going home. By then, all the other kids were drunk, goofing with each other, and joking about Mr. R's perversions and advancements. The crazy thing is, none of them seem to mind. As we pull into the naval base, everyone but us knows the shower drill. They undress with Mr. R and enter this big, steamy, shower room with several showerheads that look like the one I'd seen at Alcatraz during a Zabrecky family vacation in San Francisco. As they shower and carry on, Sully and I hang cautiously behind and discover our own victory: an adjacent shower room, where a couple of normal and sane looking navy guys are soaping up and minding their own business. "Perfect. We're safe here," Sully says with major relief. As we quickly undress and run ourselves under hot water, Mr. R appears through this thick billow of steam, wearing nothing but those thick-rimmed glasses.

"We shower together here," he says non-negoitably.

The tone of his voice has changed since escaping his perv grip. He's back to sounding like a total asshole metal shop teacher. I can hear echoing sounds of the boys in the other shower room, laughing, whipping towels, and jabbing each other. Defeated, we wrap ourselves in our beach towels, and follow him down the hall of steam to join the other naked boys, who don't acknowledge or pay much attention to us. Nor does Mr. R, who's somehow accepted we aren't going to join the action. Sully and I take the quickest and most self-conscious showers of our lives, get the hell dressed, and bolt to the rear of the bus.

It's a quiet ride home. Most of the other kids are sleeping off their buzzes while my mind cruelly replays the too recent memory of Mr. R mauling me during the Skipjack hell ride. This voice inside starts telling me I should be more assertive at school and challenge myself by taking harder classes, instead of the ones taught by freakazoids like Mr. R.

It's late afternoon, and we arrive back at Mr. R's junk palace, where my good mother is there to pick up Sully and me. "It's probably best if we keep this to ourselves," Sully says in some knowing way. He's way smarter than I am, so most of the time I try and agree with him, and later figure out what I'm agreeing with. "Yeah, you're right. I guess you had to be there," I say as we hop inside my good mother's Chevy Impala, pulling away from Mr. R's.

On Monday, I return to class to learn I'm invisible to Mr. R. He doesn't look at, acknowledge, or ask me back for another weekend adventure of extra credit, and I can't be more relieved. My grim curiosity about Skipjack mythology is dead and I just want to forget about it. But I can't. For days and months afterward, I dread these flashbacks I can't seem to shake from that day in the harbor. Mr. R is showing up in bad dreams—like the ones I'd been having, seeing Uncle Ed in the bushes pointing a rifle at me, and the others of Ray at Pinball Palace, closing in on my neck like a thirsty vampire.

***

To my surprise, at the end of the semester I receive an A in metal shop. I avoid the Industrial Arts area of the school from then on. The next semester, I take a drama class as an elective to finish off ninth grade. While performing acting exercises with other students, who are different than the kind who take metal shop, I'm learning I don't mind standing on the auditorium stage with lights shining in my face, pretending to be someone else. It's actually kind of fun. Being onstage reminds me of the innocent times I spent running around on the auditorium stage at my grandpa's Masonic Temple in Pasadena when I was a little kid, and feeling empowered to imagine myself as some dreamed-up character.

Drama class encourages all these ideas of make believe, sometimes pretending to be a piece of growing grass in a distant, rolling field in front of a bunch of other kids, other times a hobo begging for money — which beats making doorstop molds out of hot metal while being eye-fucked by a disgusting teacher. It's the end of ninth grade and I'm more than ready for a change of setting and starting high school. I have this feeling it's going to kick in at rocket speed.

JAMES & THE
PARISH INDIANS

FROM A DISTANCE, the parking lot at John Burroughs High School could be a location for a John Hughes movie. Designated as the ground-zero hangout by the hip and fad-crazed students who camp out here, it buzzes with teenage excitement and celebrates every important thing that's defining the 1980s. As the black-tarred parking lot warms up each morning, kids gather around hand-me-down cars to puff clove cigarettes, goop on eyeliner, and apply last blasts of hairspray before rushing off to class. Monday through Friday, week after week, MTV music blares from car stereos across the street from our Rockwellian campus that looks unchanged since the 1950s.

Inside the busy halls, students weave through one another — there are jocks and cheerleaders in red-and-white letterman jackets adorned with our Indian mascot; preps in brightly-colored polo shirts and Bermuda shorts; big-haired rockers in bedazzled, shoulder-padded, jean jackets; punkers with spiky hair and flannel shirts; Beatle-haired mods in vintage button-down shirts, sweaters, and drainpipe pants; and innocent kids still dressed by their parents — everyone gripping Pee Chee folders and colorful plastic binders with way too many compartments.

I might only be 15 and it's my sophomore year, but on the first day I figure out that each clique exists with delusions of individuality. So many kids want to be different and stand out in the crowd, they've all ended up looking the same. Every hundred yards or so you can spot one clique or another. I'm not that dumb to know this is also the case for me and my small clique of mods. We are, like most kids, attempting to disguise the fact that we're simply teenagers in search of identity.

After the first morning-break bell rings, we move in our packs to socialize according to our musical preferences. On one end of the campus, the Keystone Street side, the stoners, rockers, and heavy-metal kids hang out puffing cigs, smoking weed, and blaring AC/DC or Iron Maiden from boom boxes. They're known, appropriately, as Keystoners. On the first day of school, I gravitated to the other side, on Parish Street, where the new wavers, punkers, new-romantics, and mods hold court to smoke their lungs out, chew wads of Bubble Yum, chat about who's messing around with who, and learn where the house parties are on Saturday night.

Among the cool kids on Parish Street, I'm meeting new friends from all the circles and have a handful of heated crushes on new-wave babes. After long school days, I fall asleep dreaming of foxy Madonna look-a-likes and cute girls with oblong hairstyles in heavy make-up who look like they belong in MTV videos. Too often though, those dreams get interrupted, and then ruined, with eerie re-runs of Mr. R grinding my backside, Ron the Christ-loving pinball perv, or Uncle Ed pointing that damned rifle at me. I'd like to take the big pink eraser I'm using for my math homework and wipe those memories away for once and for all.

***

One day during my sophomore year, I'm in my room listening to records and doing homework and there's a knock at the door. It's my old bud James, who has gone super-punk; his hair is madly spiked and he's got on this cut-off jean jacket with metal studs and patches all over it, plaid bondage pants, and leopard-print creeper-soled shoes, and his distinctive trademark: his wire-rimmed glasses.

"So I finally got a job. I'm working nights over at the Taco Bell on Magnolia," he says, sounding less than enthused about his new gig.

"They say I can't start until I have a pair of black work shoes. They aren't cool letting me wear these babies," he says gesturing down at his creepers.

"Got an extra pair of old black shoes I can borrow?"

"Come on in, let's see what I can find," I say, as we head to my room.

I go dig up a beat-up pair of old black lace-up shoes from the back of my father's closet, figuring he'll never know they were missing.

"These okay?" I say, showing him the pair of dusty shoes. James pops off one of his creepers, slips his foot in, and wiggles it around.

"Hmm, they're a little big."

"Be right back," I say, running to the kitchen to grab some scissors. I grab a dirty sock, cut it in half, and shove one half in the toe of each shoe. He thrusts his foot back in one of them.

"Perfect. Thanks, man. I'll give 'em back after they fire me."

"Yeah," I said. "Maybe I'll take your job. I need one."

I liked James for lots of reasons, but mostly because he was kinder and smarter than most kids, and like Mike Keys and Richard, was fearless. When we met, he was this small-framed, long-haired, gangly kid in those wire-rimmed glasses who listened to Rush and AC/DC. During a brief stint as miserable benchwarmers on our town's youth tackle-football team a few years earlier, he started coming over to my house to listen to punk records and eat junk food. He was with me the night the guy with the Mohawk got thrown on my good mother's car at the Plasmatics' show at Perkins Palace. He loved talking about that night.

"I'll never forget the look in your mom's eyes after that guy rolled off the hood of the Impala. That was classic."

"She's still not happy about that. Hey, want a Twinkie?" I offer, feeling my sweet tooth kicking in.

"Sure," he says, plopping himself on my bed.

"Want yours heated up in the microwave and soaked in pancake syrup? It's better that way."

"Uh, no thanks, just regular."

For some reason whenever I offer my hot Twinkie recipe to anyone they decline.

"Ok, be right back."

I return with a plate of four Twinkies, two of which have been loaded with syrup and microwaved, and two glasses of milk.

We hung around the rest of the afternoon, taking turns talking about music and high school. I'm in my target T-shirt, pork pie hat, drainpipe trousers, spinning my latest records—45s and album cuts by the Jam, Buzzcocks, and Specials—while he's going on about his obsession with new *Oi!* groups like the Exploited, Discharge, and Crass.

"It's funny, the bands we're into now sound pretty different, but the message is pretty much the same, isn't it? Youth rebellion!" James says in this smart way. He's always saying smart stuff like that.

"Thanks for the shoes, and the Twinkies. Come by Taco Bell and visit sometime. They have me on night shifts," he says, hopping on his 10 speed and taking off.

Not long after taking the job at Taco Bell, his mother — this nice lady who'd been raising him on her own — dropped him off in the early evening for a shift he wouldn't finish. While closing up at the end of the night, James and his supervisor were visited by a former disgruntled employee who'd turned into a lunatic. He entered the restaurant on an armed and destructive mission. After stealing $650 from the cash register, he ordered James and his manager, who had fired the guy earlier that year, into a room at the back of the building. There, he cold-bloodedly shot them both execution style — once each in the back of their heads with a .22-caliber bullet — and fled the scene.

Nearby neighbors heard the shots and called the police, who found the manager dead and James in a coma. Everyone who knew James was wandering around in this messed up and confused daze, just hoping he'd pull through. Somewhere in a deep coma, James survived almost two weeks, but didn't make it. Robbed from the world was this whip-smart, sixteen-year-old, eleventh grader, enamored with new music and an underlying sensibility that let you know he was going to end up doing something interesting in life.

James was the first friend I'd lost, and it hit me hard. Burbank's this safe, boring place — nobody gets murdered at work, or anywhere. Inside classrooms, out of nowhere, the sadness of knowing he was gone, and the brutal way his life was taken, heaved up out of nowhere and I fought urges to cry. Sometimes when I couldn't hold back tears, I'd step out to the school restroom, hide in a stall, spark a clove, and absorb this unfamiliar void and confusing pain knowing his life was over. Everyone who knew him huddled around between classes to share the near disbelief he was, out of nowhere, gone.

Five days after the shootings, police arrested a suspect while he was sleeping in a car in North Hollywood. He maintained innocence throughout the trial, and was later sentenced to death for the murders. After the shock and sadness of James' passing, life moved fast into the '80s.

Friends support mother of slain boy during service

By CATHY FRANKLIN
Staff Writer

ARLETA — Bathed in soft blues, a portrait of James Michael Falconio gazed out at 75 friends and relatives crowded into a small church sanctuary Tuesday to remember the slain youth in a memorial service.

Many participants cried, clung to each other for comfort and praised the youth killed last month in a robbery.

"A fine young man," was the phrase used most by stricken classmates and teachers to describe the 16-year-old Burroughs High School student.

Other adjectives used by friends were "happy," "unique," "well loved."

"He had a keen sense of right direction. You should feel very proud of your fine, young son," one of James' former teachers wrote.

The teacher's words, along with excerpts from other letters sent to the family, were read by the Rev. Larry Bassett. The hour-long service was held at the non-denominational Galvotce Neighborhood Church in Arleta where James and his mother, Rose, attended several Sunday services.

Falconio and Taco Bell restaurant manager Lindell Hunter were shot Sept. 17 during a robbery at the West Magnolia Boulevard stand. Hunter died immediately but Falconio, a clerk who had filled in for another employee that night, lingered in a coma for 11 days.

North Hollywood transient William Kirkpatrick was arrested five days after the robbery and and charged with murder. He is scheduled for preliminary hearing Nov. 17.

Bassett spoke several times about senselessness of Falconio's death.

"I was extremely angry when I first encountered James' mother and heard the details. The first thing I asked was 'why?'," Bassett said.

See MEMORIAL SERVICE page three

Rose Falconio, flanked by the family of her son's friend Dee Dee Record, sits through a memorial service for her 16-year-old son James, killed when the Taco Bell he worked at was robbed.

Burbank Daily Review

***

"It's always boring in the 'Bank," declare its wild youth. It's like when someone says, "Where's my keys?" and Mike Keys says, "Mike Keys, I'm right here!" It's kind of stupid, but it's funny when you hear it. But kicking around Burbank can be a thrill too, and I'm not one to decline an opportunity to let loose on home turf. If fake IDs, like the one I picked up at the Pasadena Rose Bowl swap meet last month, are a bust, we stand outside liquor stores like a bunch of idiots and ask adults to buy us alcohol and get wasted in nearby alleys. We always find someone, usually a guy in his early twenties, to pimp us Peppermint Schnapps and a twelve-pack of Miller beer and then give him an extra few bucks for doing us such a cool favor. Then, we tuck back in an alley, pound everything till it's gone, and head out into the night. For me, bringing the bottle to my mouth for the first time wasn't easy.

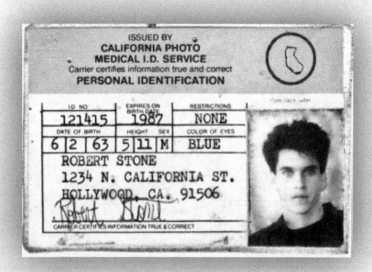

God knows how many times since the demise of Uncle Ed I've convinced myself that one sip of anything would send me down the road to becoming him. I've turned down swigs of this or that a number times, but one Friday night six months or so ago, my curiosity overpowered my fears. I took my chances with Mike Keys and a few other guys before hitting a house party. Just after dark, we pimped a huge bottle of Peppermint Schnapps at La Paz liquor store and huddled in a nearby alley. The bottle, wrapped in its brown paper bag, was quietly passed around so nobody in the nearby houses called the cops or anything. When it was my turn and someone handed me the bottle, I didn't mention it was my first time or anything, I just went for it and managed a huge mouthful down my throat. It burned going down, as it did when I was certain it was coming back up, but thank God it didn't. As it settled, I stared at the alley asphalt smelling my powerful minty breath as this warm rush washed over me. Then I started feeling relaxed and at ease. After four or five swigs I felt as good as I ever had. We headed out to couple of parties, where I had zero trouble talking to anyone or asking girls for their phone numbers.

From there, pounding alcohol on weekends and sometimes on school nights becomes a regular thing. It's hard to gauge when to stop, and how much is enough, though. A few times, I've fallen into drinking blackouts, where I don't remember what happened because I got too wasted. No matter how drunk I get, I'm pretty good at sneaking in the front door and walking a straight line to my bedroom, where I remind myself that the promise I'd made to myself after seeing Uncle Ed self-destruct was broken.

Overall, I'm digging the high-school experience — not the education aspects so much, but the social side of it. There's lots of cool kids I've been meeting up with, who gather on weekends to rally up to the Hollywood sign. It's an all night thing, where everyone camps out below the towering letters to lose their minds; some by drinking, others by smoking weed, sniffing cocaine, or taking acid.

On other nights, legions of teenagers pile into each other's cars and head to a favorite party spot, the Pickwick Drive-In Theater. The drive-in is this Burbank landmark and familiar to every kid from childhood who's grown up here, but it's seen better days. Its massive space and lack of security make it one of the easiest places to get loaded and hook up with other teenagers with zero risk of getting caught.

***

The Hollywood sign or the Pickwick, especially on warm summer nights are both prime places to let loose, but there is never, ever a dull moment when we head over the hill to Universal City, break into Universal Studios. and take ourselves on self-guided tours on the famous backlot. It's the best, free thing to do in the world.

After the police dismantle unauthorized house parties, or the lights go up at Pickwick Drive In and everyone has to leave, those of us with late, or no, curfews found a cure for night ennui by sneaking in and wandering around the old movie studio. Sometimes up to a dozen of us pile into old Volkswagens and caravan over Barham Boulevard and up the long driveway that leads to the motion-picture studio and daytime tourist attraction.

We pull in, kill the headlights, and park at a far end of the empty parking lot where everything is still and dead — like a grocery-store parking lot on a Sunday night after closing. In the distance below, the street lamps and houses of Universal City pulsate in mushy soft shades of yellowish glow.

Gaining admittance is simple, but everyone risks paying the looming admission price: getting arrested. Here's how you get in: at the far end of the parking lot there's this tall chain-link fence covered with overgrown shrubbery that, if you follow it, will reveal a clipped opening just big enough to squeeze under. One by one, we scurry under it and quietly move through a few feet of thick bushes. For a group of guys that doesn't play team sports, we're an agile bunch. Moving with this group of dudes with a single goal makes me feel like the Eagle Scout I never was.

Once in, the place is ours. The first destination is only a few hundred feet away, down a moonlit dirt road lined with tall grass. It's the iconic old house created for Hitchcock's classic thriller, *Psycho*. We move in our pack to the porch, usually with a twelve-pack of Miller or a bottle of hard stuff, trying to remain unnoticed. The Bates front door is always unlocked. In case you didn't know, the exterior of the house is, as buildings on movie sets are, nothing more than a façade. The inside, which you'd think would look like it does in the movie — with the antique furniture and everything — is nothing more than this disappointing empty shell with supporting beams going in every direction. On the Bates porch we drink and smoke cigarettes while re-enacting parts of *Psycho*, scoping out the dark lot below. I'm reminded of those times parading around the ghost light on the stage in the Lodge auditorium in Pasadena, doing something I shouldn't, pretending I'm someone else. I guess the only difference is now I'm doing it with friends.

After exhausting the thrill of creeping in and visiting the Bates residence, our pack sojourns down this steep and winding paved road used by the centipede-like tourist trams during the day to haul sunburned tourists through the sacred historical grounds of Tinsel Town. Leaving behind a trail of empty beer cans and cigarette butts, we move down this winding road in a semi-swift, stealthy manner to the famed *Jaws* set and kick around on the sandy beach created for the film. We gawk at the "Amity Island Welcomes You" sign and swap stories in loud whispers about being so frightened by the movie when it came out, how some of us were too scared to swim in pools or take baths.

Once beyond the *Jaws* set, the nerves of sliding in wear off and we wander around like we own the place. We're free to explore the depths of this make-believe world, with this false sense of entitlement leading the way. The thrill of being so close to those facades sends chills down my spine every time. This dark and shut-down world puts endless questions in our heads, wondering what films the less recognizable sets had been used in, and what it must feel like to be a movie star.

The bendy black asphalt roads lead to different corners of the world: New York City, Mexico, or Europe. Italy or France? It never matters where we end up and we don't really care. We just don't want the night to end. What matters is the adventure of it all, that we're pulling a fast one over on Universal each time we go, which somehow provides a victory.

Tonight we're under the moon, gawking at the *The Munsters'* residence at 1313 Mockingbird Lane, which is only a few doors from *The Waltons'* house, which is a few doors from the *Leave it to Beaver* house, in case you didn't know. We start a buzzed version of hide-and-seek, rumbling on the lawns of these iconic TV land sets, thinking we own the place. Everything's going great until someone decides they need to throw a beer bottle right through the Waltons' living room window. Mike Keys takes control like he always does.

"Guys! We're blowing it. That show sucks but don't break stuff! You wanna get us busted? Geez. What the fuck's wrong with you, ya'spazzy fucks? Keep it cool. Everyone needs to take a chill pill." he says in the loudest whisper-yell I've ever heard. Of course, he's right. Because the next thing we see is the sight of distant headlights from a security cart coming our direction. The headlights are the unspoken signal either to run like hell back to our mini fleet of cars, or hide in the bushes and freeze stiff like plastic army men in shrubbery until the security cart passes.

I took this girl named Shari I met at the Odyssey nightclub there for our first date. Shari's this adventurous new-wave teen from Encino with crazy big blue eyes who loves to party and mess around. We got as far as the *Jaws* set, where we started making out on the moonlit sand and put our hands all over each other. I undo her bra and unbutton her blouse, which reveals perfectly formed breasts that she's very proud of, and she unzips my pants. She reaches under her multi-layered tulle skirt, whisks off her panties, spreads open her beautifully smooth legs, and guides me to her. I'm certain we're going all the way, right there on the set from one of my favorite films. My virginity — like the movies filmed on the backlot — was about to be history. Then in the distance, slowly creeping in like the Jaws Theme Song, come the headlights of a damn security cart, forcing us to grab our clothes and make the quick dash back to her VW convertible Rabbit.

On nights like these, time stands still. The backlot and its empty streets feel like the perfect time and place to get lost and be alive. Disappearing inside Universal's fake world after dark is far more exciting than the real one I'm trying to grow up in.

***

"Robbie, have you heard?" Baba says, grabbing my arm and pulling me aside in the busy hallway. "Tyrone's gone dark psychedelic." I give him the same intense look he's giving me, then shake my head in agreement, pretending to know what he's talking about. I don't have a clue what dark psychedelic means, but there's something so intense about the way he said it that it demands my full attention. "He's quit being mod. You gotta see him—he looks totally different. He's wearing all black, full makeup, and teasing his hair up like a giant black mushroom. Now, he only listens to dark and depressing stuff like Christian Death, Siouxsie and the Banshees, and Bauhaus." Of all the mod kids, I admired Tyrone the most. Like Mike Keys, everything about him was cool. He was a spitting image of the Who's Keith Moon and played drums for a band called Sidewalk Society, this power-pop trio from North Hollywood, but now that he's gone dark psychedelic, I feel like I might never see him again.

Soon after Tyrone transitioned to looking like the living's afterlife, some other friends and schoolmates also transformed into this ghoulish new subculture that's now known as Death Rock. While other kids were changing their appearances, Mike Keys remains the king of cool and is the punk-rock James Dean of our town. He didn't make it past the first semester of 10th grade before dropping out, but shows up most days in the school parking lot around lunch in his barely running '60s Dodge Dart, looking cool as ever, to join us at Pup'N Taco or Pizza Prince.

Although I'm getting an A+ in my social life, my report cards are full of Ds and Fs. In classes my mind wanders from subject to subject of things that seem so important. What's the minimum amount of homework I need to do to squeak by? Is Sandy Smith a virgin? How much more money do I need to save to buy a car? Why did the Jam break up? Thoughts like these have led me to the easiest possible route to graduation: the Industrial Arts, better known as the home of our school's burnouts and fuck-ups.

My musical tastes are expanding. Like Tyrone, I'm bored of the mod stuff, but have no plans to go dark psychedelic. While record shopping on Melrose a couple of weeks ago I came across two used LPs I remembered from way back: David Bowie's *Ziggy Stardust and the Spiders from Mars* and the Beatles' *White Album*. One spin from both got me hooked, and I've been playing them back-to-back every night before bed. The colorful, faraway places those records transport me to, just before falling asleep, inspire new worlds beyond the KROQ playlists that are starting to bore me.

***

After a spring vacation visit to see my father's sister, my Aunt Agnes, in Flagstaff, Arizona, my father and I are unpacking the Chevy Impala in our driveway. A new neighbor passes by our house and stops for a little small talk and my father swiftly launches into a round.

"How was your trip, Ralph? Where'd you go?" he asks in this friendly, matter-of-fact manner.

"Miami Beach," my father replies without skipping a beat. I'm totally confused, but manage to play it cool, averting my attention to the sidewalk to hide my confused face.

The neighbor asks us how the weather had been. In surreal detail, my father describes a trip we didn't take, boasting of what a great time we had; the sweet flavor of roasted pig at luaus we didn't attend, crystal blue waters we didn't swim in, and a luxury resort where we hadn't stayed. He paints quite a picture, and for a moment I half thought we'd been in Miami.

Later, I ask my father, "Why did you tell him that?"

"Nobody needs to know where we were. It's none of their fucking business. Fuck 'em. You hear me? Just a little Fucky Game, that's all," he responds sharply, pointing his Roi-Tan cigar at me. That's his final answer and the end of the conversation.

And that's exactly how the Fucky Game is played. As the name implies, the Fucky Game is played to detract, confuse, or bewilder others for the sole purpose of fucking with them, and my father is just great at it. It can be played at any time, at any place, with anyone. My father and Uncle Ed are particulary fond of playing it with strangers, because if someone knows too much about you, you can't play it very well. The thing about the Fucky Game is that you never know when it starts, and where it ends.

I remembered watching them employ different versions of the Fucky Game over the years, but didn't know it had a name and everything. They'd lie to anyone about anything at any time for the sole sake of deception, as if it were some type of sport in which they'd keep mental tabs of who could tell the best detailed lies. Together, they'd perform for each other on anyone at any time—liquor stores, hardware shops, restaurants—mostly to people they didn't seem to like. Uncle Ed's whole life, posing as an FBI agent, was one big Fucky Game.

One version of the Fucky Game my father still plays takes place while he's driving. He pulls beside a random car waiting at a red light, stares down the driver until he has their attention, gives them an evil look like he's spying on them, and pretends to talk into a black telephone receiver with its cord jammed in his crotch. Anyone who has a phone in their car back back then is a movie star or undercover detective, so I guess he wants people to think he's one of the two.

Among my father's quirks he understands the value of knowing when to keep a low profile. When he happens to come across lost money on the floor of a public place, he's trained me to walk casually over to the cash, step on it, bend down, and while pretending to tie my shoe, carefully reach under it and take the money, then place it directly into my pocket without looking around. The code words were easy to remember and were always the same: "Dummy up!" That means, scan the ground and get ready to pocket free cash.

***

I'm fifteen, and saved enough money from my piddly after-school job as a maintenance guy at a place called Computerworld to pay for half of the car of my dreams, a 1968 Volkswagen Squareback. My folks were good enough to pay for the other half, and a month before my sixteenth birthday, I found one in the *Recycler* for $800—which seems like all the money in the world. The only trouble with that car is its color. Even though I'm colorblind, the orangish red it's painted is repulsive. My Squareback has *got* to be blue — like the one I saw at a parking lot in Malibu a couple of years earlier — and have dreaming about since. I take it to our local Earl Scheib paint shop and learn that I can only afford to have the exterior painted, which means the outside will be blue but the inside will remain that awful orange. So, I've become the proud owner of the only blue and orange two-tone VW in town.

On my sixteenth birthday, I barely pass my driver's exam on my third try. I'm rewarded with the independence that comes with owning and driving my first wheels. I'm no longer limited to mooching rides from friends and can go wherever I want. I know by now that sometimes my father's logic is questionable, but his advice about driving is solid.

"Now listen to me, boy, and listen good. Don't drink and drive, but if you do, keep it low. Keep it low," he said as I was pulling out the driveway for the first time, sparking a fresh Roi-Tan cigar.

"Thanks, dad. Got it," I say in an affirmative nod, letting him know he'd passed on some noble knowledge that would serve me well.

My VW Squareback is my temple, private domain, and thing to show the world who I am. It means everything to me. I practically live in it, and on many occasions, put down the back seat to sleep off a buzz if I'd had too much to drink.

After school let out, my summer days are spent working my crap job, then toiling through the hot Valley to the beach, learning to surf at nearby beaches with guys whose single objective is in line with mine: to catch waves and goof off. Gas is cheap, so at night, I can drive aimlessly around the Valley or further explore Hollywood. I stuck Buzzcocks and Jam stickers on the back window, and to the side window I attached a large red L sticker that I got from my relatives in Scotland. The L stands for "Learner," and is used in the UK as a learner permit sticker, but I just thought the big L would look cool, and they mailed me one. I made this custom license-plate frame to honor one of my favorite songs by the Jam, "Boy About Town," which appears in bold letters below the plate. I decked out the inside by wrapping a rosary around the rear-view mirror and taping a newspaper clipping of Charles Manson from his latest jail hijinks to the sun visor. I've got the coolest mismatched car, and it can't be mistaken for anybody else's.

By the end of summer, the idea of dressing like one of the early members of the Who all the time just doesn't seem right anymore. Something clicked, and I realize that I don't need to look different to think different. I'm noticing that many of the kids who look different only appear that way. Inside most of them are normal, and boring, searching for identity and aren't very interesting to be around. Most of them, but not all of them.

Although I've got two more years of high school ahead of me, I feel older than most kids from school. I'm excited by

Hollywood nightlife, where everyone is older and more interesting. I'm still a Rodney and KROQ devotee, and see as much live music as I can in Hollywood. There's a similar excitement found at new-wave dance clubs that've been popping up all over the place. The Odyssey, the Seven Seas, the Florentine Gardens, and the Valley's Hott Traxx or Phases are all good places to smoke or snort whatever drugs we can get our hands on and try to meet girls from other cities. Every kid in LA with a weird haircut who doesn't have a curfew crams inside these places to dance, get high, and hear new music among flashing lights and billows of smoke. The Odyssey, on Beverly Boulevard, is the most intense.

One late summer night at the Odyssey, Mike Keys taps me on the shoulder.

"Hey, you have a light?" I turn around to hand him some matches, and I can't believe my eyes. Just over his shoulder, two guys about our age garbed in dark psychedelic fashion are lip locked and rubbing each other while Soft Cell's "Tainted Love" is blaring. I look around, wondering if anyone thinks it's a big deal two guys with teased hair and heavy rouge can freely just make out like this. No one notices or gives a care. Mike Keys takes the matches from my hand, breaking my curious stare.

"Dude, it's rude to stare. Didn't your parents teach you anything?" he says, sparking a clove. "Big deal, they're probably bi or whatever. Get over it."

"I'm seeing things in the world. I'm growing up!" I declare, but only to myself.

***

It's the first day of eleventh grade. I wake up nervous and excited to go back to school. While getting ready, I repeatedly listen to a twelve-inch single record called, "Power and the Passion," by this band from Australia called Midnight Oil. I mow through a bowl of Lucky Charms, jump in my Squareback, spark up a Kool cigarette, and make a bee line to John Burroughs High. I pull into the parking lot which is getting packed with all the kids I haven't seen in a few months. The first guy I see is my old mod pal Chad.

"Hey man, I have a surprise for you."

He hops in my car and pulls out a small glass vial of cocaine and a smirk. We snort a couple of lines and take a couple of puffs of weed from my brother's hand-me-down pipe, and bail to home class.

As we file in among the other kids and part ways, everything starts seeming like a dream. I take a few steps before sensing this intense twitch deep in my right eye. It starts fluttering out of control until I can't see from it. These blinding flutters transform into a spasm and I start to panic. I'm struck with questions:

Was Chad's coke laced with poison?

Am I going blind?

What should I do?

Where's Chad?

Is he going blind, too?

These aren't exactly questions for the school nurse.

I have just enough common sense to get past the zig-zagging students and find my way into a phone booth near the main administrative office. I shut myself behind the accordion style door and take a moment to collect my thoughts. I'm convinced I'm having a full-blown blinding heart attack and have no idea what to do. The fluttering slows down, but only a little, and I realize I'm going to be late for my first class.

I manage to walk at a nervous pace, preoccupied with this paranoia that every person I pass knows I'm on coke and pot. Then a sweet girl named Debbie, whom I've known since kindergarten, stops me in the crowded hall to confirm my fear.

"Robbie Zabrecky!"

"Hey Debbie," I say, holding one hand over my blind eye, trying not make a big deal about my eye, or show any signs of being high.

"Are you okay? You don't look okay."

"Yeah, just having a little thing with my eye. I'm fine."

Debbie's face and voice are comforting. I remember the time she peed herself in kindergarten during story time, and just sat there after like a statue. It's clear she knows I'm messed up.

"Yeah, I'm okay, thanks. I gotta go," I respond as non-tweakishly as possible, and head to home class.

I take the nearest seat in the back of the room, and pretend I'm invisible. The spasm won't stop. I'm certain that at any moment I'm going to break into a full-body convulsion; the paramedics will be called and I'll end up in juvenile hall by lunch.

I'm wondering how I'll do in juvie when one of the lines of that Midnight Oil song starts pounding in my head on repeat and I start feeling really good: *"What do you believe, what do you believe, what do you believe is true?"*

The music playing between my ears starts making me feel great. It triggers this wave of elation, and it's like I'm living their music video. The teacher's saying something, but there's so much noise and energy pumping through me I can't tell what she's saying. All the other kids are paying attention, so I pretend to do the same. The spasm dies and the bell rings. I head straight to the boys' room, spark a fresh Kool, and tell myself it's going to be a great year.

Around campus I've noticed more and more kids dressing like they're in MTV videos. The styles are merging, and blurring the lines of the Melrose subcultures that a few years ago seemed so strict: you had to be punk, or mod, dark psychedelic, or something that could be tagged. But now it seems like everyone is in to all kinds of music and it's getting harder to tell who's into what. I'm still excited by new music, especially by bands coming from the UK like the Cure, Echo & the Bunnymen, and the Smiths.

One afternoon I'm with Sully at Ticketron in Valley Plaza, buying tickets to see the Cure at the Hollywood Palladium. This young woman in a baseball cap holding a clipboard approaches us.

"Hey, you guys wanna be in a movie?" she asks.

"Yeah, sure. I'll take a make-out scene with Molly Ringwald," Sully replies.

"It's not like that, but we could totally use you guys as extras in a background scene for a movie we're shooting. It's called *Girls Just Want to Have Fun* — you know, like the Cyndi Lauper song. We're filming in an hour at a nearby park. It should only take an hour or two. Fifty bucks cash, each."

"We'd love to," I say, answering for both us. The dough will pay for the concert tickets, gas, cigs, and alcohol. We head to the park, and for the next couple of hours, stand among 200 or so other teenage extras for some outdoor scene. It's our first job in show business, and the easiest money we've ever made.

***

I'm busy getting through high school, and my father's sustaining the Zabrecky household by hammering nails on construction sites. He leaves for work before the sun comes up and returns around 3:30 or 4:00 with his toolbox and construction hat. Like clockwork, he'd grab a frosty Coors from the fridge, take his shirt off, and lounge by the pool, puffing one of his stinky Roi-Tan's until dinner.

I pull up home from school one day while he's returning from work.

"Hey, boy, come here."

I meet him by the trunk of his aging Chrysler New Yorker. He looks a little more tired and dirty than usual. Reaching in the trunk with a half-puffed Roi-Tan gripped between his fingers, he opens his toolbox, and removes some stuff.

"You see this? It's a hammer. And these are nails. Don't ever use them to make yourself a living. You hear me? Now go inside."

He must have had a shit day on the job. This is his way of conveying a message to avoid blue-collar work.

While my father's a carpenter, and not a proud one or anything, my good mother coordinates weddings at the Castaway, Burbank's fanciest and only Polynesian restaurant and wedding location. It's way up on the hill, where all the rich Burbank people live. Like my father, she works long days and sometimes nights and the weekends.

My busy life of self-discovery, school life, and drinking doesn't always allow me to realize what my parents are sacrificing to raise Gordy, Laura, and me. Year in and year out, they work these grinding hours to ensure we are taken care of. While they're off putting in long work hours, my siblings are becoming adults; Gordy's off at college in San Diego and Laura just moved out and got a job working full time at a hospital. Most of the time I've got the house to myself. I'm free to smoke cigs, blast records in my room, and talk on the phone without being bothered.

***

I'm on a perfect streak of getting fired from every place I've worked. Finding after-school jobs is easy, but keeping them is a whole different story. Each employment opportunity has come and gone so quickly that they're all blurring into one big termination. But having a job while in my house is a requirement these days. Luckily, each one has been conveniently located within a mile or two from home base on California Street.

While pulling into the parking lot of Sizzler Steakhouse, my place of employment, to grab my paycheck, I'm nearly blind-sided by this super-sized '70s station wagon, headed toward me from the wrong direction. We both slam on our brakes and honk at each other. I jump out of my Squareback to make their wrong my right.

"What are you doing? Can't you see you're going the wrong way?" I yell, informing the driver—this extra-large woman sharing the same fashion sense as Mrs. Roper, draped in an outrageous floral print muumuu, with a cigarette dangling between her painted lips and a small white dog on her lap—just how wrong she is.

"Can't you see this clearly painted arrow?" I say, pointing to the large, directional arrow painted on the asphalt below.

"Oh honey. Honey. You do *not* want to fuck with me," she says in a slurred voice that sounds like Liberace, taking a hit off her bitch stick.

Getting a closer look at her, I notice she's a dead ringer for Divine, the female impersonator from the John Waters movies, but is definitely a woman. My eyes are drawn to her chest, which reveal a deep line of cleavage, separating the fleshiest boobs I'd ever seen up close. She's all woman and all out of her mind. A car behind mine trying to pull in honks their horn, and she flips them off. She's bananas.

For some reason, crazy people have an innately calming effect on me, so I adjust the tone of my voice and speak directly to her crazy.

"Look, lady, I work here. I'm just coming in to pick up my check. That's all. Now please move your big, stupid car so we can both get on with it, okay?"

The car behind me honks again and a voice hollers from inside. "Take it to People's Court. Move. Now. We wanna eat!"

Ignoring them, we continued our face off. She raises her painted-on eyebrows and takes another puff of her bitch-stick, blowing cigarette smoke that reeks of red wine and garlic bread right in my God-damned face.

She doesn't respond how I want her to, and knows she has me. She's been waiting all day, maybe all week, for something like this to happen.

"Oh, honey. You work here?" she asks with this cunning grin.

"Yes!" I answer, knowing I've blown it and shouldn't have told her I work for Sizz. "I'm just here to pick up my check," I say, defeated.

The car behind us honks again.

Without skipping a beat, she reverses her wagon right into the handicapped space, wobbles inside, and spends what seems like the rest of the afternoon reporting the event to my manager, Jose. I park and wait for my fate. The two of them eventually head outside and he's handing her Sizzler coupons or something.

As she's leaving with this pleased look in her overly made-up eyes, I flip her off behind Jose's back. She does the same to me.

He walks over to me and says, "You can't talk to regular customers like that. You are no good working here. Don't come back — we'll mail your check." And that was that.

Sizzler.
ROBBIE

When the new ice cream shop called Carvel Ice Cream opened in the nearby Toluca Lake shopping mall a few months ago, I applied and got the job. I had a hard time not giving away triple scoop cones on the house to anyone I knew, and even a few who just looked familiar.

"Here, you don't have to pay, it's cool. I mean, there's tons of this stuff," I'd say before getting narked out by the owner's nephew, who was a big jerk anyhow. They kept me for a couple of weeks before informing me I wasn't "counter boy material," but let me keep my work shirt as a consolation prize. Martino's Bakery hired me to load boxes of desserts onto delivery trucks, but they use this color-coding system that had me relying on my best color-blind guesses. After a week's worth of incorrect deliveries, I lost that job, too. I also lost a couple of telemarketing jobs run by these high-energy Scientologists who offered training courses to employees on how to sell over the phone. The last thing I wanted was a class to learn how to do a job that just seemed wrong. With my lack of training skills, I couldn't sell enough condo timeshares or water filters needed to make their pesky quotas, and they too, told me to hit the road. Pinocchio's Italian restaurant and deli, a Zabrecky family favorite since childhood, fired me for my continually poor counter service and reluctance to show up to work the day before Christmas. Mr. Mark, the owner, who could have been a cast member from *The Godfather*, explained why I had to go from the comfort of his cramped and cluttered wood-paneled back office.

"It's a simple. You don't a have a job a here a anymore. Now a goodbye. Get out."

One of my first jobs, Computerworld, located on the bottom floor of a one of those large, glass, multi-floored buildings on Hollywood Way near Lockheed Airport, let me go after I opted for a beach trip rather than working one afternoon last summer. Although I need a job to pay for gas and stuff, the work place is proving to be a difficult and inconvenient challenge that's cramping my style.

HERE COME
THE WARM JETS

I'M SIXTEEN, and have gone as far as third base when I meet Michelle, a devout Madonna fanatic I first saw dancing at Burbank's short-lived, all-ages, new-wave, dance club, Mr. Rogers. She sees me watching her and comes over.

There's an instant attraction between us.

"Hey you! You must go to Burroughs. You're cute."

Before I have a chance to say anything, we just start making out right there in the club. As the chorus of "I'll Melt with You" by Modern English blasts at a near deafening volume, our tongues are wiggling in each other's mouths and our hands are all over each other. Her mouth tastes delicious. It's the perfect mixture of California Coolers and clove cigarettes. She's got a nice body, big shoulder-length streaked hair, and wears lots of black plastic jewelry.

At the end of the night we exchange phone numbers. After a few late-night phone calls the next week, I find out she's a year older than me and goes to Burbank High, but not much else. I do know she's excited to meet up again and get it on. She hasn't asked if I'm a virgin and I certainly don't tell. There's no need to ask — everything about her tells me she's fucked before.

The following weekend we meet at a house party in the hills of Burbank. It's Saturday night and around ten teenagers, most of whom I don't know, pool together money for an assortment of alcohol bought from the liquor store over by Valhalla Cemetery that sells to anyone with a fake ID. After sharing a few beers, shots of tequila, and sucking down half a pack of clove cigs, we leave the party to find an empty bedroom.

The lights are off, and we leave them that way. Michelle wastes no time pushing me on somebody's parents' king-size bed and jumps on me. We start making out while pulling off our clothes and throwing them everywhere. In a matter of seconds, she squeezes her naked body against mine, and climbs on top of me.

Yep, this is the big night, and I've never felt more ready. We're getting into position. I'm on my back and she's right on top of me, and for some stupid reason I blurt, "Wait, this is my first time."

I shouldn't be saying anything, but I'm a nervous and can't help it. "That's okay, we'll change that right now," she giggles.

She straddles me like a pro, and slowly guides my ticking-time bomb of a hard-on inside her. As I slide in, I can hardly fathom how wet and good it feels and, almost as important, that I'm not a virgin anymore. I'm on my back totally inside her, and the room is spinning. There's pleasure in every direction. With her hands on my shoulders, she's moaning and gigging while we agree on a rhythm.

Just as we're really starting to get going, with zero warning, I lose control and ejaculate.

"Shit! Fuck! Sorry." My heart beats like it never has, and those feelings of elation die a sudden death. In an instant, I'm deflated and embarrassed — but still completely horny. Now my heart's barely beating and I'm relived it's over. I can't believe how quickly it all happened.

"It's okay. We can go again in a min. More drinks!" she says, as if we were re-entering a line for a carnival ride.

She puts on some clothes and leaves the dark room. The room starts stabilizing a little and my heartbeat slows back to a reasonable pace. I reach around in the dark to pull on some clothes but can't find them. I hop up and flick on the light. Looking down at my body I can't believe what I see.

There's blood all over my hands, dick, and groin area, and I don't know why.

The solid white bed comforter has blood blotches all over it, especially in the area where we'd just done it. From what I'd learned from sex education, and seen in magazines, this isn't how it's supposed to go. I'm looking at this ruined comforter thinking two things: how my dream of having sex came true, but is far from how I'd imagined it, and whoever's bed this is won't be happy when they come home and find it this way.

Then it hits me: she's on her period. Not knowing what to do, I find my shirt and underwear, which are draped over a lamp, go in the bathroom, and wash off the blood, ruining someone's parents' perfectly good bath towel. I don't want to embarrass her, and figure she must know she's menstruating, but decided not to tell me. Better play it cool, I think. For all I know, this happens to people all the time and I just don't know it. I go back in the bedroom, kill the lights, and get naked again.

A few minutes later the door opens. Light and music flood in. Her Madonnaish silhouette is there in the doorway, holding two California Coolers, suggesting the night isn't over. She's a blurred, intoxicated mess.

"I'm sooo wasted!" she says giggling, closing the door with one of her long smooth legs.

She takes a huge guzzle off one of the wine coolers, removes her clothes, and climbs back on me. There's no mention of the blood and I don't dare bring it up. We down the drinks and do it two more times without one mention of her being on her period. Each of those times, fucking a little harder, and eventually passing out on each other while muffled KROQ blasts from the living room.

In the middle of the night I wake up startled, not knowing where I am. Michelle's gone. The party is over. It's dead. All I know is that it's super late and I need to get home. I throw on my clothes, walk through the living room, which is covered in empty bottles, hop in my Squareback, and drive home.

Still half out of my mind, I'm driving west down the long stretch of Burbank Boulevard at three in the morning hoping I don't get pulled over. Two things reminded me I'd finally done it: the dried blood on my hands that are half gripping the steering wheel, and the unfamiliar sound of bloody pubic hair crunching against my under shorts.

The next morning, I wake up around noon with a bad hangover, piecing together the night before. Tossing my blood-stained underwear into the trashcan, I wonder why I don't feel like a man.

***

Most of the kids who meet on Parish Street between classes gather during lunch to smoke pot at Jeff Davidson's house, whose parents are off at work. Pot seems to be this great thing for everyone but me. It makes every other kid who smokes it relaxed and gigglish, but for some reason, has the opposite effect on me.

I took my first hit off Gordy's "sneak-a-toke pipe" he found at a Ted Nugent concert. I choked down the biggest hit I could take, and exhaled this massive cloud of smoke that dissolved into the Burbank sky. The buzz took a moment to kick in, but when it did, it came on strong. I remember my brain feeling compressed all of a sudden and that something weird was happening to my body. My eyelids felt like they were being filled with cement and my body temperature dropped. I looked around to see my brother and his friends filling a beer bong near our pool, and felt like I was stuck in some dream in which I was half awake. I couldn't tell if I was there, or just thought I was there. Then our backyard looked like I was seeing it through a fisheye lens, and I stared off into space for what felt like an hour — although it was probably only a few minutes since the same side of the Van Halen record was still playing. But instead of feeling all warm and trippy, I felt this weird disassociation with everything, magnifying everything I saw wrong with myself — that I couldn't keep a job, sucked in school, ran like girl, and besides music, didn't have any real hobbies or anything. I hate pot.

Since then I've smoked it a bunch more times, each with similar results. Occasionally, I can get that buzzed, stupid feeling the other kids describe, but my odds are about one in five — in bad feeling's favor. At house parties and outside of Hollywood nightclubs, while other kids are getting high, laughing, zoning out, I'm convinced they're secretly reading my thoughts and looking into my soul—a prospect that sends me into a sweaty panic before running to the nearest alley or toilet to vomit. I should be taking the puking and feeling self-conscious signs that drugs aren't for me. Getting high, despite the way it makes me feel, seems mandatory. Alcohol, though, is a different story.

***

One Saturday night not long after my 16th birthday Mike Keys and our bud Eric and I headed out for a harmless visit to Disneyland. We drove down in my Squareback, pounding a bottle of 151-proof Bacardi Rum with a Coke chaser along the way. By the time we made it inside, I was approaching, but not quite, in blackout mode. While waiting in a crowded line for Space Mountain, I felt like mixing things up a little for the sole purpose of entertaining Mike Keys and Eric.

"Hey guys. Watch this," I say, pulling my pants down all the way to my ankles and exposing the naked bottom half of my body to a crowd of unsuspecting Disneyland thrill seekers. Mike Keys wasn't impressed in the least, but Eric's cracking up.

"Dude, what the fuck are you doing! You're gonna get us kicked out of here. We just paid sixteen bucks to get in you idiot!"

Before he can say one more word, I somehow think it's a fine idea to whizz out the boozy concoction we swigged earlier, while spinning myself in circles. Inside the packed Tomorrowland attraction line, I start peeing my brains out in the neatest circle I can, exposing myself to the horror and disgust of all these tourists and families. People are looking away and covering the faces of their kids, who are laughing and pointing at my privates. Even

Mike Keys and Eric are aghast. It's a long pee, and I'm getting dizzy from spinning around, but my bladder finally empties.

I pull up my pants, and act like nothing happened. "You crazy bastard, I love you," says Mike Keys, who finally cracks a smile.

We wait a little extra to sit in the front seats. By the time we get on the ride, I'm just about gone completely, but I'm not too wasted to understand that if I can manage to push up my legs to prevent the safety bar from coming down as far as it needs to go to hold me in the seat, I can wiggle out of the train once it gets going and have some real fun. Once the train gets moving up the first hill and this space laser show is playing, I wrangle myself from the seat and climb out onto the hood of the train, plopping myself down belly up, with one arm around the front safety bar, preparing myself for the most thrilling space coaster ride any drunk teenager could dream of.

Once the coaster gets going, I realize *not* being secured in the seat like every other rider is a bad idea. But it's too late and the ride takes off into this dark and turbulent course through a handful of gusty meteor showers. It's dark, and loud space themed music is playing loud. We're zipping past hunderds of stars and I'm holding on for my life, wishing it to be over.

"Hold on, Robbie! You're fucked if you let go," Mike Keys says, holding on to me tightly while zipping through outer space.

The coaster abruptly pulls into the station, and there I am, still holding on for my life. The second it stops, I'm bum rushed by these two big Disneyland security guards. They handcuff and whisk me away so fast I have zero time to make plans with Mike Keys and Eric to meet up after they're done with me. I know I'm defeated, and don't resist as they escort me down a bunch of long halls before we enter a room and close the door.

They lock me inside a Disneyland jail cell, which has metal bars like real jails, and none of the fun of Disneyland. I plop down on this uncomfortable bench feeling like I'm going to puke. On the other side of the room, which is spinning, there's this wall of camera monitors where you can see everything that's going on in every part of the ride. I'm pretty sure there's no way of getting out of whatever's coming to me.

"We've got you on cameras doing some pretty stupid things. You could be facing some big charges, blah, blah, blah…"

Their words all started sounding the same. Even though I need to upchuck or take a nap, I do all I can to make the best of things.

"I didn't mean anybody any harm, I'm very, very, sorry, sirs," I squeak out in some slurred form of English.

"Come with us."

They let me out the cell, un-cuff me, take my picture, and fingerprint me. Everything's still fuzzy. Then they escort me through some back door of the park and all of a sudden we're in the parking lot.

"We've got you on file; you are not welcome here ever again. You understand?" says the one who cuffed, and uncuffed me. He gives me little sendoff push into the parking lot.

"Yes, sirs."

I find my way back to my faithful Squareback. It's the one with the rum bottle and Coke cans next to it. I hop in back and fall asleep, waiting for Mike Keys and Eric.

***

In the school parking lot, this cool senior I know, Taylor, is going on about the frustrations of trying to find work that doesn't totally suck.

"I haven't had much luck getting a job, so instead, I've been getting high and watching planes land near the Burbank airport."

Still unemployed from the Sizzler debacle, I have plenty of time on my hands. The idea of using Burbank's local aerospace company, Lockheed, as the background for a little recreational after-school activity beats driving around Burbank looking for Help Wanted signs and filling out crummy applications.

"Mind if I join you?" I ask.

"Sure. My spaceship boards after sixth period."

After the last school bell rings, I leave my Squareback in the school parking lot, jump in Taylor's ride, some restored muscle car that's immaculate — and reminds me Uncle Ed's Chevelle — and head north on Hollywood Way. We circle around the airport, which looks shabby and has seen better days. It looks nearly forgotten and abandoned, which is a good sign we were probably safe from getting busted. Taylor parks as close possible to where the incoming planes are slowly descending onto the weed-lined runways.

He fiddles with some cassettes in his glove box, reviewing homemade cassettes of Public Image, XTC, and Bauhaus, before deciding on one by Tangerine Dream. We're sitting there and chain-smoking inside, not talking much, just listening to the tape. As this dreamy synth Krautrock blares from inside, we're waiting for the next massive airliner to descend from the smoggy sky. It's kind of like fishing.

As the first plane appears in the distance, he reaches under his seat and produces a brown, lunch-sized, paper bag. What is probably a pipe and bag of weed, or vial of coke or speed, but it's something I'm not expecting. It's a can of aerosol brake cleaner.

"What's that?" I ask, knowing what it is, but not knowing what he's planning on doing with it.

"After school special," he says under a quiet grin, shaking the can.

He sprays the inside of the bag with a blast of brake cleaner and brings it to his mouth. He breathes it in deeply, and holds it in as if his life's depending on it. Just as I'm getting my head around what was going on, all this stuff happens in succession; he releases his breath, his head falls back against the head rest, his neck muscles seem to quit working, and he giggles like a little kid. Just then a jumbo jet heads straight for our windshield. We're parked so close, it creates this illusion that the aircraft is going to crash into us and blow us to bits. The scream of the engines and brakes is explosive, and quickly replaces the sound of the Tangerine Dream cassette. The plane hovers just over our heads and hits the runway as he regains consciousness, wipes his eyes, and laughs like an innocent boy stepping off a roller coaster.

"That's how that works," he says, explaining his guilty pleasure in four words.

When the next jet comes into view, he sprays another hit of cleaner into the bag and hands it to me. I'm nervous, but totally in to a new high. I do as he did, taking the bag to my mouth so that no extra air can sneak in, suck in every bit of brake cleaner, and hold my breath until I no longer can.

In case you're wondering, it doesn't take long to feel the effects of huffing brake cleaner. It's not like pot or coke, where it takes a minute or two before you feel something. The initial numbness is pretty overwhelming. Then the world melts into one large audio blob and the buzzing sensation is rattling my body as this jumbo jet is heading toward us. It's like the craziest 3D movie but instead of just seeing stuff, you're feeling it too. My brain's bulging against my skull, and my blood's pumping so hard I can feel every heartbeat loudly between my ears. My vision starts blurring into melting layers of color; it's like looking through a kaleidoscope for the first time — you just fall into it and trip out like you're in some nice dream. Just as I'm feeling elated and blissful, the joy starts morphing into guilt, and I'm envisioning the passengers on the plane seeing us in the car below, judging us for not working at the local pizza parlor or ice cream shop. But the good outweighs the bad.

"This is incredible," I let out after regaining some form of speech.

"Beats working for Sizzler, I bet," he replies, refilling the bag with a blast of fresh fumes.

We huff a couple of more times — each time with similar but lesser effects. I recognized the common diminishing pattern drugs seem to have. My first experiences with pot, coke, amyl nitrate, and speed all had one thing in common: this pyramid-like effect; the first times were always the strongest, and then it was a matter of trying to capture that elusive, inaugural buzz.

The sun was starting to go down when he drops me off at my car back at the high-school parking lot.

"Thanks man, that was pretty cool," I say, wondering if I should give him five bucks for brake cleaner. I get this sense it's no big deal so decline offering.

"Any time. I'm there every day. Weekends too. Plenty of arrivals between 3:30 and 5:00pm," he says, as brake cleaner junkies who know the landing schedules of airplanes do.

I have this nasty headache coming on as I'm driving home, looking for Help Wanted signs on Magnolia Boulevard.

***

It was just another summer night, after the cops broke up a Burbank house party, when I see Mike Keys and Richard getting inside Mike Keys' beat-up Dodge Dart. I stick my head in on the driver's side and use my lighter as a makeshift flashlight to light their faces, pretending to be a cop.

"Do you boys know it's after ten o'clock? Do your parents know where you are?"

"Yo ese! Night's just getting started. It's still early, bro. Let's head back to Richard's and keep things moving," Mike Keys says, in this way that starts off as a Cholo, but ends in surfer talk. He's the only guy who can pull off both dialects in one sentence. He and Richard look shady as hell. They've both got bandanas tied around their foreheads and Pendleton shirts buttoned all the way up.

"Sounds good. Meet you there," I say, nodding in agreement.

"Cool. Give me all your money. Party favors — la Cocaina," he says, in this devilish sing-songy Mexican kinda way. I've had a few rum and Cokes at the party and like the idea. I reach in my pocket and hand him the last 25 dollars I have in the world.

"Meet us at Richard's house in half an hour," Mike Keys says, popping in a Suicidal Tendencies tape and pulling away.

Mike Keys and Richard dropped out of high school and are pretty deep into BPO gang stuff, and could probably pass as the youngest member of Echo & the Bunnymen or the Smiths. It's funny to think that only a few years earlier, all the same things mattered to us, and now they're on this tear, being gangsters and wearing bandanas covering their foreheads and talking like Cholos, and I think I'm in a band from England.

The back guesthouse at Richard's father's house is BPO headquarters. It's just a converted garage, but the walls are covered in gang graffiti. There are a few crummy chairs and makeshift table that look like discards from Goodwill, and a mattress in the corner. It smells of beer-drenched dirty carpet and this slight paranoia that at any time, BPO's despised North Hollywood rivals, FFF, might swing by on a shooting rampage.

Whatever impact gangster life was having, it was aging them. They were 16, but looked 19 or 20. They looked and sometimes even talked like Cheech & Chong, except their faces were still as white as white could be. Life's so weird, I think. But one thing hadn't changed: When we were with each other, it was like old times, and when I was with them, I felt invincible.

Mike Keys reaches in his buttoned-up Pendleton shirt pocket, removes a few small plastic baggies of drugs, and tosses them onto a graffiti-covered, wooden, cable-spool table. From his other shirt pocket, he pulls out a syringe and drops it next to the drugs. Though buzzed from the party, I sober up a little, thinking these guys are into some next level shit. Richard hovers in with a metal spoon and a Styrofoam cup of water. Mike Keys pulls his belt off and the mood goes dark — our days of our youthful innocence are behind us, and there's no going back.

I sit back in one of the barely useable chairs and observe; I don't want to make a big deal about them using needles or anything. I thought shooting drugs was a thing reserved for outlaws, rock stars, or low-lifes. But they're not, it's just my two old best friends getting ready to party Sid Vicious style. Mike Keys goes first. I watch him sprinkle a small amount of cocaine from one of the bags into the spoon. He adds a few drops of water, and lights the spoon from below, boiling them together. He removes the lighter from the spoon, drops a small piece of cotton to absorb the boiled drugs, and sucks out the contents with a syringe that has a slightly bent needle. Somewhere along the way, he's become an expert with using needles, as if he'd been doing it his whole life, but that's how Mike Keys does everything, like a damn pro. Somehow he's gifted with this ability to look cool doing the most mundane tasks, with this impressive ease. Unlike me, it's impossible for him to appear awkward. It's like he's immune to looking like a fool or something. With his usual confidence, he ties off his arm with his leather belt and injects a dose of coke into his forearm.

My heart's racing — I've never seen something so intense.

He drops the belt, looks at me, and smiles blissfully as his eyes are bulging from their sockets. He lights a cig, and starts pacing around the room. The drugs had done their job.

"It's really good," he says with that third-grade smile on his face. He gets busy cooking up the next batch for Richard, who has a similar reaction.

"Fuck yes," Richard agrees.

Then it's my turn. I'm nervous, but before I have any time to chicken out, I thrust out my forearm. Mike looks at me with a lit cig dangling from his lips.

"Sure you're into this, Robbie?" I detect it's more of a warning than a question, but can't blow the vibe and ruin everything.

"Hell yeah!" I blurt out, trying to sound like I've been shot up a million times before, and before I can change my mind.

Mike plunges the dose of coke into my right forearm, which doesn't hurt at all, and pushes in the loaded syringe. As he removes the needle, a small stream of blood drips down my arm and onto the dirty carpet.

"It's okay. Happens. You're fine. Just hold your finger over it for a sec," Mike Keys says with the confidence of a doctor.

With my thumb held down on my forearm to stop the bleeding, the belt falls from my arm and the drugs kick in. All of a sudden I need to stand up. Then pace. Then smoke.

Then I enter another state of mind. Under my skin, fireworks are shooting off and there's this intense ringing between my ears. While my heart races faster and faster and faster, I want to jump out of my skin. If it had its own pair of legs it would've left my body and run around the block a few times. Trying to keep whatever cool I might have left, I'm taking these big breaths while Mike Keys and Richard are sitting back and laughing, remembering their first times and how they reacted similarly.

"Dude, you're pacing like you have to take a shit. Just kick back, ese," Mike Keys says, sort of demanding. As the intensity lessens pretty quick, I lay on my back on Richard's mattress to catch my bearings while Mike Keys sets up the next round. Shooting up with Mike Keys and Richard — who were beginning to feel more like distant brothers — is a rite of passage. An innocence vaccine.

We shoot a few more loads, chain smoke, and reminisce a little about elementary school.

"Remember that time I socked it to that Nazi bitch, Ms. Dawson, on the playground?" Mike asks, drizzling more coke into the spoon.

"Dude, that was classic," adds Richard.

"Yeah, she was the worst. She's probably dead by now, or something," I throw in, not really agreeing but wanting to sound tough and go along. Mike Keys changes the mood by remembering our murdered friend, James.

"Sometimes I wish I could go back in time. I'd go right back to that night James was headed to clock-in at Taco Bell and stop him. And if I saw that guy who shot him, I'd have showed him what was up."

"Me too, bro. I still think about him all the time," adds Richard, dropping the Cholo accent and sounding just like he did back in grade school.

"Wish there was some way to bring him back. He was way too young, and way too smart to die. Bet he would've gone to college and everything."

I can't think of anything insightful to add, so I stay quiet with every memory of James I have racing through my mind. Out of nowhere, a TSOL gig flyer just falls off the wall and onto the floor. The three of us look at each other like we're in some jacked up Scooby Doo episode. After a long beat Mike Keys breaks the silence.

"Well that was goddammed weird."

It was weird. No argument. As we lay there drugged out of our skulls, looking at the flyer with some notion that James' ghost popped in to spook us for a second. I see a vacancy in Mike Keys and Richard's eyes. They look like zombies, and if they do, I must too. I bail just before the sun comes up and head back to California Street.

I wake up that Sunday afternoon more sick and dehydrated than ever before. I sneak in the kitchen, pour a huge bowl of Lucky Charms, and head back to my room, where I obsess on the three little needle marks. I stay in my room all day, listening to records, and talking to girls on the phone, wondering what adventures might possibly be ahead.

KING FOR A DAY

GOOD SURFERS ALWAYS make surfing look easy. They make it seem like an effortless and exciting dance, like some Zen thing where they and the wave are at one with each other. I'm a barely okay surfer, and even though I must've crashed a million times in brutal whitewater while learning, I got just good enough to eventually catch my share of long rides on the shores of Zuma and Malibu. But dragging my board back and forth to the beach on weekends isn't doing it for me anymore. It's become more of a chore than this thing I feel like I should love doing. Although I used to be totally excited by surf culture, I've come to terms with the fact that I don't love surfing, and surfing doesn't love me. I'm just not that great at it, like I used to be at Pac Man.

With my board and wetsuit collecting dust in my bedroom, I made the easiest decision I ever did by swapping my multi-colored, tri-fin surfboard and wetsuit for a barely playable, 1960s electric bass guitar with Chad — my neighborhood friend who gave me that nearly blinding coke the first day of eleventh grade. Music's been such a huge part of my life, and it's time to find out if I'm musically inclined, or not.

With four strings instead of six, the bass seems easier to learn than guitar. I started taking bass lessons at the nearby ABC Music Center and have been learning the fundamentals of the instrument as fast as I can. I connected with a couple of school friends who are just getting started on guitar and drums, and formed a band, calling ourselves the Castaways. We started practicing in the drummer's garage after school, learning covers of TV's *Batman*, *The Munsters*, and riffs by Echo and Bunnymen, the Jam, the Kinks, and Bauhaus. We've even come up with a few of our own songs, but so far, they mostly sound like stuff we're trying to emulate.

The past few months we've been practicing a lot after school. I've been getting the hang of playing easy bass riffs and singing at the same time, and now we've got a handful of covers and originals. We got offered our first gig, and changed our name to something more British sounding: Image Generation. Our first show is at this all-ages rec room called the Sun Valley Sportsman's Hall on Saturday night. We're opening for Burbank's one and only hardcore punk group, Urban Decay, who've played a handful of Burbank house parites.

A few days before the show, Urban Decay's drummer broke his arm so it's up to us to pull off the headlining spot. I'm plugging my bass into the amp and walking up to the mic in front of about 100 drunk valley teenagers who are expecting something great. Holding on for my life during the show, my nerves are so overpowering I feel zero joy barreling through our set. We play every song three times faster than we practiced them, performing our half-hour set in fifteen minutes. It's all over so quick, and now I'm covered in sweat and just relieved it's over. I figured we were about as decent as any garage band of teenagers could be for their first gig.

Although we're far from being good or anything, performing music feels right, and I can hardly wait to do it again. A few months later we invite a couple of seniors from Burroughs to join us: an arty keyboard player who makes weird sounds on an old synth, and a New Romantic, Bowie-obsessed singer named Ted, who not only sings better than me — which wasn't too hard — but looks cooler than any of us. We practice up a storm and somehow get booked for our first and last gig at Madame Wong's West in West LA. After a month of solid rehearsals, we make it through the show, playing to an empty house on a school night. Pretty soon being in a band seems like more trouble than it's worth, and we call it quits.

For one of my school electives, I enrolled in music class at school and learn the basics of upright bass. On my search to continue to play music, I join a new-waveish group of guys about my age called LIVE. They have a set of songs that are already written, and rehearse at this house in Hollywood where the Go-Go's were rumored to practice in their early days. Musically, it's not the best fit, but I want to keep playing bass and keep my music dreams going, so I join. After playing a handful of shows, I realize it's a lot of work just being someone's bass player and bail. Music is the path I want to pursue, but I'm not sure, or really ready, to start my own band.

***

By twelfth grade, I'm cruising through the '80s feeling pretty good about things. I mostly wish I'm in a band from England and can find a job I can keep for more than a month. Every day before school, I puff up my dyed, jet-black, short hair, and wear my trusty jean jacket like my life depends on it. Beneath the denim I wear every day on the high school campus I mostly look forward to attending, I'm scared about the way forward, and don't know what I'll do with myself after graduation. My siblings, Gordy and Laura, had these immediate college and work plans when they finished, and I hear other kids talking about going off to college or working for their parents' small businesses and stuff like that. But anytime I wonder about my future, all I can do is dream of having my own band, performing in night-clubs around the world, and getting far away from Burbank.

Certain parts of high school can be a real pain. On the Burroughs campus, there is no shortage of authoritarian teachers and mean-girl cliques who parade around campus between classes with sticks up their butts. It also has its share of jockish school spirit, but that stuff doesn't interest me in the least — it only recalls my early days of playground embarrassment and sucking at sports.

Although I'm friendly with kids from all the cliques, the one thing I couldn't care less about is school spirit. I'm not anti-patriotic or anything, it's too all-American for me. I get jazzed socializing between classes, as well as cutting out on them. I've embraced this role of taxi driver, cramming stray kids in my Squareback to ditch classes, and drive around, smoke our lungs out, and listen to KROQ at high volumes.

Sometimes, to break up the monotony of the sacred high-school lunch hour, I round up a few friends, motor through the Pup 'n' Taco drive-through, and head to Forest Lawn Cemetery, where the view of Burbank is unbeatable. We sprawl out on the huge lawn embedded with gravestones, annihilate barely edible chilidogs, and wash them down with cherry Slush Puppies and clove cigs. From up there, I always sense that life after high school is somehow gonna be okay.

I've made twelfth grade as easy as possible, creating a curriculum that includes little homework and lots of time to socialize and party. I used three of my elective classes to help print the school paper, *The Smoke Signal*. Our print shop teacher, Mr. Davidson, is an easygoing hippie. If the paper is delivered on time, he allows us to smoke cigs in the darkroom and goof off as we please.

My social turnaround from being the shy elementary school kid to the guy who's friendly with all types of kids makes me uncomfortable at times. Because I was so shy and introverted early on, it's become my unwritten mission to be friendly to any kid I meet, especially if they're different. I'd say I'm friendly to pretty much everyone in school and appreciate it when they were friendly back, which has made me a pretty popular guy on campus. During this last year of high school, walking the halls between classes has become a thing of its own; students I don't know say hello and call me by name.

I'm fearless about who my friends at school are. One of my best and certainly most interesting friends is this unusual boy/man I call Peculiar Chris. Peculiar Chris and I met in junior high, after he transferred from a special education school, and have been good friends ever since. I was drawn to him right away. He was the ultimate freak, geek, and rebel, and didn't even know it. Everything about Peculiar Chris was special, but not all the other kids agreed — especially the jocks. He's got this thinning black wiry hair and theatrical thrift-shop wardrobe and looks like he actually might be in his twenties; by noon, his round face and dark eyes reveal a full-on five o'clock shadow. He's the only kid who wears sun hats and scarves, and uses every chance he has to share his flamboyant vocabulary.

His excitement and encyclopedic knowledge of musical theater and sci-fi & fantasy are unparalleled. Out of the blue, he just loves offering statistics on that stuff. When you're with Peculiar Chris, you never know what he's going to say or do.

"Did you know *West Side Story* was inspired by *Romeo and Juliet?* It's so much more fabulous once you know that. And if that's not enough, I just read that Ray Bradbury has a distant relative who was tried at the Salem Witch Trials. Oh, darling, now everything makes sense! Oh, and did you hear? The cafeteria has the nerve of serving Sloppy Joes and tater tots again at lunch! What's this world coming to? Oy!"

The other day, I'm walking with him down the hall and in his distinct, squeaky, and perverse voice, he's spouting his sexual fantasies about girls…and boys, with sharp innuendo, a little louder than usual. Unabashedly queer, he couldn't care less how the other kids see him. I think he's pretty punk — the '80s embodiment of a teenage Truman Capote. But this day he's a little over the top, even for Peculiar Chris.

"You know what I'd like for breakfast? Fresh squeezed PUSSY! And for lunch, ASS, and for dinner, well, I'd better not say in front of all these HANDSOME…"

Out of nowhere, one of the over-fed jerks from the football team slams Peculiar Chris up against a locker and it makes this loud clank that resonates down the hall. His hat and scarf go flying off. He's got Peculiar Chris' neck pinned with his forearm and looks like he's ready to beat his ass. The hall quiets and everyone crowds around.

"I've had it with all the fag shit. Stop looking at me that way, you hear me?" he says, between his clenched teeth. Peculiar Chris knows exactly what he's talking about, but even though he's about to get pummeled then and there, he can't help but being Peculiar Chris. That's part of the reason he's so special.

"Your wish is my command, MASTER!" And right when he says, master, like he's Judy Garland or something, I butt in.

"Hey man, leave him alone. He's not hurting anyone. Just leave him alone. He doesn't mean it," I plead. After a few long seconds, the dude gives in and, while still holding Peculiar Chris in a death grip, looks at me.

"Okay, Zabrecky, but if this guy so much as looks at me again, he's dust. Got it, queer boy?" he says releasing Peculiar Chris from his grip.

I pick up Peculiar Chris's hat and scarf, the hallway crowd disbands, and there's Peculiar Chris, unfazed.

"Someone didn't have their Cheerios this morning! My lord! Where's the sense of humor here people?!" he says almost too loud, re-adjusting his hat and scarf.

"Just keep it down, especially around those guys," I say.

The thing I love about Peculiar Chris is that he, like Mike Keys and Richard, is comfortable in his own skin, which makes me proud to be his friend and usher him in to my social circles, and remind kids he makes uncomfortable that he's cool.

His unpredictability is a sure-thing cure for temporary boredom, and always great for comedy relief. At the end of class, with the teacher's permission, he sings these incredible acapella verses of the "The Time Warp" from *The Rocky Horror Picture Show*. He parades around the classroom singing and dancing around the teacher's desk as if his life depends on it. His presence and fearless passion for performing make most kids uncomfortable; but it brings me pure joy, wonder, and great relief from boring class assignments. His impromptu performances are as good as, or better than, most live shows I've seen in Hollywood. Peculiar Chris, more than any kid I'd ever met, has a magical talent — this kind that can't be taught. He's got to be destined for a huge career in Hollywood. His classroom performances have inspired me to back him on acoustic guitar, which I can barely play.

After school, Peculiar Chris and a handful of stragglers that don't have wheels pile into my Squareback and I drive them home. Even though I paid for half of my car with money I worked for and saved, some part of me feels bad for these kids who live far from campus and are stuck walking. Peculiar Chris lives the farthest away, so he's always the last one I drop off. Sometimes he gives me these, "lemme unbutton your pants and make you feel good eyes," but I'm just his driver and occasional protector. I'd never accept a blowjob from him.

We recently formed a little music duo. I pluck simple guitar riffs and strum the three open chords I know while he jumps around and dances around my room like a banshee. We've got these songs called "Night Wind of Living Damned," "Glass Rose," and "Ballad for a Dying Vampire." Last weekend, we went down to the boardwalk on Venice beach to play them live. It was fun playing them and a total thrill seeing Peculiar Chris totally unleashed and running around the boardwalk singing at the top of his lungs, but beach tourists passed by us like we were a pair of nut jobs.

Although I'm popular, most of the time I still felt like the wart-monger living some other kid's life. At night, after taking the needle off the last record and hitting the covers, I still have my sleepwalking fits. Last week I found myself standing in the middle of the backyard in the middle of the night, thinking I'd been chased by Uncle Sniper, and guided myself back to bed, trying to erase that memory once and for all.

***

As fall turned to winter that year, I experienced my most unconventional high-school moment. I knew I was popular, but didn't
know exactly how liked I was until the student body informed
me that I was a nominated as Homecoming King of our twelfth-
grade class. The news was surprising — a Homecoming King
seemed like a title that was rewarded to someone who'd earned
it, like the football quarterback, the highest-scoring basketball
player, or the president of the yearbook committee. But me? I
hadn't done anything to *deserve* it. I had no clue what the title en-
tailed, and could've cared less. What I did know was that results
were going to be announced at the school dance that winter and
that I was supposed to be there in case I won.

A week before the dance, I decide to go with a group of
friends. Having donated all my mod suits to Goodwill, I didn't
have a shirt, tie, or jacket, so I opted for my brother's hand-
me-down suit from his high school dance days. That night, I
showed up half wasted in the JBHS gymnasium with a group
of friends as the members of the Associated Student Body announce the winner. Inside the dimly lit gym decorated with balloons and streamers, they're announcing the nominees through
an echoing PA system, and announce the winner: me. I'm the
new king, whatever that means, and I'm half out of my mind.
People cheered and made me feel like I'd done something good
and someone placed an absurd-looking imperial crown on my
head as I stood beside our queen, the school's most vivacious
and foxy redhead, Cyndi.

After the fuss is over, I sneak around the side of the school
gym for my first smoke as king, and there's Mike Keys and a few
dudes from BPO pounding tall cans of Coors. It's a little weird
seeing him on campus, since he dropped out a year ago, declaring
high school was nothing but a waste of time. But since it's night,
we're at a social event with people we've known forever, and a
muffled version of "Whip It" is playing, it seems normal.

"Homecoming King? What's that about? Isn't that like a jock and cheerleader kind of deal?" he asks. He's as confused as I was a few weeks ago.

"Not sure, entirely, but has something to do with staying in school and *not* being a dick to other kids," I say, feeling awkward but holding my ground. Saying that made me realize why I was king.

"Aww, burn dude!" chimes in one of the other guys.

"Whatever dude. Catch you on the flip-side, Robbie." He says, as he and his croonies hop in back of a lowered white street truck with their beers and storm down Parish Street, off to terrorize FFF. I go back in the gym, where kids are now spazzing out to "Hearbreaker" by Pat Benatar — a song that was popluar like five years ago. What a weird night, and this DJ is *way* behind the times, I think.

As king and queen, Cyndi and I were required to make an appearance at some big football game a couple of weeks later, where we'd ride in the back seat of a classic convertible around the high school track during halftime. On the night of the big game and my JFK moment, I agreed to pick up one of the other kids from the homecoming court and take us to the game. Jason was a blond-haired, blue-eyed guy who drove every girl crazy with his handsome surfer looks and Jeff Spicoli vocal inflections.

"I just need to stop at my dealer's house to grab a bag of weed before we head over, that cool?"

"Of course," I reply.

As we pull up to an apartment not far from school, he hops out and says, "Be right back, bro," and disappears into the dealer's house. If I have one respectable quality, it's that I'm punctual. Each minute is like an eternity as I'm watching the clock tick on my Squareback dashboard.

After a couple cigs, he eventually emerges with a smile that says he scored. "Sorry dude. Man, that guy can really talk. I'm sure we're fine," he says, handing me a lit joint, as we race to get to the school.

We arrive at Burroughs to a full parking lot and the sound of the marching band in full swing, reminding us just how late we are. As the band plays some semi-out-of-tune brassy number, the bleacher seats are filled and the halftime event is almost over. Very stoned, we park in someone's driveway, and race up to the gate, where my good mother and Auntie are staring me down with disappointment. The fancy car I'm supposed to ride in is half way across the football field with the queen, Cyndi, sitting alone in the back seat.

"You run and get in that car right now!" Auntie insists.

As stupid and high as I am, it's the only thing to do. I sprint down the track, jump in the car, and apologize for being late. Together, we're driven around the last stretch of the track while the crowds of school-spirited Burbankers wave us on, celebrating a moment most kids would've dreamed of, but one that makes me feel out of place.

***

Near the end of my senior year, I'm in print shop goofing off when I receive a notice to report to the administrative office. For the fiftieth time, I made the mistake of smoking weed at lunch and was more stoned than I wished to be to face school officials. I use the confidence learned from Mike Keys and Richard as I step into the dank principal's office.

I haven't the slightest clue as to why they want to see me.

With a paranoid reluctance, the pot backfires and sends me into a panic, like when you suddenly know something heavy is about happen that you have no control over, and there's no time to think, let alone cope. All I can do is go with it and ride it out.

Inside, a Burbank cop in full uniform and two important-looking people in suits sit and survey me with concern. Surely, I thought, they must have known I was high, or that I hid a box of cigs in my jean jacket pocket, or that I know the local drug dealers at school, or that I'd been cutting classes, or a handful of other scenarios. One of them speaks.

"Do you remember attending Mr. R's metal shop class at Luther Burbank Junior High?"

Crap. It's about that.

"Um, yes, I do."

"According to our records, you took some extra credit while in his class and went on his private boat, the Skipjack. Is that true?"

My throat goes dry and tense, but I manage to squeeze out my answer.

"Yeah. I did. Once."

"We ask you this because some of his former students have come forward and reported him to the police. He's done some very bad things. One of the student's parents are charging him with rape. He's in a lot of trouble. We need you to tell us everything that happened between you and Mr. R."

My mind's spinning in a million directions before settling on a solid panic. I'm in no shape to give a report on my trip aboard the Skipjack to anyone. I hated Mr. R and what he tried to do to me, and I wanted to tell them everything. But I just couldn't. The last thing I wanted was to go on record about what happened that weekend.

"That was a long time ago. I barely remember it."

"Can you give us *any* details about your experiences that day on the Skipjack?"

I quietly replied, "No."

They look at each other, realizing I'm not going to talk, and let me go. The news of Mr. R's arrest spreads like wildfire in small-town, Mayberryesque fashion. Before long, everyone seemed to know some poor boy that'd said he'd been molested by that creep.

Mr. R went to jail. He was the first real convicted criminal I knew. The people of Burbank talked about him like he was famous. As his name and boat became legendary, my high school world was starting to feel claustrophobic and too insular to enjoy any longer. Some kids heard I'd been on the Skipjack and asked me about it, but I always shrugged it off, saying it was no big deal and nothing happened.

The rest of my senior year went fast. Despite low grades, I graduated, and was more than ready to start living.

PART TWO

HOT FREAKS

I'M RUMMAGING THROUGH A BUNCH OF JUNK at the American Way Thrift Shop wondering what miracle is going to save me from joining the 9-to-5 work force. While high-school friends are heading off to college or jumping into full-time work like Mike Keys and Richard have, I'm flipping through a stack of dusty Perry Como and Barbra Streisand LPs feeling stuck in post-high-school purgatory. I don't normally come here to look at records, there's hardly ever any good ones. Today, I'm just killing time. I mostly come here to hunt for random, inexpensive objects to decorate the garage of the Zabrecky household into an art studio I'm calling "the Lab."

I've painted the walls a color I can see with no problem, dark grey, found matching carpet — at least I think it's dark grey, but it could be blue — installed some track lighting, and now just need a couple of stools and lamps to make it feel complete. The Lab is a space I use to create and listen to music and try my hand at painting, drawing, and making collages. But mostly, it's is my place to dream, and understand art as a form of communication. I'm learning how to interpret ideas and apply them to different mediums, sometimes jamming a bass riff, or spray painting an imagined city skyline I've never been to on canvas, other times gluing found objects onto existing photos I've found right here inside this musky second hand palace, which was once the Thrifty Drugstore of my childhood, and combine them to create surreal Dada inspired collages. Living at home and assembling the Lab is economically effective. My generous folks don't charge me a dime to use the space, keep my bedroom, eat their food, swim in their pool, or tie up their phone line. I've got a pretty good deal going, I say to myself as I pick up a funky 60s lamp with an op art lamp shade. It's $4.99. Score.

While putting last touches on the Lab, I daydream I'll go to college and become a high-school teacher, just to put my parents at ease, but those daydreams aren't enough to motivate me to earn some unwanted degree and pay for it through student loans. That type of plan seems like the first stage of a long-term failure for me. All I want to do is start my own band, make records, and travel any place I can to get out of Burbank and perform music. I've found a part-time job teaching art classes to kids at a daycare center in North Hollywood and am taking a few general classes at Los Angeles Valley Community College.

An actor friend who thinks I've got an interesting look suggested I try going out for TV commercials and TV shows. Other than the two acting classes I took in school as electives, I don't have any experience as an actor, but feel like it's worth a shot. Every couple of weeks I've been going out on casting calls, but can barely handle the energy of all these guys my age, desperately pacing around stuffy audition rooms in Hollywood wanting to be the next Tom Cruise or something. After a bunch of demoralizing auditions, I was cast in something, and faked my way through learning lines and pretended to act in an awful courtroom reenactment show. The experience was enough to educate me that acting isn't for me, and stopped going to auditions shortly after. Even though it seems like it'd be exciting to be in movies, my mind is fixed on playing music and starting my own band. There's gotta be more to life than graduating high school, going to college, and settling down in the same place I grew up. I know I can't go on too long with my low-paying, after-school, daycare-center job and putting around Valley College. In the meantime, my preoccupation with music has led me to engage in Hollywood nightlife.

Many of my what-the-hell-am-I-doing evenings are spent hanging around the Lhasa Club. Located in a one-story brick building in seedy Hollywood just off Santa Monica Boulevard, the Lhasa Club is my sanctuary. Inside, visual artists, poets, musicians, writers, and artsy hipsters pack in to sit around dimly lit junky tables and on the floor, drinking from Styrofoam cups and bottles in paper bags, to hear the latest poetry by Exene Cervenka, Henry Rollins, or Lydia Lunch through a crummy microphone on a small stage. A month ago I caught an art show by this radical DIY artist Mark Gash, who showed these sexually fierce, large-scale, surreal paintings. His paintings were like explosions on canvas. They're some of the most provocative things I've ever seen.

I caught something I wasn't expecting when a performance-art group called the Afro Sisters took the Lhasa stage. At first glance, you'd think they are just a few raunchy drag queen hookers who wandered in off the street to accost audience members, but then you start to understand they're a concept group like KISS. On a dirty white sheet pinned to back wall of the Lhasa, they projected this totally weird and subversive movie they'd made, of them running around Hollywood like this screwball, skanked-out exploitation version Charlie's Angels, and then performed a set of lo-fi trashy punk while berating audience members. Then came equally fascinating performances by the Holy Sisters of the Gaga Dada, a spooky, transcendental version of the Go-Gos; a set by bizarro punk cabaretists, Tyrants in Therapy; and an introspectively existential monologue by this terrific nut called John Fleck.

The Lhasa Club is magic.

The Lhasa has become the perfect distraction for my uncertain future. The more I go there, the more I realize I can do anything I want with my creative life. It's got punk's spirit, mod's smartness, and a DIY ethos that holds no creative boundaries. Everybody at the Lhasa is living a life that's fueled by art. It's like Zurich's gift to performance art, the Cabaret Voltaire — but instead of being in Switzerland in the middle of World War I, I'm in Hollywood in 1987. Driving back to Burbank from the Lhasa, I'm always inspired, heading deeper down the path to make my mark on an art map.

I show up for an art opening some weekend night with a bottle of Southern Comfort jammed in my pants, anticipating another evening of artful distraction. I tuck myself against a brick wall in the back, soaking it all in, feeling like I'm in some Beatnik movie, when two attractive girls about my age with brightly-colored hair in tutus and leather jackets stroll by. One of them asks for a cigarette, the other for my name. It's impossible to tell whether they think I'm cool and want to meet me or if they're just jocking me for a smoke.

"Robbie? Really, Robbie? That's kind of cute, I guess," one of them condescends. The last thing I want, or need, especially at the Lhasa, is to be cute. Fuck cute, I think. I'm at the Lhasa. I need to be cool.

Suddenly, Robbie is the name attached to the guy from Burbank who was going to live and die there, so I lie.

"No. No, I said it's Rob, not Robbie," I say, lighting the real cute one's cig, hoping for a phone number from either of them.

"Thanks for the cigarette, *Robbie*. See you around." Ouch. And there they went.

Right there in the back of the smoky and dim lit Lhasa Club, in my mind at least, I dropped the cute last syllable from my name and became Rob.

My last name is a whole different story. My father told me that Zabrecky, in Polish translation, means "in the trees, behind the bushes, watching all," or something like that. As a kid from white bread Burbank, where it seemed like most kids had last names like Smith or Jones, my last name was one more thing that set me apart from them. I wasn't crazy about it and sometimes got teased for being a Polack. For a short time I shortened it, calling myself Robbie Z, since that's what people like to call me anyhow, and even Robbie Zee for a few months, before realizing they both sounded stupid. By 19, Rob Zabrecky sounds like the name of the person I'll be in the future, and Robbie Zabrecky was the guy from Burbank.

Maybe it's no coincidence that while I'm searching, I've been falling into a spiraling pattern of blackout drinking. Although I'm still under legal drinking age, getting drunk and loaded is chalked up as "tying one on" in the Zabrecky household. Last weekend my brother Gordy came up from college in San Diego, went out partying and blacked out. We spent the better part of Sunday morning driving around Burbank, looking for his motorcycle. As of yet, we haven't found it.

One thing's for sure: a night of hard drinking guarantees a solid night of slumber, free from the nightmares of my sniper relative and sexual predators.

***

It's Friday night and I've just finished painting a huge, black, worker ant on the back of the Lab door. I'm draping some colored Christmas lights over a dozen or so masks I've been collecting, which are hung on the wall next to the door with the big ant. There's all kinds—old Halloween masks I wore as a kid, African Voodoo ones, and a couple I found at the thrift store that go on mannequins that look they're from *The Twilight Zone*. It's definitely starting to look like an art gallery in here, I think.

The phone rings, which I drag into the Lab from a long cord in the house. It's my friend Melissa, this sexy girl I know from Valley College who has an obsession for '60s fashion and talks like a total Val.

"Hey! What are doing tonight? I'm hitting a club in Hollywood with this guy you've *got* to meet from North Hollywood. His name is Sellso.

"Sellso?" I ask, wondering if that's even a name.

"Yeah! Totally cool name, right? You say it like, *sell*—like I'm going to *sell* you my car, and *so*—like *so* what. But fast. But it's spelled with a C. Celso. And it's like, really his name, I swear. I know you guys are going to be, like best friends. We're coming over to pick you up right now," she says all in one whoosh and hangs up the phone. I guess I'm going out tonight.

Twenty minutes later an old Dodge Coronet with huge back fins and chipping paint pulls up and honks. Melissa's in the passenger seat. I hop in back and sit back on the sprawling, rotting upholstery as we bail over the hill into Hollywood. Melissa's totally in charge and calling like *all* the shots.

"So, we're going to this totally underground club called Ground Zero that changes locations, like, all the time. It's run by these cool old Hollywood hipsters that used to do that cool place, the Zero Zero art gallery thing. Anyways, this is like, their new thing, so it'll be totally rad, because they're totally rad. And so are you guys! Oh my God, I haven't even introduced you guys yet! Duh! Robbie, this is Celso! Celso, Robbie!" Her voice, and the intonation of her words sound just like Moon Zappa's in the song, "Valley Girl." She doesn't know I changed my name to Rob, and somehow it's not worth correcting her so I let it slide.

I look in the rear-view mirror and catch a glimpse of the guy driving, smile and nod.

"Hey man. Cool car. Need some gas money?" I say, introducing myself, wanting to get off to a good start.

"No man, it's cool. You can buy drinks or something later. Yeah, thanks. Just got this thing from the *Recycler*. 700 bucks. Had to go all the way up to Seattle to buy it and drive it back, though. Got it from this weird old hippie who lived on a farm. It was smooth sailing the whole way back, but when I pulled up in front of my parents' house the radiator blew. It's still a little messed up," he says, like it's no big deal.

I get the impression that not too much is a big a deal with this guy. He's a quicksilver of a dude, with this great smile that reveals the same stained and chipped teeth as the punk kids I'd met in Scotland. His dark eyes are darting all over the place through a pair of thick, black-rimmed, 1950s glasses and he drives like a total maniac. I'm not sure he even has a driver's license, or if he does, how he could've gotten it by weaving through cars and slamming on the brakes the way he does.

I use my faithful fake ID to pick up a pint of Southern Comfort from a rundown liquor store in Hollywood, and we park in an empty parking lot behind that old post office on Selma Avenue and Cahuenga Boulevard. It's the part of Hollywood that looks nearly abandoned — like Burbank did in the early '80s — but it's safe to conduct our pre-club drinking there before venturing into the club. There's no sign to advertise it, just a red-light bulb outside the brick building on Selma. Some cute girl sitting on a stool with big hair who probably also works on Melrose takes five bucks from each of us and we head inside.

The club is packed. "Bang a Gong" by T-Rex is cranking so loud we can't hear anything else, so we shuffle around, buying each other cheap drinks, smoking cigarettes, and gawking at local celebrities; Danny Shades, Tequila Mockingbird, and Ruben Blue, who are famous in local rags like the *LA Weekly* and *Scratch* magazine, are out in full force — it's the jackpot of Hollywood nightlife. Even Mark Gash, the artist who made those explosive paintings from the Lhasa club, is here.

We find a back patio outside where the music is still loud, and huddle in a corner, soaking in the '80s-underground night action. Out there, me and the guy with a name I'd never heard before from the next city over are pulled to each other like magnets. He's the most fantastic young lad I've ever met. He's a living character — a Frankenstein mash-up of 1920s silent film star Ramon Navarro and 1950s silver screen actor Sal Mineo—that is, if they gave birth to a slightly disheveled, music and art-obsessed teen who fell off the screen of a Jim Jarmusch film. He looks famous, or like someone who should be. Melissa's off getting the next round of drinks. That's when Celso and me have a chance to get some words in with each other.

"I'm from North Hollywood. Went to Notre Dame High School. A bunch of my old cronies run with FFF, but that scene isn't for me, you know? I just wanna play my guitar and see the world, you know?" he says through the greatest smile I've ever seen.

"I'm sort of in the same boat. Grew up in Burbank. I can't get into going to a real college and most of my old buds are doing things I don't want to do," I respond.

As outgoing and upbeat as he is, there's an inner darkness lurking behind that smile. Something tells me we'll be friends forever.

We hang around Ground Zero a few more hours. By the end of the night, we've probably had five drinks apiece. Melissa's pretty gone, and already nostalgic about introducing Celso and me.

"I knew it. I just knew it. You guys, you guys are fully going to be beeeeest…" and then she collapses against a wall and passes out. Celso and I take it as our exit cue, and carry her to Celso's car, where she vomits all over the front seat, then falls asleep like an angel.

Our best plan is to get her home, prop her barely standing body on the porch of her parents' home in the Sherman Oaks, ring the doorbell, and bail as fast as possible. Heading back to my house, Celso shows me one of his favorite tricks.

"Watch this," he says pulling into someone's driveway. He floors the accelerator, makes a sharp turn and starts tearing across a dozen or so manicured lawns of quiet houses in North Hollywood. Tearing over nicely manicured shrubs and manicured rose bushes, I can't believe I hadn't thought of trying this before.

"Oh man! Hope there's no cops around," I say half panicking, but feeling the best thrill I've had in a while.

"Me neither!" he says like he's Han Solo navigating the Millennium Falcon through a meteor shower. We're heading full speed toward a lattice fence when he makes a turn so sharp that for a second I'm sure we're on two wheels. The Coronet shakes and bounces like there's an earthquake inside, and somehow we're stabilized at end of the quiet street.

We look at each other and burst into laughter.

There's something off — the perfect kind of off — about this guy and I can't hardly wait for another adventure with him. He drops me off and we exchange numbers.

***

Like me, Celso's a big dreamer. He wants to start a band, make records, and go on the road, rather than take the path of everyone we know by going to college or getting stuck at some job we hate. On weekdays we start hanging out together between classes at Valley College, or "13th grade," somehow believing our destinies are different than the other students rushing from class to class.

As far as my old comrades go, Sully and I are still close, I've seen less of Mike Keys since high school, and even less of

Richard. Yesterday I received a phone call from the mother of my old high school friend; the guy I dubbed the Truman Capote of John Burroughs, Peculiar Chris. She called with horrible news. She said he'd suddenly become ill with a rare flesh eating virus and passed away. I could hardly believe it. His spirit depicted the idea that unusually talented individuals such as he could grow and prosper, even if he was from a town like Burbank. Except for Sully, Mike, Richard, and the spirit of Peculiar Chris are starting to represent the past, whereas Celso represents the future. My Burbank life's over. It's dead and I need to move away from it.

Sully and I are sitting in a booth inside our late-night go-to place to dream, the Copper Penny. It's a 24-hour restaurant and coffee shop with this dark wood-cabin-esque atmosphere that's just across the street from Warner Brothers Studios. Over coffee and smokes some Friday night he gets an idea.

"Man, I'm so fed up with Burbank. We should go to Europe this summer. We could get around for pretty cheap and see a bunch of cool cities. Wouldn't cost that much if we start saving now."

It's the best idea he's ever had. There's nothing stopping us, and a few months later we're kicking around Amsterdam, Denmark, and the French Riviera. At the end of the trip we end up at Heidi's place, this foxy foreign-exchange student we'd met while in high school.

One night in her living room, Sully and I perform a few songs we've cobbled together from a cheap acoustic guitar I brought along. The tunes are short and minimal, inspired by '60s surf and spy riffs, with narrative lyrics with content inspired from our walks back home and from our trip. With Sully on guitar and me singing and bopping around, we play this handful of nearly improvised songs for a few friends we'd met in Copenhagen. When we're done, there's this long awkward silence — nobody knows if they should laugh or applaud. Even though it's a pretty safe bet it's so awful they don't want to say anything, it reminds me of jumping around freely on the stage at the Lodge, and feels kind of great.

On our last day, I remembered that before I left, Celso asked me to send him two postcards from Amsterdam, with a chunk of hashish sandwiched between them. I found the perfect one that read "Groeten Uit Amsterdam." It had all these cheesy images of monuments and tourist stuff. I bought two, smashed some hash I picked up from one of the million hash bars near my hotel between them, just like he asked. Below the stamp and his return address, I wrote, "Let's start a band."

***

Three months later I'm in the Lab on some forgetable week-night, looking back and forth at an open schoolbook I'm supposed to be reading, and a painting I'm almost done with. The phone rings and saves me from trying to understand either of them.

"Hey man, it's Celso. What are you up to?"

"Not a thing."

"Me neither. Hollywood?"

"Yeah, Hollywood."

"I'll be by in 15."

Some people are just made to be friends. When me and Celso are together, lightning can strike. Tonight, we're breaking Groundhog Day monotony by motoring over the Cahuenga Pass into Hollywood in Celso's Coronet.

I'm not sure who said it first, or how we decided tonight is the night, but we're trying crack together for the first time. We're here at the corner of Yucca and Ivar in Hollywood—the epicenter of drug activity — with fifty bucks we pooled together. It's overrun with dozens of black and Hispanic drug zombies, all swarming around one another, buying and selling all kinds of stuff. It's a late-night farmer's market, but for drugs.

Everything about this intersection looks like a movie set—the run-down buildings tagged with occasional graffiti, faded signs with missing letters from past decades, and the grand Knickerbocker Hotel and iconic Capitol Records building looming as a backdrop. It's my favorite type of LA weather. Santa Ana winds are sweeping the smog someplace else for a change, but are still blowing here at a steady pace. Gusts of warm wind come along every few minutes and blow fallen palm-tree branches or fast-food wrappers up in the air, and they do a little dance. Tonight, run-down Hollywood is crystal clear, pulsating, and perfect. As the palm trees rock back and forth, I have a feeling we're in for a night we'll remember.

We park Cel's less than inconspicuous Coronet on Yucca and weave in and out of this crowd of shady druggies, trying to keep our anonymity. Somehow it's apparent to everyone why we, two Valley boys, are among them. In thrift-store overcoats, we want to believe we're fitting in, but we're not fooling anyone and we know it, sticking out like a pair of novice chumps.

Soon, every other peddler is trying to make a deal with us. We pause in crack traffic and look at each other, not knowing whom to buy from. There are so many options, and it's impossible to tell who's got the best stuff and won't rip us off. I'm getting paranoid, and my heart's racing with a premonition that we can get busted just for being there.

"Man, this looks like a bust. Wanna bail?"

"Not yet. Follow me," Celso says, kicking into high gear. We walk half a block down Yucca, where out of nowhere, this enormous, thirty-something gangster appears like a genie from a bottle. He must be seven feet tall.

"Hey, hey, hey, what you boys looking for?" He's wearing a baseball cap, sunglasses, and an over-sized sports jersey that hung over his crotch. It's hard to believe they make clothes that big. He carries himself with the same assurance as a fancy maître d', providing a confidence our order is on its way — and when it arrives, it'll be excellent.

Without needing to exchange words, we know he's our guy. Celso quickly hands over our fifty bucks. The dealer slips me a small plastic bag that contains a half dozen small rocks of crack. I don't know if we're getting a good deal or ripped off, or whatever, but jam the rocks into my pocket as fast as I can. Then comes a new voice.

"Welcome to Hollywood, boys! I'm Ms. Sheila. Now, what'choo nice-looking boys gonna smoke from? Huh? You need a pipe. Look at you! You some fiiiiine boys."

I turn around and there's this disheveled and nearly incoherent black transvestite, tweakishly adjusting her long platinum wig. I'm not sure why, but I trust her with our lives.

"Oh yeah, we need a pipe. You got one?" I ask.

"I've got one for each day of the week, sunny boy."

As the four of us are standing on the corner, waiting to make our next move, this small hunched-over black dude with white hair appears out of the darkness. He's missing his two front teeth, probably more, and his eyes are bulging from his little head. His t-shirt, which is way too big for him, says, "D.A.R.E. TO KEEP KIDS OFF DRUGS."

"Where you fools gonna smoke dat? You need a good, I say a good, safe place to smoke dat. I got a place, just down MacArthur Park. You gimme a ride down there and I'll set you up." Everything's happening so quickly that there's no time to doubt a thing. We just have to go with it. Suddenly, Celso and I are sharing the role of Dorothy on the road to Oz, and we're with the Tin Man, the Scarecrow, and the Cowardly Lion. It's time to party.

The wind's blowing everywhere as the five of us are in Celso's Coronet plowing onto the 101, heading south to MacArthur Park. I wonder again if Celso has his driver's license, but now's not the right time to ask. The inside of his car starts reeking of a foul combination of human urine, feces, and nasty perfume. I light two cigarettes to kill the smell and hand one to Celso, as our unlikely alliance heads south on the Yellow Crack Road. I'm in the back seat, riding bitch between the drag queen and the gangster, while the nearly toothless old man spouts gibberish, giving Celso directions to Oz.

"I know you've got our vittles. Our tender vittles," Ms. Sheila says, grabbing at my pocket, and then my crotch.

"Hey, take it easy," I say, handing her the stuff, and watching her meticulously pluck a yellowish crack nugget from the little plastic bag. She tightly presses it into this cigarette-shaped glass pipe, and hands it to me.

"Here you go, honey," her sweet baritone voice whispers. It's one of these all or nothing moments. I look around the moving car, feeling the excitement and energy of that short second, knowing there's no time to waste. I put the loaded pipe to my lips and ignite the rock. As I suck the fumes through the glass tube into my lungs it glows like a piece of Krypton shrapnel. The taste is the most unnaturally horrible thing I'd ever inhaled, but like so many things I've never done before, I know I need to muscle through it. The taste makes me gag, and my lungs felt like they're going to erupt. I hold it in for as long as I can before blowing a massive cloud of toxic smoke that disperses everywhere. I'm saluted with a unanimous cheer. Someone grabs the pipe from my hand and this party is officially on.

When you're high on crack, the world transforms into this whole different place. It's hard to overstate the primal euphoria of that first hit, but the inside of my head shakes with the biggest head rush — like the feeling you get during the first drop of a roller coaster. Then my entire body is absorbed with this crazy floating energy, like I've been sucked under a crashing wave, plummeted into an exciting new zone, not knowing which way is up. Then comes this major tingling in my groin and an unexpected erection. A throbbing erection is the last thing I want, or need, especially in present company, but there's nothing I can do to stop it. I light another cigarette to distract unwanted attention from my pants and push my knees together so tightly that they almost make me shoot a wad into my tighty-whities. As I start to stabilize, my ears start hearing this high-pitched ring that tells me everything is right in the world and I feel this smile on my face.

Now, I've got a pretty good understanding why crack is so popular. I'm off the map of everything I've known before and am living somewhere outside my body.

Ms. Sheila takes the pipe from me. With the expertise of a career professional, she reloads and hits it hard without missing a beat. "Um, needed that!" she says, bursting into huge baritone laugh.

"Hey, up here!" chimes in Celso from the driver's seat. She passes him the pipe. He takes his first hit from behind the steering wheel in the fast lane. "Oh yeah!" he exclaims while releasing the smoke into the warm night air, somehow continuing to drive. For all Celso's reckless driving tendencies, he somehow obeys the rules of the road like a driving instructor while he's on crack.

Now everyone in our crack-smoking crew is on the same page and we're headed toward downtown at rocket speed. The pipe makes its way to the backseat again and I reach for it. "Oh, thanks, doll," Ms. Sheila giggles, while intercepting the pipe into her large manicured hands. Somehow we're not going in order. Tonight isn't about being fair, though. She takes another hit and hands it back to me. The mouth end of the pipe is smeared with pink lipstick that smells of burned plastic.

I take another hit, holding in the smoke until it erupts out of my mouth like a volcano. My logic and wit are gone and now I'm so high I don't care if I live or die. Here I am, living some dream, not caring about anyone or anything else, feeling like I'm in some Lou Reed song or John Waters movie. In my thundering head, I've transcended the regular world for this one where there are no consequences, just pure, selfish, late-teen hedonism, and it feels unbelievable.

The pipe makes another round and comes back to me. I'm so revved up and hypersensitive to sounds and gripping the pipe is almost too hot to hold. It feels like a sizzling French fry just out of the vat. I almost drop it, transferring it hand to hand until it cools down and take another huge hit. Now I'm ready to fuck or fight. I'm so excited I don't know what to do with myself; I'm stuck inside the back of this racing car, where it stinks to high heaven and my dick is still hard.

We arrive at MacArthur Park and take the lead from the little old man. He's the only one who's in control. "Pull over here. Right here, ya fool. Now kill da engine, kill da engine. And da damn lights. Da damn lights!" We're sitting in the car for an uncomfortable moment in silence, waiting for our next order of business.

Instead of barking out a plan of some sort, he confuses everyone by yanking Celso's keys from the ignition and bolts out of the car, and disappears into the dark park. Celso takes off after him and tackles him near a palm tree that's ready to blow over from the strong wind. It's a tornado of bewilderment, and I'm paralyzed in the back seat, still sandwiched between Ms. Sheila and the gangster. My erection and the joy of the first few crack hits are gone. Ms. Sheila starts to panic.

"Take me back to Hollywood, take me back to Hollywood!" she whimpers, shaking her massive knees like a little girl who wants to go home after peeing her pants at a slumber party.

The gangster gets fed up with us and loses his temper. He removes the last thing I expect to see: a small pistol from under his jersey. He starts waving it around the back seat.

"I'll take down all y'all motherfuckers if ya don't just fuckin' relax! Don't nobody move. We just gotsta stay put, and be coo. Be coo."

I see the gun and freeze. My heart's nearly pounding out of my shirt. Not since Uncle Ed shot me have I felt this kind of high alert panic, where the idea of death is so imminent. We're all going down, I'm certain. All I can do is await my destiny.

The three of us watch the old man, as he escapes Celso's clumsy half nelson and scurries off into the park, where the silhouettes of crack zombies lurking around a picnic table are illuminated by a distant wind-blown campfire. They're off in the darkness, and I'm stuck in the back seat, barely being able to comprehend what was going on and obeying my orders to stay put by the gangster. All I can think is that I'm the world's worst wingman. I close my eyes and start praying my own version of "there's no place like home," like Dorothy did at the end of *The Wizard of Oz*. All I want is for us to return to Kansas—the Valley—where the fridge is stocked and everything's fine.

Every minute is like an hour. Celso finally emerges from the park. He's dazed and out of breath, holding his keys, with that incredible smile of his. He hops in the driver's seat and gives us the play by play.

"I chased that dude half way through the park. He's way faster than he looks. Kept saying, 'Got me a new car, got me a new car!' Out of nowhere he just stops and says, 'Looking for these?' and hands them over. Then he grabs a 10 speed with two flat tires that's laying there and takes off."

Just then a cop car rolls by and flashes a light in our car. Everyone manages to stay cool. Celso looks at them and flashes his million-dollar smile while the rest of us drop back in our seats. They flash the brightest flashlight into our car and survey us inside. Figuring this is the part where we get arrested for possession of crack and God knows what else, luck is on our side, and they continue up the street.

This party is over and we all know it. Every bit of energy is deflated. Celso, the drag queen, the gangster, and I head back up the 101 with zero of the excitement we had while going down. They helped get us high, but after seeing the gun and everything that happened with the old man, the spirit of the adventure was dead and they had to go. With a mutual sense of relief, we return to the intersection where we'd met and drop them off.

We had a little unfinished business: a few chunks of unsmoked crack. Neither of us were ready to call it a night. It's nearly 2am, but we hit Playboy liquor on Yucca and Wilcox, using my fake ID to pick up a bottle of Southern Comfort. There's only one place to go — the place where people with no place to go after midnight go: Errol Flynn's spooked-out nearly demolished mansion at the end of Fuller Avenue. It'd become a destination for night-timers to drink, take drugs, and take in a perfect view of Hollywood. It's only a cement foundation with an empty swimming pool covered in graffiti and broken glass, but it's got the best view of Hollywood and there are no cops.

Fighting the winds, which are still in full force, we jump the tall, black, iron fence and head up the dark driveway. As the warm winds continue to blow, the city lights glow below like a cliché from a film. Smoking our last bits of crack, we laugh like hell about what'd just happened, and share our dreams and visions of playing music. Up on that lookout while most of city is asleep, we decide to form our own group.

Long after midnight we smoke the rest of the stuff, kill the Southern Comfort, and run out of cigarettes. We head back to the Valley with the satisfaction of knowing we're going to change each other's lives. In some stupid way, we've just proved ourselves to each other. Elements from earlier—stupidity, unabashed dreams, naivety, and fearlessness—form an invisible outline for an ethos and foundation to getting started.

***

The next morning, I wake up with the most explosive, toxic headache I've ever had. My tongue rolls over half a dozen blisters on my dry lips and I need water. Bad. As my head lifts off the bed, I realize my face is tightly glued to my pillow by bloody scrapes. I sit up in a panic, and race to the bathroom mirror with the pillow still attached to my face. I slowly peel it off, revealing four or five quarter-sized bleeding sores. The floor's spinning and my body is aching all over as I stick my head under the faucet, and then suck down a quart of Gatorade, trying to stabilize.

While applying Band-Aids to the open wounds that look like pepperonis from Dino's Pizza, I take a moment to discern what'd happened last night. I start seeing rapid snapshots and eventually piece it all together. After Celso dropped me off, I wanted a cigarette, but was far too wasted to get in my car, so rode my bicycle to 7-Eleven to grab a pack. On the ride home, I was so far gone I'd crashed into parked cars and collapsed on my face every few houses. I missed my classes again that day, and it's totally worth it. Now, I have something to look forward to: forming a band with the greatest guy I know.

JABBERJAWING

WHILE BIDING TIME at Valley College, I met this couple about my age named Gary and Michelle. I appreciated their ability to show up for school costumed as if they'd stepped off the set of a Russ Meyer movie. He resembles a teenage Tiny Tim and she styles herself like a lost cast member from *Barbarella*. After becoming fast friends, we've agreed that Hollywood nightlife takes precedence over Sociology 101.

Between mind-numbing classes, and sometimes instead of them, we meet on campus to scour the *LA Weekly* and hatch evening plans, which always culminates in sailing over the Cahuenga Pass in Gary's lopsided Galaxie 500, with Michelle riding shotgun, to explore LA's music and art worlds. These nights usually begin by heading inside Hollywood Boulevard's cavernous Raji's to see bands, or checking out downtown art-loft parties before engaging in late-night people-watching at coffee houses like the PikMe-Up or Onyx/Sequel, where inspired casts of late-night art people are alive and well.

About a year into this routine, it was unanimously decided among the three of us that LA needs a venue where John Waters and Lou Reed can be honored as kings and Keane big-eye paintings can be viewed as high art; a place with a menu that features Pop Tarts, sugar cereals, assorted coffee, *and* live performances. After a little brainstorming and a loan from their folks, they've become motivated to create the clubhouse we can claim as our own, and it'll be called Jabberjaw.

After spending much of the spring and summer on obsessive scavenger hunts at garage sales, thrift shops, and flea markets across LA, a selection of retro décor has been procured. All we need is the right venue. After checking out a handful of available spaces, a former machine shop on the desolate 3700 block of Pico Boulevard near Crenshaw Street is secured as the location. I've volunteered every free moment to scrape and patch holes, hang drywall, and drench the interior with high-gloss turquoise paint. This prospect is the most exciting thing that's happened since I met Celso, and has become a solution to my conundrum of having a creative outlet besides music to pour myself into.

Across LA, record stores and art galleries have been plastered with flyers advertising Jabberjaw's opening night, finishing touches were added, and a business license was procured. Opening night was a hit, and Jabberjaw becomes a dimly lit melting pot for art-minded LA hipsters, Redd Kross fanatics, disaffected USC kids, trust-fund Satan worshippers, KXLU disc jockeys, and collectors of obscure records and videos. It's also been attracting curious, drunk, Latino hustlers who wander in from the nearby gay disco, Catch One, as well as hipster alumni from the late '70s punk world. You couldn't have dreamed such a colorful cross section of characters converging, but here they all are.

A steady stream of articles about LA's newest and only coffeehouse-art gallery-micro movie theater have been appearing in the *LA Weekly*, *Bam*, and the *LA Reader*, bringing in new and interesting patrons every week. Seeing the wonder and amusement of new customers revel at worn VHS screenings of *Pink Flamingos* or *Desperate Teenage Lovedolls* playing on repeat inside the Micro Movie Theater, or discovering the sounds of Martin Denny or Arthur Lyman in the club's Tiki Lounge, is a real kick. Almost overnight, Gary and Michelle have become the Sonny and Cher of the LA underground, and I, its punkish Norman Bates.

I can hardly wait to arrive each night to make coffee, serve cereal, and bus tables for this colorful cast of LA music and art people I've been admiring from a distance. I've also been helping Michelle book live entertainment and find new art shows. Art students from Otis Parsons and Cal Arts have been queuing up to show new works, and now, there are far more artists inquiring to show work than the available space and dates on the calendar. Every night seems to attract a new cast of characters, and I love catching glimpses and knowing looks of those reveling in our unique late night happenings. Even Red Kross shows up a few times a week with their ultra-cool entourage to drink cappuccinos and chitchat about obscure TV stars and the latest Japanese garage bands.

Exchanging college years for art dreams, and finding ourselves deep in the LA music and art world adored from the steps of Valley College, is the smartest thing any of us has done. Even though I'm nearly broke and still living at home, Jabberjaw gives my ideas a place to live. I've hung a couple of my paintings: one being a 3' by 5' canvas of a bloodied surgeon closing in on a patient, painted from the perspective of the patient; the other, a multi-colored self-portrait of me in some paranoid state, afraid to open his door because he can't face one more day of his life, which he hates. Hearing validating comments about them from customers who have no idea I'm the artist as I ring up their orders makes working the cash register all worthwhile. While bussing tables, I chuckle to myself while overhearing trash talk from the mouths of those who'll probably be future rock stars.

***

Someone is singing a lullaby right in my ear and rubbing my head.

> *Rock-A-By-Robbie*
> *On the Tree Top*
> *When the wind blows*
> *The cradle will rock...*

I have no idea where I am or what time it is. I pull my eyes open, and I realize I'm in fetal position, being tightly cradled in the enormous black arms of Hollywood's underground trans-favorite, Vaginal Davis. She's rocking me like a newborn, batting her long eyelashes at me like I'm her baby, while adjusting her long platinum wig. She's calmly stroking my hair, just singing away. I think I might be dreaming, but as I start to regain vision, I sense we're in the back courtyard outside Jabberjaw. There are others seated next to us. We're joined by *LA Weekly's* favorite queer, six-foot-seven, Christian, drag punker, Glen Meadmore; and the transsexual, polio-ridden, Goddess Bunny, along with her James Dean-ish, teenage, hustler beau, dolled up and whispering to each other. I squeamishly release myself and thank Ms. Davis for her hospitality, and drive back to Burbank, trying to piece together what happened before blacking out.

My blackouts are becoming a regular thing. I never intend on blacking out, but I've fallen into a habit of losing control and ending up in compromised places, like with what happened with Ms. Davis. Just couple of nights ago I showed up on a night off, with a few old Burbank friends. I took the liberty of ushering us into the Tiki Lounge to host a small crack-smoking party. Even Michelle, who has a high-tolerance for pushing things to their limits, doesn't condone crack.

"What's that horrible smell in here?" she says, busting in, just after I've taken the hugest hit I could. Then she sees the glass pipe coming out of my mouth.

"Oh no! Not crack, no way, baby! Jabberjaw is *not* a crack house, Robbie. Not cool!"

A minute later she comes back with her trusty broomstick — the one she uses to chase out vagrants who come in asking for change — and chases us out like vermin.

"Out! Out! Out! All of you. How dare you! Jabberjaw is NOT a crack house! Get out, and stay out!" she says, with the same disgust as Mink Stole, battling Divine in *Pink Flamingos*. Something about the madness of her swatting us out like flies tells me that Michelle and me have become the John Waters characters we'd previously deified — we'd graduated, or devolved, from watching weird movies to living them. And at least for tonight, I add Jabberjaw to the list of employers who can no longer use my services.

AMERICA'S MOST WANTED

"A ND NOW, here they are, for the first time anywhere. Please join me in welcoming Possum
Dixon!" Celso and his huge beautiful smile strums
an aggressive two-chord repetitive riff on an acoustic guitar
like his life depends on it. It's loud, and tinny, and distorted,
because it's been miked and is coming through the crummy old
PA speakers. I grab the mic from its stand and we launch into
our first song, "Six Times."

Six times I thought I was getting old.
Time to time it happens when I'm out alone.
My past begins to tell me of all the things that I should have done.
Please God, just forgive me that I'm only 21...

Twenty minutes earlier, Celso and I are standing in the alley,
behind Bebop Records & Fine Art, sharing a bottle of Southern
Comfort and chain smoking to help relieve the pre-show tension. Richard, the club's proprietor, peeks his head around the
corner and discovers us standing there.

"You guys are on. Now," he says politely, but like he's talking
to a couple of fuck-ups.

As ready as we'll ever be, we go inside to discover a surprising number of around thirty curious onlookers and friends, who
were mostly there to catch the headliners — our favorite new
band, Lazytown. After Richard's introduction, I feel the weight
of it all and pray I can pull off the show. I go into a near blackout, knowing that my ass is on the line. By the end of the show
we'll know if we have a band or not. After Celso bursts into
the "Six Times" riff, my nerves calm and but I'm overwhelmed.
Then comes the last thing I expect, an elated freedom.

Throughout the show, stuff was thrown around and broken, and the audience stayed back to ensure their safety. At the end of it, which added up to a whopping twenty minutes, I'm drenched in sweat from singing and flopping around, and Celso's right hand is bloody from playing the guitar three times as fast as we had rehearsed. Meanwhile, our other two band members, my Jabberjaw co-hort Michelle and the drummer are wearing fewer clothes than they started with. As my heart slowed down to its regular pace, I couldn't help but thinking it was the most exhilarating 20 minutes I'd ever lived.

Afterward I'm just relieved it's over. Having no idea what anyone thought, I'm prepared for the worst of reviews. Much to my surprise, Richard smiles at me and shakes my hand.

"Wow. That was interesting. Let me know when you can come back and headline your own show." Whatever we did, he liked it enough to ask us back, making it one of the happiest nights of my life.

***

That first gig happened between working long nights at Jabberjaw and boring days at Valley College. I'm making the time to make it all work, and Celso and I have been rehearsing in the Lab, where we've sandwiched every idea each of us has ever had. After we have the seeds of a twenty-minute set, this handful of simple songs, jammed together by disjointed riffs and theatrical outbursts, we've rounded out the group by enlisting my Jabberjaw cohort, Michelle, to play tambourine, and the drummer from my high-school garage band to bang on pots, pans, and assorted junk. Songs with no bass, others with two guitars and one repetitious riff, free-form trumpet solos, and short monologue/ spoken-word sketches are all part of this musical experiment.

Every newly formed band has rules. Some band's rules are that there are no rules. Ours are this: we'll be devoid of the conventional rock-band blueprint, which'll provide us the creative latitude to make the kind of music we want to hear. So far, we've created this mash-up of music made from people who listen to too much B-52s, Pere Ubu, Violent Femmes, Iggy Pop, and the Velvet Underground. These songs and musical fragments — fueled by Dada and punk ethos — are the basis of our set. We've added a couple of theatrical interludes in which I've incorporated a few props: a tattered Ken Doll I found at a thrift shop that I sing to and shake around like a voodoo doll, a BB gun pistol that looks so real that in a few months it will be borrowed by a friend of Celso's for an actual bank holdup — yes, an actual bank hold up in the Valley — and a handheld industrial light which we use as our only light source.

Together with these ingredients, we've created a mini-series of musical outbursts and fast-paced songs played with spastic urgency, San Fernando Valley style. We costumed ourselves from things found in thrift stores, creating a look inspired by the characters seen in early John Waters movies. Even though our set of music is under thirty minutes, and we don't know exactly how it'll play out, but we are committed to putting on a show that we'd like to see.

Opportunity struck when our friend Matt called, offering us the opening slot for his band, Lazytown, at BeBop. Celso and I both know Matt from different places; I'd met him at Valley College, where we bonded over a love of Redd Kross and kitschy '60s and '70s stuff and Celso knew him from high school. Matt's got this incredible encyclopedic knowledge about music, and can tell you more about obscure and cool underground music than anyone. His band Lazytown channels the killer energy of Husker Dü and the Replacements, and write their own songs that are always getting stuck in my head. He's on this streak of turning me on to music that's been changing my life. He just gave me two LPs that have shaped my musical influences immeasurably: Television's *Marquee Moon* and Richard Hell and the Voidoids' *Blank Generation*.

Even though we're far from being ready, we accept the gig. We don't have a band name, but need one for the pending *LA Weekly* live-show listing. I ring Celso.

"So, the *LA Weekly* needs to call us something for our Bebop show with Lazytown."

"What? Hey, hold on a second. Lemme turn the TV down."

"*The Weekly* needs our band's name for the Bebop gig. Any ideas?"

"I'm watching *America's Most Wanted*. There's this nut job out there murdering people in the South named James Dixon. The dude looks totally insane, and has the word 'possum' tattooed across his fingers. How about Possum Dixon?"

"Hmm. Okay. I'll let them know. Talk to you later."

While I dislike the name because of its hickish twang, I can't deny Possum Dixon sounds like a band name. It rolls off the tongue easily, but can't sound further away from the music we're creating. It evokes the name of a band that might share a bill with Lynyrd Skynyrd or Creedence Clearwater Revival. Since I can't think of a better name, we stick with it, at least for one show.

If you've never been to Bebop, you're missing out. It's the Valley's gift to independent music, a unique and magical place located in a small storefront right in the middle of stinking Reseda. Inside it's packed with cool records, hand-Xeroxed poetry zines, and a small performance space. It's been established as the Valley's destination for underground musicians, poets, and visual artists to buy records and perform to small but enthusiastic audiences.

At the helm is its artful proprietor, Richard, who's embraced the independent music community with open arms, giving them a place to sell their records and play shows. On the cramped walls, the past is alive with artwork from previous shows from the Minutemen, Jeffery Lee Pierce, Exene Cervenka, Wednesday Week, Downy Mildew, and my newest favorite group, the Victor Banana.

***

While we're figuring out who we are as a band, Jabberjaw's gaining recognition as one of LA's newest places for radical live shows and out-there art shows. This new band, who call themselves Hole, has been rehearsing there by day. They're fronted by Jabberjaw's most ambitious, skank-chic hipster, Courtney, who works at a vintage clothing place in Hollywood, right around the corner from the PikMe-Up. She also strips at Jumbo's Clown Room. Her special powers allow her to command any conversation on practically any topic, and leave you with this impression that she knows more about it than you. Anyone disagreeing, debating, or disputing her is subject to having loose ashtrays, coffee cups, or lit cigarettes thrown in their direction. While Hole uses the space to rehearse during off-hours, Cal Arts kids and shock-artists like Father Larry are lining up to show new work on a rotating basis. I'm amazed how fast Jabberjaw has become an integral part of the LA music and art world. It's like LA needed it all along, and now it's here as if it always had been.

Bebop and Jabberjaw are the perfect venues for us to perform, and explore the boundaries of what a band can be. During our first string of performances at BeBop and Jabberjaw, members have come and gone—sometimes playing only one show, and others members quitting and bailing out halfway through. The whole thing is to incorporate at least one new element per show to keep things fresh and interesting while we're discovering who we are. The chaos and uncertainty brought on by our noise interludes and monologues have become more miss than hit, while the songs we're writing are slightly more consistent and easier to play. The musical experiments come with their consequences. We seem to fall into one of two categories with audiences: excellent or awful. While some people have lauded us for putting together a risky, highly energetic, live show, others have painfully booed from the back of the house. Post gig emotions can range from joy to pain—the accolades feel good but the boos leave me wincing every time, reminding me my skin needs thickening.

***

After the excitement of those chaotic first shows, we do what all new bands do: annoy club bookers with crummy demo tapes and phone calls in hopes of securing gigs. We don't have much trouble getting nearly non-paying opening slots at Raji's, Club Lingerie, the Shamrock, and the Gaslight. But the real venue we want to play is the crown jewel of LA's post-punk underground, located in a desolate area of downtown LA.

Al's Bar has been going strong since 1979. Bands we love like the Fall, the Replacements, and the Residents have all performed there. All sorts of fascinating graffiti cover walls that lead to a small stage tucked under a low ceiling. Industrial sized, metal, support beams that block views of the stage are all part of its intimate allure, where people who look like they belong there congregate in small groups.

Sometime in 1990 Hole, along with my favorite live band, the Imperial Butt Wizards, have an upcoming show there and ask us to open for them. We zip through a twenty-minute set, playing to around thirty Al's Bar locals. Hole plays to a growing group, and eventually, the Imperial Butt Wizards pack the place and nearly burn it down when, during their finale, they set a bunch of stuffed animals on fire.

After that gig we felt like we'd made it, and started playing Al's on a regular basis. We met the staff and locals, including the newest booker, this college-smart fox with long black hair in curls, called Naomi, has been championing us amongst the straight-ahead punk bands and who regularly play there.

When it seems like the only thing missing from our band is a second guitarist, Sully's the perfect candidate. Here's why: I've known him forever, he loves good music, and is probably smarter than you. We're brotherly, and he's the only guy I know who thinks I'm someone who might actually do something special in life. While Celso and I have this way of being lofty, abstract dreamers, developing a different kind of friendship, encouraging mindless and sometimes reckless behavior in each other, Sully engages in the craziness of things, but knows when to keep the peace. In some ways, he's overqualified. He's been attending our shows, likes what we're doing, and can play guitar better than Celso and I combined. We meet up at the Lab, and he, Celso, and I have an instant chemistry.

We'd been through a handful of drummers and finally settle on one we know from Burbank, named Rich. We also add an accordion player for a brief period, but before long settled on being a quartet: Sully on guitar and now keyboard; Celso on vocals, guitar, and trumpet; Rich on drums; and me singing and playing bass.

From trial and error, we're slowly headed in the direction of "verse-chorus-verse" pop-formatted music, with added noisy instrumental breaks. I'm playing this stand-up bass I found in the *Recycler* for 200 dollars, which creates these dronish, noisy sounds when its bowed, while Sully and Celso are creating similar atonal, abrupt blurts of sound on the electric piano and guitar.

We don't want to look like a rock-and-roll band, especially not like the ones gaining popularity during these days of what's being called grunge. Most of those groups remind me of the burned-out Keystoners from high school. Visually, we discover our own sort of anti-rock image—a slightly disheveled, 1950s college-student look—not too different from one of the bands we totally worship most from the LA music underground of the '70s, the Human Hands.

The band is coming together and it's becoming everything to me. All I want to do is stay on course; define our sound and aesthetic, create our own flyers, T-shirts and stickers, book shows, and continuing getting mentioned in local papers. The efforts that go along with the dreams to make them pan out are happening and, for once, everything feels right.

One night after a show at Al's Bar we met this music fanatic our age named J, who hosts a late-night radio show at UCLA. He offered to sell our T-shirts after the gig and soon became our manager, even though we don't need one at this point. He joined forces with an ambitious young woman from the LA music world named Holly, and the two of them have become a management team. Now there are two people we barely need, but are glad to have them help sell T-shirts after shows, place flyers in record shops, and encourage people to come see us.

***

I've taken a survival job stamping mail and running errands at a TV production company. It's a daily grind to show up on time, make coffee, distribute mail, and deliver checks to television studios in Hollywood and Century City, but provides steady work as the band takes small steps to playing better gigs. Although it's a dead-end office gig, it's been providing fodder for a batch of new songs I'm writing. One of them is a surf-inspired guitar riff called "Nerves," which includes lyrics I scribbled on a piece of paper one hung-over morning while driving around LA, delivering checks.

Landlord.
Church.
Car crash.
Work.
My head aches.
And Silverlake.
You Nerve Me.
I hate work.
I'm a mailroom clerk...

While I'm spending my 9-to-5 hours catering to these over-paid TV writers and producers, Celso's putting himself through junior college as a one-man taxi service driving strippers around to private shows. A few nights each week he escorts strung-out naked dancers with names like Daisy and Medusa, along with a scratched-up boom box, from party to party in his rusty Coronet. Although he isn't a big guy, part of his job is to provide security for the girls, which means that regularly he's fighting off intoxicated douche bags getting touchy with the talent. At band rehearsal, he shares stories about some of the drugged-out strippers he's carting around. Yesterday he showed up at practice with the biggest black eye I've ever seen.

"So last night I'm in the dining room of this swanky USC frat house escorting Daisy, who looks just like my old girlfriend, Donna. I hit play on the ghetto blaster and 'Wicked Game' from Chris Isaak starts playing, and she stands on the dining table and starts this slow dance and removes her skirt —which I grab from the floor like I always do — and these eight or so jar-headed morons, who must be football players or some shit, are all jacked up on something. They start getting touchy with her. I try telling them a few times that physical contact isn't cool, but they don't listen. Two of them are putting their hands on her legs, and look like they're ready to pull some shit on her. She starts scream-ing for help while the song's still blaring. I grab some chair and swing it at them like a bat, which knocks them off the table and breaks'em out of their rape spell. Then it propels them into kick-my-ass mode. We run for our lives, but not before one of them gave me this," he says, with that great smile, pointing to his eye.

"Fuck, it was crazy. Glad they paid in advance."

***

I'm standing on the small stage of the PikMe-Up, performing my first reading from my self-published chapbook, *Music for Deaf People*. It's a collection of lyrics and prose I'd written about working in the mailroom. I'm nervous because although I've seen a bunch of readings, I've never done one myself. It's not like singing over music or anything like that, it's more like reading a school paper, but for the cool kids.

I'm getting a few chuckles and applause from a few tables, but mostly it's the regular crowd who are going on, chatting and what not, and I'm fine with it. I'm just glad to be there on this Sunday night. Out of the corner of my eye, I catch the owners Tawny, who to me is the personification of LA thrift-shop underground cool; and her artfully queer partner, Jerry, a combination of Dick Van Dyke and John Waters, sitting behind the counter gossiping. Andrew, the PikMe-Up's booker, who carries himself with the gentleness of Warhol, stands by the entrance giving me his full attention.

The storefront-turned-coffeehouse has served LA's hipster elite for the past few years, defining itself by its super-kitsch interior, eclectic art shows, and performances. It embraces everything I've practically ever known to be cool—all in one cramped storefront space. It thrives on patrons who love live music and art, and love to be seen doing it. It's the go-to place for LA music vets and spoken-word artists like Exene, Viggo Mortensen, Kristian Hoffman, Phranc, Vaginal Crème Davis, John Fleck, as well as newcomers Hill of Beans and Glue. Sometimes Rodney on the Roq even shows up for art openings. Mostly I like it because it reminds of me of the Lhasa Club, but now I'm onstage instead of in the crowd.

At the PikMe-Up, this small and fascinating group of diverse LA artists work in several mediums, creating music and art for what seems like the sole purpose of sharing it with fellow Angelenos. Pleasant Gehman is one of them, and she's up next. Plez has a black belt in LA music and poetry, and her specialty is celebrating LA's most subversive and strange. Since the late '70s, she's been writing and performing, known for her lurid stories of hanging with the Germs, the Cramps, and the Go-Go's at places like the Masque, the Canterbury Apartments, and the Sugar Shack. Struck by her sense of adventure and ability to present poetry readings, rock shows, and write for LA publications, we became friends after being introduced by my girlfriend, Annette.

Plez and Annette are singers in the LA poetry/rock collective, The Ringling Sisters, and produce live shows and readings around town. They also present a yearly orphanage fundraiser with some of LA's most talented musicians and entertainers. I've been joining her on her latest scavenger hunt exploits: finding and hanging out in dive Mexican transvestite bars in east Hollywood. I've kind of become her fake kid brother.

She just walked on stage and is reading a poem about the contents of her purse and everyone's loving it.

The PikMe-Up crowds have been responding well to our music and we've been gigging here around once a month. We created a semi-acoustic set just for the space, in which I play my stand-up bass, Celso plays acoustic guitar, Sully plays an electric Rhodes piano and Vox organ, and Rich plays a stripped-down drum kit. We've been playing our songs, extending middle sections with bursts of experimental bowing noises from my stand-up bass and Sully's organ. On nights we don't perform we come see other acts and performers. You can't go wrong hanging at the PikMe-Up.

One night after one of our shows, my friend Steve, who's one half of the acoustic duo Hill of Beans, introduces me to his friend. He's waif-like and looks even younger than me.

"Hey Rob, this is Beck. He's a singer/songwriter who just moved back to LA from New York City."

"Hey man, nice to meet you. You ever play here?" I ask, noticing his big blue-eyed, million-mile stare.

"No, but I'd like to. Mind if I open for you guys next time you play? It's just me and my guitar and banjo. I've been busking in subway stations and playing around lower Manhattan for the last year," he says in this gentle tone that also has this air of self-assurance. I'm not sure what his music sounds like, but since there's little at stake, it seems like a good idea to have an opening act, instead of being one for a change.

"Yeah, sure. We're back here in couple of weeks. I'll let Andrew know. You have a band name, or just go by Beck?"

"Just Beck. Yeah. Beck. Thanks."

Two weeks later, I'm tucked in the corner of the PikMe-Up watching Beck. He's playing the trippiest, most surreal songs I've heard, sung in this nearly deadpan, serial killer tone. He trades off from acoustic guitar and banjo, and then reaches into his wrinkled button-down shirt and pulls out a harmonica. He plays this solo piece that sounds like hell, and I love it. At the end of his set, he says, "Hey Rob, come join me for this one. It's in E." I'm on the spot but have nothing to lose, so I lug my stand-up in to my arms and follow him as best as I can on the tune. Once we get going, I'm pretty sure we're both improvising. He's going on in this weird croon about working at a video store for the couple of dozen onlookers, of about half which are paying attention.

Another local band that's caught my eye at the PikMe-Up is a group called Glue, who celebrate the late 1970s recklessness of the CBGB glory days like it's just getting started. Their songs are short and fun and mostly fast. You get the feeling they're written about their friends who are there to see them. Their raunchy thrift-store-chic aesthetic, combined with the black cross-dressing singer, Sean DeLear, who embodies the essence and glory of Diana Ross and Joey Ramone, sets them apart from any other group I've seen.

Next door to the PikMe-Up is the vintage clothing that store employs Hole's singer, Courtney, who never seems to be working. It's an amusement of its own, stopping in to visit her there. She's like a living cartoon from a Gary Panter comic strip, piling on makeup, trying on dresses she's there to sell, and talking nonstop about her band. If Sid Vicious' girlfriend Nancy Spungen had a younger sister trying to make it in Hollywood, it'd be Courtney. We usually end up praising some forgotten band from the late 70s or 80s, or expound the genius of post punk Liverpool groups like Echo & the Bunnymen and the Teardrop Explodes. Courtney might even know more about cool music than Matt, I'm not sure. But I do know the PikMe-Up and its surroundings are fertile ground for the alt-rock explosion that's just ahead.

IN BUILDINGS

"*S*HE *LOOKS LIKE AN ACTRESS, who's late for an audition. Is she Catholic or Jewish, or the Devil? Half Catholic,
Half Jewish, or the Devil...*" I found these words on a
scrunched-up piece of paper in my front pocket after a long
night of working and cutting loose at Jabberjaw. I must have
written them since they're in my scribble. I'm in the Lab, still
fully dressed, with my head still on fire. I grab an acoustic guitar
that's missing a couple of strings and put the lyrics to music,
with a chorus that repeats, *"In buildings, she makes me shake now,
in buildings, in buildings, in buildings."* I drift back to sleep, praying
I remember how it goes when I wake up. I open my eyes to a
knock on the Lab door. It's my good mother, and she looks like
she's got news.

"Little Fellow, your father and I have decided to sell the
house. We're moving to a new housing development called
Palmdale. It's hot, but nice there. You are welcome to move with
us if you'd like."

"Palmdale? Where's that?" I ask, with zero intention of relo-
cating with them.

"An hour north from here."

"Ah. When's this happening?" I ask, wondering if I'm dreaming. It's a weird thing when you've lived in the same house your
entire life and one day your goood mother tells you you've got
to move.

"We've got two months."

I get my head together and realize their decision to bail out
of Burbank is one of the best things that's happened to me. I'm
twenty-one and way overstayed my days here. High school was
another life ago, and the idea of college still seems like a trap,
especially while I'm getting what's like a PhD in LA's DIY music

and art world; playing gigs, booking art shows and bands; and making cappuccinos for LA's underground music and art sect.

In a matter of a week, I pack up the Lab, and find a room for rent in a spacious, Mediterranean-style, two-story, furnished house in the hills east of Hollywood, called Silverlake. Among palm-tree-lined hills, charming low-rent bungalows, and old apartment buildings — mostly inhabited by Latino and old-school left-wing gay communities — I have a newfound anonymity. It's an idyllic setting to get started in life; nobody knows me here and I'm as free as I've ever been.

***

My first time shooting heroin was there. I'm with a girl I've been seeing, a privileged, Jewish-American princess, Valley-girl-gone-mad named Melanie who's too pretty for her own good. She's drifted off the college path since I'd met her at Valley College a few years earlier and has become a real dope fiend. One night she shows up to see me at my new east-side abode with a cache of drugs and syringes.

"Cool place, dude. Congrats on making it out of the Valley," she says, in the most dull and nonchalant fashion you've ever heard. We go in my bedroom and close the door. She removes the stuff from her purse and, like it's nothing, nonchalantly shoots herself up on my bed. She sparks a cig and gives me this dead-in-the-eyes sexy zombie look that lures me in, slowly making my dick harden.

"Now what?"

I'm torn between taking my clothes off, then hers, and getting it on, and wondering how those drugs are making her feel. Without thinking too hard, I pick a lane.

"Mind if I get high with you?"

"Are you sure? You know, they say this stuff's addicting," she says in a taunting effort at humor. Sometimes druggies like to pretend they're Nancy Reagan.

"I'll take my chances. I'm a big kid now," I respond, getting more curious about how this is going to go.

"Okay mister, the first time's free," she says in the relaxed voice of a movie star from the 1940s. Then, sort of like the way Mike Keys did the night we shot coke in high school, she prepares a dose for me. She takes my arm like a sexy nurse and uses this fancy scarf that's tied around her neck to tie off my arm.

"Oh, so you know, the first time makes most people puke," she says, pushing in the syringe plunger, injecting a small amount of dark brown liquid into my forearm.

I'm guess I'm part of the "most people" equation; the nausea comes on so strong and so fast I throw up in my hands on the way to the toilet. My head's spinning and what's left of the burrito I had for dinner is spinning down the bowl. I'm still not sure what hit me. Everything's blurry when I return to my bedroom where Melanie's on the bed sitting like a purring cat.

That's when a tidal wave of warm bliss washes through my insides. Instead of having sex, we just laid on my bed for a long nap. I awoke feeling as good as I ever had, still elated and comforted from the drugs, like I was in this breezy dream. I didn't mind the nausea one bit; I thought it was a small price to pay for feeling that good. We woke up, played some records, injected more drugs, smoked cigarettes, and fell back asleep. That warm and fuzzy feeling was the high like no other and great trying once, but there's no way I'm getting hooked.

***

My job duties in the mail room also entail daily deliveries to an offsite videotape warehouse. After making a drop off one afternoon, I get an idea that the space could serve as a decent place to rehearse. It's in a quiet industrial area of North Hollywood, and after 5 p.m., its devoid of human life. I have the keys and security code and am not scared enough not to give it a shot, knowing it'll save the band money on rehearsal space. That night after work we drag in our amps and drums and play for a few hours.

Afterward, we carefully cover our equipment with empty boxes and leave no trace we were there at all. From then on, after dark, it's Possum Dixon headquarters.

We continue to meet a few times a week there before lugging our gear into Hollywood to play clubs. There's this juvenile appeal to the nightly ritual of opening the door and killing the alarm code. It feels like we're pulling a fast one, which slightly sets us on edge, knowing that any time, my boss might come along and pull the plug on the whole thing, adding one more entry to my long list of jobs I'd been fired from. It's the greatest deal we've ever had — we play as loud and long as we wish without paying a dime.

One late night while rehearsing at the video vault, I launch into an improvisation rant, singing the lyrics to as many of the popular Madonna songs as I can remember over an instrumental section of one of our songs. Celso and Sully get a chuckle from it, which encourages me to take things further. I put down my stand-up bass, unbutton my shirt, and whip off my belt, thinking I'm Madonna, whispering into a distorted mic, "*...You must be my lucky star, cause you shine on me wherever you are.*"

At our next gig at Al's Bar, I go into the Madonna thing. Everyone recognizes the lyrics and cheers me on. From then on it becomes known as the Madonna Medley — an absurd aside that audiences either love or hate, but always provokes a reaction. It's screwball theatrical moments like these that get us booed off the stage or asked to come back for headlining spots.

Inside the warehouse, we tirelessly play, work on flyers, and book the next shows. By now, the group's post-punk style, crude and bold Dada-inspired artwork, and messy, vintage wardrobe choices place us on a unique tier in LA. While band ideas start informing each other, more people are coming to see us, and fanzines are reacting accordingly. While some local music critics write us off as bratty art-pop, others are writing favorable reviews and rooting us on like a small-town band that might get a shot at the big time. Last month Pleasant described us the best anyone has in a *BAM* magazine article. "Possum Dixon are like *My Three Sons*, if Lou Reed directed them," she wrote.

In the nearby musical landscape, it's a big deal to the independent music community when Seattle's Nirvana got signed to Geffen Records. While kicking around LA after recording their LP, *Nevermind*, they played at Jabberjaw, drawing the biggest crowd it'd ever seen. With Iggy Pop in attendance and rooting them on, their performance became the most talked-about show in Jabberjaw's short history. A few months later, *Nevermind* is released and the music industry is turned on its side. Suddenly FM rock radio stations and magazines at 7-Eleven who'd been promoting hair-sprayed hard rockers like Guns N' Roses bombarded music fans with this new "grunge" music they say is erupting from Seattle's independent music world. Bridging punk and metal and dominated by super loud, distorted guitars and screaming vocals, grunge is taking the music world by surprise. Grunge is inescapable; every other conversation was about this new brand of rock that does nothing for me, but at least it's killing hair metal. In a matter of months, Nirvana, together with Mudhoney, Soundgarden, and a legion of other bands, provide tired hair-metal fans something new to listen to and talk about.

✳✳✳

Amid a fast-paced schedule of playing shows and handling band duties, I move from Silverlake into a three-story Victorian house, not far from Downtown LA, called Ellis Island. I learned of it after meeting a curiously stout and broad man with fluorescent green colored hair and glasses — who goes by the name Rush — outside the Cover Girl Club one evening at a performance by the San Francisco experimental-noise music collective known as the Caroliner Rainbow. The following night we met up at Jabberjaw and became fast friends, bonding over bowls of Cap'n Crunch and our common obsession: the LA art and music world.

The next week I attended a weekend Ellis Island party, and learned it had served as a hippie commune in the late 1960s and housed a colorful cast of musicians, writers, and visual artists who attended, or dropped out of nearby USC. I fell in love with its Animal House, free-for-all aesthetic, and its surrounding residential area characterized by streets lined with other magnificent Victorian mansions. The neighborhood is oddly juxtaposed in a sketchy gang-graffitied area with liquor stores you wouldn't want to enter after dark, about six blocks north of the USC campus.

Many of the houses in the neighborhood are in a state of disrepair, and Ellis Island with all its worn, artful charm is no exception. Its semi-dilapidated exterior is perfect: a vintage car covered in enough grime to obscure its make and model is parked on the front yard, which, other than a few patches of barely living grass where there once had been a lawn, is nearly devoid of life. A couple of windowless sills adorn the front, where paint is chipped off the walls here and there, and a circular sign carved of wood is mounted above the porch, reading "Ellis Island."

When a room became available on the second floor, just above the living room, I dragged in my few belongings and called it home. It's in an amazing historic neighborhood in an area I never knew existed, but connected with immediately. I feel like I've won the lottery by scoring a room and being part of its trippy legacy.

At Ellis Island, anything goes. Inside, some of the long-time residents are still recovering from the '60s—some of them are former followers of the '70s Indian mystic, Bhagwan Rajneesh, and have trippy and friendly names like Tantra, Lotus, and Woofie. There are other radical USC students who'd been living there since the late '60s and are now in their 30s. If Silverlake was a far cry from Burbank, moving into Ellis Island feels like renting a room in the Twilight Zone.

Rush is Ellis Island's head honcho, a former hippie turned first-wave punker who's been kicking around the LA underground music world since the late 1970s. By day he holds a long-time job at the Los Angeles Department of Water and Power, and by night, he's a full-on underground music fanatic. He can't be missed by the shock of green, blue, or orange hair, which he seems to change every couple of weeks, sporting a local band

T-shirt and travelling from one gig to the next. Recently, he part-ed ways with LA's satirical, rock group Green Jello, with which he performed, and I'd been following. These days he's interest-ed in producing and running his own independent record label, Pronto Records, to record local bands out of a studio he's cob-bled together in the commune's large and dusty, third-floor, con-verted attic he calls We Bad Studios. It's the most inspired attic I'd ever stepped foot inside: a cross between the coolest record shop you've ever been in, a low rent New York art gallery, and the living room of Sanford and Son.

Between staying on top of band life, showing up for my day job Monday through Friday, and keeping my room tidy at Ellis Island, I'm somehow getting out on dates with some intrigu-ing girls. Jocelyn's a brilliant and impossibly cute playwright who lives in New York but comes to LA plenty. Tiffany speaks faster than she can get her thoughts out. She's got the prettiest long black hair you've ever seen and is always up for an adventure, and Annette's a cool and gorgeous platinum blonde who's been a mainstay in the LA music world since the early '80s. Each of them would make great girlfriends, but the band comes first and the way things are going, I can barely keep up.

Sully's girlfriend, Jean, who's totally obsessed with the Talking Heads and anything French, is like the kid sister I never had. She just came by to film me kicking around my newly decorated room at Ellis Island for a mini documentary on LA nightlife she's making called "Five Nights Out." She's full of ideas to cap-ture this corner of the world in LA music. We agreed: it's no mid-70s CBGB music revolution, but it's something we can call our own. Over the past few weeks she's been taping live shows and interviews with Possum Dixon, Beck, Glue, and some other musicians and performance artists kicking around.

***

Pronto Records releases Possum Dixon's first 7-inch record, "Watch the Girl Destroy Me," with "Friends" on the B-side. To

celebrate the release of this first vinyl effort, we play a record release party at Jabberjaw, asking some old friends from the Valley
who are debuting their band called Sugarplastic to play. That
night at Jabberjaw is a milestone for the band. We're in the center of what seems like a perfect time and place: performing and
soaking in the thrill of the burgeoning local music community by
signing records for friends and new fans.

We followed that release with a box set containing three
7-inch singles called *Music for a One Bedroom Apartment*, containing
six songs on three colored vinyl 45s, which gets played lots on
college radio. Our next recording is another single. It's my personal favorite that sums up the band, "Nerves," and gets co-re-
leased by Flipside Records and our own imprint label we called
Surf Detective.

The band is on a roll, gigging and getting regular airplay on
KXLU and KPFK, and receiving recognition from the LA music community. We've been opening for touring bands we love
and admire, like local faves fIREHOSE; Olympia, Washington's
gift to do-it-yourself music minimalists; Beat Happening; and
the Dead Milkmen, who've had a video on MTV. Last weekend
we made our first out-of-state show, driving to Arizona to open
for Phoenix's gift to punk, the Meat Puppets.

A few months later we book our first mini-tour. We're going
all the way to Austin to play this music conference called South
by Southwest. Since the late '80s, the conference has been estab-
lishing itself as a grass-roots music event, featuring new groups
as well as established bands promoting their latest records. We
perform as part of the conference's "new band night" in this
cavernous warehouse outside downtown Austin. The gig is disappointing — we play for a crowd of about thirty people in a
space that holds 300. It's been a long haul to play for so few
people, but getting out of LA to play has been another great
bonding experience for the band. We play our best, pack our
stuff, and head home.

THIS TOWN

FEW DAYS after returning from Austin, J calls with uplifting news.

"So this new record company out of LA called Interscope Records, who saw you in Austin, just called. They're cool, and signing new bands, giving them creative control to make records however they want. They wanna see the next show. Cool, right?"

We're excited by their interest in us and invite them to see us at our next Al's Bar gig. We learn fast that when one record label shows interest in signing a band, word in the music industry quickly spreads, and suddenly other labels become interested, too. It's not because they necessarily like your music, but don't want to miss out on a business prospect. The show is packed — not with the typical Al's Bar patrons but music industry types looking for the next big band to sign. At the end of the night I've got a handful of business cards from all sorts of record labels.

The next week Interscope invites us to their offices for a meeting. Coincidentally, the production company I work for has just moved offices to Wilshire Boulevard, catty-corner to Interscope's offices. From the window of the fifteenth floor, I'm still delivering mail and stealing copy paper to print our flyers, and I can see into Interscope's bustling offices. It's a little strange and surreal, standing before this large panel of glass window at a job I need, to look across the busy street, where bustling people are working away promoting bands.

It's our first formal meeting with a large record company and we're nervous. After arriving at their twelfth-floor offices, we notice something not often seen in Westwood: an imposing, large, black bodyguard, at the door. He's protecting employees from enemies of the gangsta rap artists Dr. Dre and 2Pac Shakur, whose records were distributed by the label and have been stirring up all kinds of ruckus. "These guys are okay, Geronimo," a label rep says, ushering us in, as if we're entering a Black Panther meeting in northern Idaho.

We huddle inside a dark conference room. It's a near match to the one I'd just wiped off with Pledge, dusted, and set up with a bagel spread across the street. We sit on one side of the epic conference table, politely accepting soft drinks, and popcorn, barely saying a word. The room fills with executives and employees and the lights dim as they screened a VHS copy of a low-fi video we made at our secret rehearsal warehouse for "Watch the Girl Destroy Me." When the video's over, the lights come up to reveal each of our previous 7-inch records, a self-released seven-song cassette, bumper stickers, and a copy of my poetry/lyric book, *Music for Deaf People*, neatly laid out on the table.

The heads of various departments take turns speaking, making it clear that they had done their Possum Dixon homework and were fans of the band. Then, the co-owner of the company, Ted Field, takes the floor and the room goes dead quiet.

"We like your band. You've got your own thing going, and we'd like to help you sell some records. We would very much like Possum Dixon to join our roster and be part of this label. We are not interested in any sort of bidding war. Please consider our offer, and if you think it's fair, let's get a contract signed right away."

And that's exactly what happened. We like the idea of reaching a wider audience, and think we probably won't be able to without the help of a larger label, so under J's advice, we sign a two-record contract. According to J, they're offering us a solid deal and are also interested in buying the publishing rights to our songs — all of which seemed agreeable. From our goal of playing Al's Bar on a Friday night, we've entered a new, unknown dimension in the band's history. Our Possum Dixon world is about to thrust into overdrive.

Shortly after we sign the contract with Interscope, the *LA Reader* publishes an article, written by local music critic Thomas Edward Adelman, titled "Possum Dixon: They're Invisible, They're Bulletproof—and They're Signed."

He wrote, "Here's hope for struggling young iconoclasts: Los Angeles Possum Dixon has just signed a two-record deal with Interscope Records. And just think—all it took was four years of gigging shitty dives, rehearsing three to four times a week, stealing copier paper and postage from work, designing and printing their own T-shirts, bumper stickers, and chapbooks; all it took were three self-produced singles, a seven-song cassette, and a triple 7-inch box set."

Our Artist and Relations go-to guy at Interscope is called Chuck, and he's become the band's new best friend. He's this baby-faced twenty-something guy with a friendly, trusting face who spent his teen years touring with Los Lobos and Lone Justice. These days he's the right-hand man of the label's co-owner, Jimmy Iovine. Now all we want to do is make a great record.

In addition to signing our Interscope contract, we also sign the publishing deal with them for what seems to be a ton of money. We hire a high-power music lawyer, sign our contract, and celebrate by quitting our jobs. I have more money than I've ever had, and buy my parents a huge TV for their Palmdale home. With my only concerns making a record and paying my low rent at Ellis Island, and with some money in the bank, for the first time ever, I feel like I'm on top of the world.

The only thing we need is a producer. One night at Jabberjaw we're mulling over some ideas.

"It'd be amazing if Earle Mankey produced you. He's so LA," suggests my friend and teen idol, Michael Quercio. Earle's name is synonymous with great LA music. He was an early member of Sparks, and produced the Runaways, the Dickies, 20/20, the Pop, Concrete Blonde, and Quercio's former group, the Three O'Clock. Michael's impulse is right, and Earle is our only choice.

However, Interscope has different ideas; they're suggesting we go with a producer with recent success, one associated with the new grunge and alternative bands, following Nirvana's success. But we have our hearts set on Earle, and after learning he's interested, it's Earle we get.

We start pre-production at Hully Gully Studios in shady Frogtown. It's an LA rehearsal studio institution that when you enter, you can't help but feel like you're in some lost scene from *Repo Man*. Since the late '70s, it's been the hub for cool bands to run their sets and use as a place to hang and score drugs. For a couple of weeks, we show up at noon and play until late at night, working on arrangements, and experimenting with song ideas. The spirit of our band has never been more alive. Earle's this calm and mild-mannered guy who's smarter than all of us combined, making excellent suggestions to strengthen our club-tested material and turn it into our first record.

***

I'm making a little drug pit stop en route to band rehearsal from Ellis Island to Hully Gully —a heroin drive-thru of sorts—just around the corner from MacArthur Park. Just north of 6th Street on Bonnie Brae, I'm slowly patrolling rows of low rent apartments in my less than inconspicuous green and white '70s Ford Bronco, until I see my guy standing on the sidewalk; a Mexican dude around my age, decked out in a Dodgers cap, wrap-around shades, extra-large pants and T-shirt hanging off his men's medium body, and puffy white sneakers. Recognizing my car from previous stops, he knows this repeat customer when he sees me. We exchange quick head nods, like we have before, and he runs up to my car with laser focus, popping his head in my window. He spits out a rainbow assortment of tightly bound balloons, each about the size of a chickpea, packed with black tar dope, into his hand.

"Three for forty?" I say all as one word, meaning I wanted three of his balloons for 40 bucks, and in a jiff.

"Yeah, yeah bro, tree bor borty, tree bor borty," he fires back even faster.

In one motion, I fork over two crumpled 20s as he plucks three balloons from his palm and plops them into my mine. There's no time or need for small talk or fuss, just a quick transaction with excellent customer service. I shove the drugs inside my pocket, jam the gearstick into first gear, and tear off to band practice, cranking "This Town" from a worn-out Go-Go's cassette at full volume for the hundredth time. Right now, in my world, everything is fine.

During a break while running our live set in the big room at Hully Gully, I casually slip into the bathroom to get high. In the filthy and graffitied bathroom stall, I bite open one of the balloons and smear a small wad of the sweet-smelling black tar on a torn piece of tin foil I'd brought along, roll up a sweaty dollar bill and place it in my mouth. I torch the drugs from underneath the foil to chase the dragon—the street term dope fiends use to refer to smoking heroin from tinfoil—and marvel at its magical transformation from thick black goo to this glorious sweet-smelling vapor trail, which I inhale from the bill. Over the muffled sounds of two bands practicing at once in nearby rooms, I spend the next couple of minutes sucking up every bit of smoke through the bill and head outside.

As the warm effects of the drugs are taking hold I join the rest of the band at our meeting spot, a seedy area behind the rehearsal studio that houses an ever-buzzing gargantuan power-line tower. It's a large open space that looks like it could have been a film location for an action scene from *Adam 12* or *Starsky and Hutch*; it's overlooking the LA River and littered with broken glass, aborted shopping carts, and an occasional soiled baby diaper. It looks more like an apocalyptic crime zone than some place four guys from the Valley should be loitering at night. I kneel near the guys between a couple of tall weeds to nonchalantly blend in and listen to their conversation, but as they carry on, I can't help but drifting in and out of consciousness.

"Rise and shine, princess," Sully says, nudging and waking me from some deep dream. Time passed, and I have no idea if I've been out for one minute or ten. I look around, slightly startled to see it's just Sully and me. Celso and Rich are gone.

"Man, you okay? You look pretty wasted," he says, concerned.

"No man, I'm fine. Just a little tired," I reply, in my best lying voice.

"Huh. You're telling me you're not high?"

"Nope."

With a disappointed and concerned sadness he presents a question to which he knows the answer.

"If you're not smoking heroin, then what's the deal with the rolled-up dollar bill and piece of tin foil hanging out your sock there?"

I follow his gesturing eyes, revealing the tightly rolled bill and folded-up shiny foil popping out of my sock.

"C'mon man, I'm not stupid. Since when do you keep dollar bills rolled up in your sock? And, that's no Ding Dong wrapper."

Even though I'm busted, and hate every fiber of my being for lying to him, I stick to my guns, denying what we both know. Painfully aware of the frustration and grief I'm causing him, I respond like a defensive sibling. "I'm not high. I know what it probably looks like, but I'm not. Think I caught the flu or something."

We both know what a useless lie I was attempting to sell him.

"All right. Well, I'm done rehearsing tonight," he murmurs, heading back toward the studio.

As the moonlight barely illuminates the myriad of spray-painted tags on the LA River's cement walls, compliments of old school LA gangsters, Frog Town, the volume of the buzzing power lines grows louder and louder. I'm starting to blow the career I've worked so hard to establish for so much of my life and causing one of my best friends a pain he doesn't need. The band and our friendship are starting to take a hit because of my using and he and I both know it. But if I'm high, everything's fine and works itself out, or that's what I tell myself at least. Amongst the weeds and trash in that vacant armpit of LA, I have another cigarette and drift off into another nod.

***

Located in the middle of drab Van Nuys, a boldly painted 1970s-era banner reads "SOUND CITY" above the entrance door, outside this innocuous warehouse-style building. Sound City Studios is the place we've chosen to record after surveying a handful of studios in LA. The interior reveals an enchanted rock-and-roll maze, all of which evokes the nostalgia of the '70s which immediately grabbed our hearts. It's the home of many of my favorite recordings I remember as a kid; ones by Tom Petty & the Heartbreakers, Fleetwood Mac, Neil Young, and most recently, Nirvana. Although none of those bands directly impacted our sound, they all have one thing in common: each one sounds great.

We arrive with our songs in the best shape they've ever been in and head to the studio like clockwork for a week and record our basic tracks. We're smart enough to realize that each band only gets one shot at making their debut record, so keep the drinking and drugging down to a minimum while taking our existing batch of songs and magnetizing them to two-inch tape. Earle's production ideas, like recording pianos and keyboards through guitar amps, and going for like-minded sounds he'd made on other records, make each session exciting.

After a week of tracking at Sound City we save some of our recording budget by recording the remainder of the record at Earle's home studio. He lives in residential Thousand Oaks— not exactly the rock-and-roll environment Hully Gully or Sound City provide, but it serves its purpose. It feels like the summer camp I never attended, hanging out in Earle's guesthouse, which had been converted into a recording studio. Between takes I flip through old issues of *Rolling Stone, Creem,* and *Music Connection,* taking cigarette breaks and dreaming about the way ahead. After a few weeks, we have our album and song listing in order, which clocks in at around thirty minutes.

We settle on opening our record with perhaps our most narrative and rigid track, "Nerves." With my vocal narration delivered over Celso's strangled and surfy guitar riffs and a solo accompanied by Sully's dramatic all-keys-at-once piano pounding, it's the right song to kick off the record. We also record two of our favorite covers, a keyboard-driven version of the late 1960s Yardbirds radio single, "For Your Love," and "Days of Wine and Roses" from the Dream Syndicate.

It's a thrill to record all the songs, especially our only ballad, "Invisible" — a song outlining of my day-to-day world from the year before: my mad but impossible crush on this talented and beautiful young New York playwright I'd fallen for named Jocelyn; and a recollection of the time I visited Mike Keys in the hospital after a near-death experience from stage diving off a stack of amplifiers during a show at the Hollywood Palladium, that landed him on his head and put him in a coma for a week. But Mike Keys being Mike Keys pulled through and was back on his feet like nothing happened. On the recording, we used the same crummy Casio keyboard I bought at a garage sale for a buck.

On the day I record the vocals for "Invisible," which are done in Earle's bathroom to get a natural echoish feel, he left the tape rolling at the end of the song. Meanwhile, I'm peeking in his medicine cabinet to see if any pills are laying around. The shelves are empty, but as I close the door it makes this great clanking sound. "What's that sound? It's really good," says Earle in my headphones. I take that as a cue and start slamming the door open and shut at irregular times as a percussive effect, which ends up sounding perfect in the final mix.

***

We complete the record and nervously turn it over to Interscope for review. The label informs us that we did good, and made a solid retro-sounding record with hit singles. They're primarily focused on the third track, "Watch the Girl Destroy Me," our jingle-jangle pop song they're certain will become a sure-fire hit on the FM dial. They invite us to their offices to share their excitement, where we experience moments of nearly unbelievable encouragement, making us feel like we'll be the next Beatles.

One of the tracks on the record, "In Buildings," surprises us all after KROQ got an advance copy and started spinning it multiple times each day. We're thrilled they're playing it because they think it's a good song. The "In Buildings" airplay defines a brief window when I could turn on my car radio and hear a song I wrote played on KROQ and KXLU. Hearing Possum Dixon on the radio always feels like some big accomplishment, providing a sense of temporary validation for my twenty-four-year-old unsettled mind. It doesn't take more than a month before KROQ doesn't see a big boost in phone requests and stops playing the song. Meanwhile, KXLU decides we've become too commercial to be played on their station and stops playing us, too. In what seems like a blink of the eye, neither station is interested in playing our music. Once again, we're in between here and there, trying to find our audience — and our record isn't even out yet.

Waiting on a release date, we kick around LA rehearsing our live set a few times a week. We're offered a gig on a local bill opening for another Interscope Records recording artist: Orange County's No Doubt. They've amassed a large Orange County following and the label is curious to see how we'll go over with their crowd. Also on the bill is Battery Acid, a hard-rock alt outfit featuring former members of the Three O'Clock and Mary's Danish. Although the three bands are stylistically different, we're eager to play with new bands, especially at the venue where the show is booked — just around the corner from BeBop Records where we'd played our first show — at a decent-sized venue called the Country Club.

It's a dream come true to play at the Country Club, where I've seen some of my favorite live shows as a teenager in the early '80s; shows by Wall of Voodoo, Agent Orange, R.E.M., the Dream Syndicate, the Three O'Clock, the Pandoras, the Question, the Untouchables, Sidewalk Society, and all the others that've have left indelible musical memories and helped shape my musical path.

On show night, we walk out to a few hundred young music fans, who've packed themselves inside the Reseda venue, and burst through our set, performing for a group of enthusiastic new faces who carpooled up from Orange County for the show. The night marks a personal triumph — I remember anytime I'd seen a band there, I just figured they'd made it. Driving back to Ellis Island, I think the show was a blast, but I realize playing the Country Club is not the pinnacle of our career, or anyone's. We still have a long way to go.

***

We've earned enough of a local following to book our record-re-
lease party at the Roxy Theater on the Sunset Strip. After securing the date we invite our two favorite acts to open the show:
Beck and Glue. Beck's been playing a ton of shows around town
and his star is rising fast. He's shrugging off the attention as if it's
some big fluke and just signed a contract with Geffen Records.
Glue never fails as a good live band, always bringing their loose
and reckless energy and raw punk madness, so we figure that between the three of us, it'll be a strong show with lots of variety. A
couple of years ago, the three of our acts combined could barely
fill the PikMe-Up, and in a few weeks, we'll get to take our acts
to Sunset Strip with big lights and sound and see how we go over
with a larger audience.

    After our sound check that afternoon, I hang around the
club and take an hour nap in the dressing room, reflecting on
the music world we've found ourselves amongst. From the tint-
ed bay windows upstairs at the Roxy, I watch this long line of
music fans form a jagged line along Sunset Boulevard, waiting to
see our show. I can't help but be reminded that for many years,
I was waiting in lines like the one I'm seeing, making me feel
like I've finally accomplished something in life. Recapping the
band's past, we've come a long way from those frenetic Bebop,
Jabberjaw, and Al's Bar gigs.

As the crowd fills the club, Beck and his new band spread out all over the stage, exploring musical realms far beyond his acoustic material. Every song uses different instruments as he's venturing into surreal hip hop and country-infused punk with drum machines. He performs what's becoming a hit song on KCRW, "Loser," for one of the first times, and the crowd loves him. Thirty minutes later, Glue is playing their best loud and queer proud, cross-dressed, punk rock. Sean DeLear is glowing, channeling Diana Ross and Joey Ramone tonight more than she ever has, and the lights illuminate the band members, turning them into stars.

A minute before taking the stage, I look out to the sold-out house of longtime friends and fans of the band, among patches of new, eager faces, and like our first show at BeBop, feel like my ass is once again on the line. We take the stage and perform our new record as if our lives depend on it. Tonight, I have to be good. Celso's to my right, pounding his guitar with his great big smile, Sully's banging his keyboards with double fists and chiming in with background vocals, Rich is sweating over his kit, playing as hard and fast as he ever has, as I'm just hanging on, having the time of my life. This time, as far as I'm concerned, I made it.

THAT DECEMBER

IT'S AROUND MIDNIGHT, and I'm scrunched between the other members of Possum Dixon at some famous restaurant in Little Italy in New York City. Even though our plane from LA landed an hour ago and we're all a little grumpy, here we are. Everyone's beat, but the label and J insisted we need a nice meal before our show tomorrow night at the College Music Journal Music Marathon. We've learned quickly that dining with them means exuding polite enthusiasm as they tell us about their big plans to break our record. On one hand, it's exciting to hear how they are getting some of their other acts out on the road and touring Europe and doing all the stuff we wanna do, but on the other hand it makes me uneasy since it hasn't happened yet, and nothing is ever as easy as it seems.

We're waiting for our food to arrive, and I can feel one of our label representatives staring me down. I picked up on his vibe as soon as we sat down and have been trying my best to ignore it by counting the Chianti bottles hanging from the dining room's ceiling. His vibe's getting heavier and is starting to push me over my already irritable edge.

"Okay, okay, I'm just gonna say it." The table goes quiet. "Rob! I could dress you. I could really dress you! Please, just let me dress you!"

Apparently, my 1950s, threadbare, collared shirt pulled under the moth-eaten V-neck sweater, high-water trousers, and beat-up, black, work shoes I'm wearing aren't cutting the mustard; too shabby and not enough chic for an up-and-coming rock singer. He's is officially calling me out, offering a Zabrecky makeover. I guess he has something in mind, perhaps something like what he's wearing: a floor-length snakeskin jacket from the '80s, tight stone-washed jeans, and snakeskin cowboy boots — Paul Stanley from KISS in his post-makeup era.

I look down into my plate of vegetarian pasta to keep from bursting into laughter, and the band follows suit. It's probably not a good idea to laugh at the idea that this guy is offering his services to become my new fashion guru, even though it's totally absurd.

"Well c'mon, what do you say? Huh? Deal?" he says, persisting like a persnickety grown-up geek.

"Um, how about a raincheck. Is that an answer?" I respond.

"Okay, okay, I see. I'll break you, Zabrecky! You'll see."

Since that dinner, the label's been trying to convince me they can use what good looks they think I have to sell records. I've declined their ideas to use my likeness on the cover for our record, feature me in press photos, and other stuff. The notion of me as some kind of Alternative pin-up boy isn't what we signed up for, and makes me wonder if we've made the wrong decision signing with them.

***

That December we're invited to play one of the headlining slots at Hollywood's Palace Theater for the annual Ringling Sisters Benefit. This year's show features a bang-up lineup of bands and poets including X, the Circle Jerks, Dave Alvin of the Blasters, 7 Year Bitch, Babes in Toyland, and Jim Carroll. Sharing this bill at the Palace, a renowned Hollywood concert venue, with these bands and artists, is a landmark event for us.

I'm particularly excited to see Jim Carroll perform. I've read his memoir, *The Basketball Diaries*, twice, and am a fan of his poetry and music. While rehearsing for the show, we've learned a version of his Ramones-ish single from 1980, "People Who Died," in hopes of playing it live with him.

Just after sound check on show night, I run into a foxy girl I've seen around at Jabberjaw and the Ellis Island parties whom I've had a crush on for a couple of years. With a wild-eyed look in her eye she grabs me and pins me against our dressing-room wall.

"Trick or Treat?" she whispers with these wild flying-saucer eyes.

"Treat," I say, feeling some rousing occurrence about to commence.

"Follow me." She drags me by the arm into an empty bathroom and digs through her purse for a minute that seems like an hour. She eventually finds what she's looking for—a tiny, glass, barrel-shaped vial—and dabs two small piles of methamphetamine between her thumb and forefinger. She lifts the pile to my face and gives me an ear-to-ear smile. With every nose muscle I have, I suck up the powder as hard and fast as I can. It burns like crazy, making my eyes water and my body clench.

"Damn! Strong batch," I say, a little embarrassed at my immediate physical reaction and after I can see straight.

"I told you it was a treat," she replies, vacuuming the remaining mini-mountain of stuff up her pierced nostril. As she looks up and wipes the last few bits of crystal from the rim of her pretty little nose, we catch each other's eyes, grab each other by the backs our necks, and start feverously kissing.

In one swift swoop, without disrupting our tongue dance, we waddle inside a toilet stall and slam the door. In rapid succession, she pulls off my belt and yanks my pants and undershorts down to my ankles and I reach under her polyester op-art dress and maneuver her panties down to her platform shoes.

Everything is happening like a video on fast forward.

The impact of the drugs kicking in at full speed, the feel her smooth curving body around mine, and the exchange of our hot saliva make for, hands down, the fastest erection I've ever had. I lift her from the back of her legs as she guides me inside her sex tunnel, and in an instant, we're on our way to quite possibly going halves on a baby.

We finished almost as fast we started, and then it all just died.

We level out from the initial drug rush and with slight embarrassment, re-adjust ourselves, and smile at each other awkwardly.
She curtsies and I bow, as if we'd just performed a soft shoe
routine for the sink and mirror, whiff another hit of meth each,
and go our separate ways.

Leveling out and containing myself as much as possible, I
remind myself I still have to perform a set of music. Flying high
among the backstage buzz, while the bands and friends of the
bands are chatting and hanging before the show, I realize I've
been talking non-stop nonsense to every person who'll listen to
me. I've cornered Dave Alvin from the Blasters and am in the
middle on a stream-of-consciousness rant about how we're sharing this time and place in life together, and how important music
was to me as a kid growing up in Burbank, and God knows what
else. The whole time, he's is looking at me like I've got two heads.
Halfway through my pointless vomit, he goes, "Okay, man, you
gotta take it down a notch or two. I need another beer," and
disappears. I'm there alone looking down at a plate of deli meat
wondering what to do next. I kind of hope someone just hits
me over the head with something heavy and knocks me out for
a while.

Out of nowhere I'm struck with this overwhelming desire to
meet Jim Carroll. I can't control it. It's life or death. For my own
self-important, drugged-up reasons, I can't wait, and suddenly
I'm walking upstairs to his dressing room. Outside the door with
the piece of paper that says, "JIM CARROLL," everything's quiet and tranquil. My hand just starts knocking on his door and I
can't get it to stop. My mind's racing and my body's still, but my
hand just keeps knocking. The door slowly opens, and there he
is greeting me with a most vacant stare, as my hand is still knocking. Not even a second passes before I launch into a big gushing
run-on sentence: "Hey Jim I'm from one of the bands on the
show tonight and I love, I mean, I really love your work and also
loved your book *The Basketball Diaries* so much I read it like five
times and wanted to meet you, my band, we're called Possum

Dixon, we took our name from this serial killer who's still on the loose but that's a long story but we learned 'People Who Died' God I love that song it's so good and it's for sure one of my all-time favorites and wanted to know if you'd sing it with us tonight wow I can't believe I'm standing here with you I love your work did I say that, anyhow it would be amazing if you'd you play that song with us tonight. Um, would you?"

He looks at me like I'm a stranger from another planet. He sees I'm not just some crazed weirdo fan looking for an autograph, but perhaps something worse: a crazed weirdo fan who wants to perform onstage with him. After what feels like a lifetime of gazing into my eyes, he speaks. "Yeah. Yeah, that sounds okay. Let's do it at the end of my set."

"Yeah? Okay, alright, great, thank you and see you later." I race downstairs, trying to keep my cool as I tell the rest of the band 20 or 30 times we'll be doing the song with him.

We walk on stage to an exhilarating roar of hometown applause. My heart's racing so fast it just might burst. I do all I can to keep my cool, doing one thing at a time, and overthink everything. I plug my bass in; yes it's plugged in, definitely plugged in. I look into the lights; yes, I'm onstage and this is totally happening. Are my shoes tied? Yes. I move my body to the mic stand at center stage, and wait for the drums to kick in and start our set.

By now I've learned to play under the influence of all types of drugs, but this time I've gone too far. I start feeling this out-of-body experience, seeing flashes of myself watching the band from various angles of the theater, all in quick cuts. Unaware I'm noticeably high, I continue playing while fighting selfish urges to stop for a cig break in the middle of a song. A cigarette sounds so good right now. Then come these rushes and waves of elation and all I can think about is the girl I had sex with in the bathroom a couple of hours earlier, and if she's up for going again after I'm done playing. It's as if I've dived into a pool with no water, suspended in air, waiting to shatter on the concrete. But song by song we get through it and 15 minutes later we are done.

Later, after what seems like an eternity, Jim Carroll finishes his set and we, along with mighty Circle Jerks front man Keith Morris on background vocals, join him through our zippy version of "People Who Died" for a raging Hollywood crowd. After the show, I have this great sense of triumphant relief, until J tries talking some sense into me.

"Hey man, over the past six months, we've gone from performing at the dozen or so clubs we've been playing for the last four years, to making a really good debut record. By everyone's account—Interscope, press, and everyone we know — things are hopeful for the band. This ain't the time to blow it. You gotta get your head together."

I know he's right, but can't get my head around the idea of taking this ride sober. Looking at him dead in his eyes, I deliver a bold-faced lie I somehow think he'll buy, "You're totally right J. After tonight I'm done. Not another drink. Not another drug."

"Really?" He says, knowing I'm bullshitting him.

"Really," I respond, ending our near buzzkill pep talk.

Now if can just find that girl from earlier and get a little higher, everything will be okay.

***

Our debut LP is becoming a favorite on college radio stations nationwide, and I'm being asked to give lots of interviews. Most of the publications, college newspapers, fanzines, and arts & entertainment mags, request me as the band's spokesperson — a task I'm not entirely comfortable with. It's one thing playing live shows and being onstage with the band, but when it comes to the band's history, dissecting how we function as a band, or talking about the creative process, I naturally retract into my inner shell.

From day one, the songwriting process has been an enigma. The only consistent element is that I need to be in this curious and inspired mood that I can't induce, and it's guaranteed to be short and fleeting. I'll grab a guitar or bass and riff and something comes out, and then words come out in a melody, and the basic structure is done. I bring the structures to Celso, Sully, and Rich, and we work them into songs. But they can't be overthought. Anytime we labor over anything too long, it loses whatever I loved about it in the first place. But explaining this to music journalists isn't something I'm comfortable with. It lowers the veil a little too much.

To offset confrontational moments when writers are looking for the facts they need to get their jobs done, I rarely give them a straight answer. No matter how easy the writer is to talk to, I usually end up feeling like the self-conscious, shy kid from Burbank who has no place being in a band or talking about music at all. Something about going on record makes me uneasy, especially I'm when asked about my personal history, the songwriting process, or personal views.

At times like these, the Fucky Game comes in handy.

It's easier, and much more entertaining, to employ those Fucky Game tactics learned from my dad and Uncle Ed. Playing the Fucky Game and giving abstract answers makes interviews more manageable, and makes for a more interesting article. In an interview I did yesterday, I told a reporter that Possum Dixon was the name of an American car from the 1950s, like the Plymouth Satellite. I told another writer I was born in Scotland, and trained on the bagpipes. I said I'd written all the band's songs on them, and I'm almost certain he believed me.

As part of this new world of full time rehearsing and giving interviews, the band meets with the label, lawyers, and business managers a couple of times each week. In fancy Westwood offices, I drift off into my deep fogs as J and middle aged men in polo shirts throw around numbers and timetables that bore me more than high school math. Occasionally I'll look around and pretend I'm engaged in the changes of one contract or another, noticing Celso half asleep or looking out the window, who like me, is waiting for night to fall and the excitement to begin.

***

I'm swaying back and forth on my hammock, on the second floor outside deck at Ellis Island, daydreaming of the places we might go to support our record and the phone rings. It's Beck.

"Hey man, it's Beck. Was wondering if you'd play a little stand-up bass on my new record, the one I'm doing for Geffen."

"Yeah. Totally," I say, thinking maybe we'll rehearse it with his new band or play it live to feel it out or something, and then record it at some place like Sound City.

"Cool, we're recording at this house in Silverlake in an hour. You have a pen? I'll give you the address."

Thrilled for the guy we probably would've voted least likely to succeed in 1991, I lug my stand-up bass in my Bronco and show up at the address; a two-story Spanish-style house way up in the fancy hills of Silverlake — an area we call the "swish alps," cause that's where all the people that've made it live — where he's recording. With my bass in tow, I'm greeted by these guys who are recording the session called Tom and Rob. Beck's plucking a banjo and singing to a cat. He sees me, nods and smiles. I sense he's got a pretty good idea about how this is going to go.

"Hey man, thanks for coming. Here," he says, gesturing to a closet nearly filled with someone's clothes. "This should capture a nice, acoustic bass sound."

"Okay," I say while pulling me and my bass inside, still having no idea what we're recording. With Beck, it could be thrashy hardcore or a lullaby. Tom and Rob start wiring mics around the room and look like they are ready to start recording. Beck grabs an acoustic guitar.

"It's called 'Black Hole.' Goes like this," he says, strumming the acoustic in this drowning Appalachian way that feels a little witchy. There's no time think, just play, so I start bowing the root notes of chords he's playing as best as I can over a couple of takes. He starts singing, and is off on some fantastical surreal melodious rant that gives "Lucy In the Sky with Diamonds" a run for its money. There's no telling what he's singing about, but the lyrics—stuff about lightbulbs, clouds, and glass walls—all sound like they belong together and are delivered with sincere conviction.

When we're done, they play me some of the other stuff he's working on, and like "Black Hole," it's this strange blend of wonderful music. I'm amazed at how diverse his tastes are, and how his stuff is coming out. Stylistically, it's all over the musical map — one song sounds totally different than the next. He's working in this infinite music universe where there are no boundaries, which is inspiring but also makes me second guess myself a little. I think about how narrow-minded and rigid our record sounds, how every song's been arranged through this singular late '70s rock lens.

I bail, and take myself on a leisurely drive through the Silverlake hills, feeling optimistic about all this recording stuff that's happening on this almost unimaginable scale—making records for Geffen and Interscope and playing the Roxy—when just a couple of years earlier we were putting around LA, gigging at the PikMe-Up and Al's Bar for a handful of people.

WE'RE ALL HAPPY

I'M STRETCHED OUT on my bed at Ellis Island, reading *The Catcher in the Rye* for the third time when J rings. He's always calling.

"So, the Dead Milkmen are offering you guys a slot opening for them on their upcoming US and Canadian tour. It'll end up being like three months or something and you'd hit every big city in the U.S. and Canada. Plus a shit ton of smaller cities."

This is the kind of tour we've been anticipating. I call the other guys and share the news. Everyone's in. Being fans of the Dead Milkmen and having hit it off with them after opening for them at the Palomino a couple of years earlier, we can hardly wait to start. We think they're a great role model for a band. They've been together for a bunch of years, and seem to do things on their terms. With the same lineup from the early '80s when they formed in Philadelphia—Joe Jack Talcum, Dave Blood, Dean Clean, and Rodney Anonymous—they also seem like the perfect band to show us the rules of the road and learn about touring. We enlist one of Celso's high school buds to help with guitar tech and roadie duties, a fearless adventure seeker and guitarist named Craig, and a seasoned tour manager who's memorized the U.S. highways from years of touring named Denny, and are ready to go.

Before meeting up with them, we open a string of shows for X in the Southwest. They're out supporting their seventh studio album, *Hey Zeus!*, headlining theater-sized venues. After finishing our sets, we watch them like we're on a paid vacation. Seeing them perform songs I've loved since the early Rodney on the Roq days leaves me in awe every time. When X take the stage, they're this unstoppable and incredible force. Being in X's world makes us seem special. On top of being a great band, they're encouraging to us as a new band and treat us kind of like kid brothers.

Playing our set has become a breeze — maybe too easy — and might be getting easier than it should be. Last night at the El Rey Theater in Albuquerque, I climbed on my stand-up bass, pretending to ride it like a surfboard. I lost my balance and fell onto it, snapping its bridge and neck. Looks like the rest of the tour I'm playing electric bass only.

During the X shows we've been alienating homophobic members of every audience. To mix up our live set, we've using the middle section of one of our songs to revisit my Madonna Medley. I usually start with a few verses from "Like a Virgin," and end with "Lucky Star," at which point I've unbuttoned my shirt and yanked my belt off, swinging it like an amateur burlesque dancer, occasionally getting heckled by the audience.

Later in our set, Celso takes over lead vocal duties for our distorted version of the '60s Bossa Nova-infused club classic, "Girl from Ipanema." He removes his shirt and ties it around his waist like a cheap hustler, exposing his brown and bare mid-section while wandering through the crowd gripping the mic, flashing his famous smile and revealing those tobacco stained teeth, engaging audience members in Spanish. A couple of nights ago he traded his eyeglasses with a guy in the audience, and took a hit off his cigarette. It's impossible to know what might intrigue him, and he, like X, is a mysterious thrill to watch. Playing in a band with one of your favorite performers is a gift. While we're up there under those lights, watching that big smile of his light up every room we play, being in this band is way more than I could have ever imagined. It's a dream come true.

***

The tour with The Dead Milkmen is better than we could have imagined. They've been generous and kind, sharing their wicked sense of humor and dedicated fans with us. City after city, legions of their fans line up long in advance to push themselves against club stages to see the band up close. From the Bottleneck in

Lawrence, Kansas, to the Covered Dish in Gainesville, Florida, loyal fans pack inside theaters and clubs to jump around and sing along to songs about toxic waste, UFOs, conspiracy theories, trendy cars, and punk-rock girls.

The Dead Milkmen are responsible for showing us how to keep the other twenty-three hours of a show day interesting. In each city, they fill in their time giving college interviews, visiting with fans, and finding absurd things to amuse themselves with to keep things fresh. They have a terrific tour manager named Dan who makes touring feel like one big party, and a dry-witted soundman we get on great with named Matt. The Milkmen call him the largest Jew in captivity. They come up with the best pet names. Between their crew and ours, we've formed a friendship and bond that enables us to cut loose each night. The whole thing feels like a travelling summer camp I never attended, but wished I had. Over the past few shows, they've generously shared their stage time with us, and we've been joining them on-stage to sing background vocals on their hit, "Punk Rock Girl," sometimes only in our underwear. We love being on tour with them.

We made our first visit to the Midwest, for a one-night stop at a venue called the Ranch Bowl in Omaha, Nebraska. It's this well-known bowling alley/rock venue that can pack in a few hundred kids on a good night. Although our record is climbing the college radio charts, we're still a new, unknown band to the sea of faces staring us down as we take the stage. One of those faces is a disgruntled teenager standing in front of the stage, just in front of my microphone. Both his middle fingers are pointed high in the air as we walk on stage.

"You suck!" he hollers, before we've even played one note. Crowd members try hushing him but he keeps on. And on. And on. After one too many times of him yelling, "You suck," I've had enough.

"Look you little queer-bait, meet us in our dressing room after the show and we'll give you something to suck on."

I ignore him for as long as I can, but he keeps his middle fingers up and continues heckling us, like it's his only mission in life. His commitment to hating us is so inspiring and commendable, that when it comes time for my Madonna Medley, I dedicate it directly to him. The audience is roaring and cheering me on as I swing my belt at him, singing the chorus of "Like a Virgin" into his furious eyes. He's determined, and holding his ground like a stealth soldier; arms held high, giving Possum Dixon the double bird.

We blaze through our set, once again playing our songs faster than we recorded them. Before our last song, I quip into the mic, "Hey, throw us your change — we need the money!" I didn't really think they'd do it, but they do, and now, nearly every kid in the audience is pelting us with every nickel, dime, and quarter in their pockets. For our entire last song, "Elevators," we encounter this heavy rain of coins. By the end of the song, the stage is littered with layers of Oklahoma pocket change. We share a good laugh stuffing our pockets, grabbing our instruments, and head backstage.

There in the Ranch Bowl's makeshift dressing room is the "You suck!" kid from the audience. He's pacing and talking to himself and looks crazier in person than he did in the audience. He sees me come in, and before I have time to exit he approaches me with a stare that says, "I'm totally crazy," and corrals me into a corner where I can't move. He pulls up his shirt, revealing a large black pistol protruding from the boxers that overflow from his dirty drooping jeans. He points it at my chest. Too afraid so do or say anything, I freeze, feeling my heart beat like it never has before. My father's golden life lesson number three — the one about throwing sand into the eyes of an attacker—isn't going to come in handy right now — there's no sand backstage at the Ranch Bowl.

"No one, I say NO ONE, talks to me like that, you fucking understand?" he declares, with the gun still aimed at my chest. I think my life and what I know of it will soon to be over. The sight of the gun induces a barrage of awful Uncle Ed flashbacks. I look around, hoping someone will help me out this mess, but the only person around is Chuck, our faithful representative from Interscope Records who flew out to surprise us on the road. He's on the other side of the room, stuffing his face with hummus and reading band graffiti, completely oblivious to my dilemma.

"Yes, yes, I understand. That'll never happen again. I'm really sorry." He mutters a few more nasty things under his breath and leaves. I take a cab back to my hotel room, counting my lucky stars he didn't pull the trigger.

***

Before joining the Dead Milkmen for this tour, I decided to wear the same clothes for thirty days and thirty nights without removing a single garment. Part endurance test, part Fucky Game, it just seemed like the right thing to do. If I follow through, it'll mean playing around twenty-five shows in the same shirt, pants, underwear, and socks without taking them off once, not even to bathe. I just happen to be in the right mind frame to make that dream a reality. I'm three weeks in and going strong.

My shirt — a light blue, long-sleeve, button-down shirt from Goodwill — was already paper thin when I got for a buck. I've also got on a pair of old '50s, high-water, wool trousers held up by a thin black belt, black dress socks, worn-out work shoes, and tighty-whitey underwear. It was warm in LA when we left, and I forgot to factor in we'd be traveling into colder areas of the country, including the beginning of a New York City winter.

The stages of old theaters and nightclubs are dirty places. Musicians and roadies with filthy shoes drag in the soil and grime from wherever they've been. Dirty amps and drums are dragged across them and all types of spilled alcohol soaks deep into the carpets or wood floors. My shirt and pants have become a sponge for these ingredients and are, gig by gig, picking up scuzz from each stage I've been rolling around on. Between my dirty clothes and non-bathing pact, I've started smelling bad.

The Dead Milkmen, who've been supporting my goal and all, have appointed me with the pet nickname "Egg Boy," because they say I smell like rotten eggs.

As the shows are moving along, my shirt's been ripping and tearing in various places. Using the easiest repair tool I could find — small strips of silver duct tape from Craig's toolbox — the shirt has taken on its own vintage, Richard Hell, punk-rock aesthetic. In my neatest scroll, I've written Egg Boy along the front pocket in magic marker.

Now we're on the last few days of the tour, before we've got a week off, and I smell so bad that nobody wants to be near me, let alone sit next to me for any length of time in the van. But quitting isn't an option; I carry on with proud stink, and finish the tour in my nearly demolished outfit.

A few days later we turn up for a show at the Capitol Theater in Flint, Michigan. After sound check, Celso and I meet a group of young and excited Dead Milkmen fans who claim Possum Dixon as their second favorite band of all time. Huddling in a tight pack, they remind me of myself at their age, showing up to the gig early to catch a glimpse of their favorite bands.

"Been listening to your record non-stop. Know every word. What are you guys, new wave or something?" one of them says, having no idea what new wave is.

"Is it true you guys took your name from a serial killer? My brother's in jail for killing someone. Says he didn't do it, though," says one of the others, who looks like he could be River Phoenix's stunt double. They're going on and on with questions and know almost as much about us as we do. The thing is, they don't seem to care if we answer or not. They just like asking about stuff. "Is LA like it is in the movies? Are there movie stars and hot chicks, and palm trees everywhere? That's what it looks like in the movies. Hey, you guys want us to drive you around and show you the ruins of the crumbling Motor City? Looks like the end of the world. C'mon let's go. We'll show you."

We like the way they just kind of decided we should go, and jump in their barely running Ford Falcon wagon. Before we know it, we're zigzagging through the outskirts of town. There are destroyed and abandoned building structures everywhere. They're mere shells of their former selves, only intact in their basic structures — large windows have been bashed out and their walls are covered with graffiti, nearly hidden by tall, dry weeds. He's right, it looks like the end of the world. As much as I love weird and dark stuff, this is too real and too depressing to get a kick from. It's just sad. I've never seen anything like it, and when the shock of all the destruction wears off, it leaves me scarred. While passing blocks of abandoned buildings, the kid driving is tells us about it.

"This piece of shit we're cruising in was made here. Look around, it's like a bomb went off and everyone died, but we're somehow still here. We got the shit ass end of this whole deal. First were the race riots in the late '60s and then by the '70s the auto industry died and the motor city turned into a this, a ghost town. At least we're not working zombies like our dads. And thank God for fucking music," he says, as we're passing by a slew of colossal shut-down automotive plants that once employed their folks.

The bunch of us pull into a run-down pancake house for a pre-show dinner. Inside, a large group of churchgoers in matching T-shirts that read, "I'm with Jesus! The Youth Connection," are seated by the entrance. The presence of one of the kids in our group, who's sporting blue hair, must be miffing them by his appearance, and suddenly there's a mounting tension coursing throughout the restaurant. They're staring, shaking their heads — like he's going to hell for his blue hair or something—and he's just staring back, becoming increasingly bothered by the God-fearing maddoggers. After a minute of this, that feels like an hour, the tension finally breaks.

"That's it," he says, dropping his fork into a plate of barely eaten pancakes. He gets up and walks over to them.

"Fuck you and fuck God!" His strident delivery catches the attention of every diner in the place. Every fork and knife stops clanking and the whole place goes silent. He lights a cigarette, drops a lit match on their table, and walks out.

We finish eating as fast as we can and bail. We're exiting and Celso gives them his million-dollar smile as we skirt past them, offering a "Have a good night," but they don't so much as look at him, or me. We head back to the Capitol Theater and usher the kids in as our guests, where later, they go totally bonkers during the Dead Milkmen's set.

***

During the party-every-night Dead Milkmen tour, Interscope launches our first single from our record, "Watch the Girl Destroy Me." The label insists the song is an FM radio hit. We understand that song is part of the reason they became interested in us in the first place, and it's always made us a little apprehensive. I'd written it when I was twenty-one after getting dumped by this super-babe I was seeing who was employed at a Melrose record store. She was, in every way, out of my league, and after she realized that, left me in the dust. After writing it, I haven't had any real emotional attachment to it, and never thought it was anything to bank my future on, but now, it feels like the success of our band is riding on it. It's the sound of our other songs — the surf-inspired ones with angular spy riffs and narrative vocals— for which we'd like to be recognized. I suppose if "Watch the Girl Destroy Me" has the success they say it will, then fans will discover the other songs on our record.

The label started their radio promotion launch and alternative rock stations around the country have started playing "Watch the Girl…" in regular rotation. Driving into unknown cities and hearing our music sandwiched between Nirvana and FM newcomers Green Day on our van's radio is a real kick, and guarantees packed club shows. Last year at this time we were playing clubs in LA and opening for some of our favorite bands, and now we've made a jump to the medium time that's surprised us all.

***

After making a name for ourselves from our string of independent singles, press in independent publications, and roots in the College Rock community before signing with Interscope, Possum Dixon still has some gravitas in the DIY community. But since signing with them, we've been thrust into the sell-out category to a new regime of Indie Rockers who think success is poison.

Sully, Celso, and I were at some stupid party in Silverlake and bump into a guy from the local music community who's been kicking around the past few years. He's transformed as one of Indie Rock's sheep and just starts talking to us.

"Oh right, I know your band. You're those guys from one of those Interscope bands, aren't you? Aren't you guys on MTV or something?" he says, pretending not to know our names, even though I'd bet 50 bucks he does.

"Yeah, that's us," Sully replies. "Our band is the Archies, and we're going on tour with the Beatles next month."

Sully's the best at dealing with idiots.

"Then we're recording an album of duets with Aerosmith on the French Riviera," Celso chimes in. He's pretty good at it too.

"Lemme guess, your new band sounds like Sonic Youth, Beck, and Pavement, but is somehow totally original. I'll bet you have a lo-fi, cassette only, release you made on your four track and won't play for more than 20 people at a time. Man, it must be so cool to be you. Take a hike, loser," Sully says, brushing him off with ease.

"Whatever. Have fun partying with No Doubt, Weezer, and the Wallflowers. Sell outs." he says, trying to burn us.

My father's golden rule about not everyone liking you had never been so true. The stupid terms and labels being thrown around make my stomach turn.

We've been continuing to make waves in the press and are gaining national popularity. The *LA Times* recently favored our new record, noting our '70s new-wave/punk influence and clean-cut aesthetic as this fresh new thing. Other local publications have generously granted us long interviews and cover stories, often using words like "pop-punk" and "brainy" to describe the band. Some articles are labeling us as the "next big thing"—which seems way more like a curse than an accolade. While Grunge singers are screaming and crooning across the FM dial, we're defined by my sometimes overly deadpan vocal delivery, Sully's abrupt clanky piano jumping in and out of the songs at unexpected moments, Celso's abstract and tightly wound catchy spy riffs, and Rich's deft drumming. It feels like we're the head of a revival class that doesn't exist, which if nothing else, gives critics something to write about.

FAN MAIL

A LL THAT AIR GUITAR PLAYING and rock stuff I dreamed about as a kid is happening in real life, and for the most part it's glorious. The past six months have been a blur, appearing on a dizzying number of stages across the United States. We've been introduced to the country through its nightclubs and theaters, playing to hundreds, sometimes thousands, of excited music fans each night. Hauling ourselves from one major city to the next, we're slowly building an audience of our own. Our live set is better than it ever has been, and we can easily zip through our first album, along with a cover of the Yardbirds' "For Your Love" and the Dream Syndicate's "The Days of Wine and Roses," in under thirty-five minutes. Seeing the country through our van windshield by day, and playing by night, an anticipated future awaits us.

After having a day job for the last few years, I've never felt more free staring out the van window, daydreaming about the next stop on the tour. Throughout the Midwest, bucolic farmlands and never-ending skies are a welcome relief from nightclub madness. Conversely, pulling into new cities and meeting club owners and fans is a welcome break from looking at Midwest farmlands all day. The whole thing feels like a long vacation.

In New York, we've made appearances on a new talk show, *Late Night with Conan O'Brien*, as well as MTV's *120 Minutes*. These brushes with fame, where fans of the band are asking us to sign records, CDs, and magazine articles we've appeared in, are becoming regular. But more often than not, self-doubt kicks in and leaves me wondering if this is all too good to be true, and if it's just some good dream.

I felt as cool as I ever did when I walked inside Max Fish — New York's East Side go-to hipster bar — and heard our music blaring through the jukebox while this couple who looked like they'd just wandered in from Warhol's Factory are dancing nearby. It's moments like these when it seems like we might be starting to leave our mark on the music map.

The worst part of being away from home has got to be the food. After reading about how awful eating red meat is for people, the thought of swallowing and ingesting cooked animals started making my stomach turn. I took the path of vegetarianism, and quickly changed my diet altogether. I traded munching hamburgers and pepperoni pizzas for a non-dairy diet, known in small circles as veganism. Although I smoke too many cigarettes and do plenty of things that aren't good for me, the idea of eating killed animals and animal byproducts has become a huge turn off. Every night on tour, I'm grossed out by deli trays of sliced meats and cheeses that await the band in our dressing rooms. As a result, I've been surviving on an unsteady diet of oatmeal, hummus, bread, coffee, and cigarettes.

***

We've made a couple of stops back to the West Coast to play some shows in LA. One of them was a couple of nights ago, when we did a one-nighter at this new nightclub in the heart of the Sunset Strip called the Viper Room, that's owned and run by Johnny Depp. The Viper Room's become the talk of the town — even among the most jaded Silverlake hipsters — after Tom Petty and the Heartbreakers played on opening night. Since, it's become a hangout for rock stars, movie stars, and old-school Hollywood elite. Nestled between Tower Records and the Whisky a Go Go, the venue has had former lives as the Sunset Strip staples, the Central and Filthy McNasty's, but now, it's the Hollywood nightspot where pretty girls who look like they've just stepped off a *Vogue* cover shoot work as cocktail waitresses, serving thirsty patrons. Plus, I heard it's the location where the Plimsouls performed one of my favorite songs, "A Million Miles

Away," in the movie *Valley Girl*. There's nothing about this place I don't like.

Wanting to reconnect with my brother Gordy, I invite him to the show. He just graduated from UCLA and found a real job. He's got this great wife, and they just had a son. Our career paths can't be further from each other's. He came down early, and after my sound check, we picked up a bottle of Southern Comfort and planted ourselves on a nearby bus stop just up the street from the Viper Room.

"I was driving here thinking about all the crap I gave you when we were younger. You only deserved about half of it," he joked, while the sun disappeared behind Sunset Boulevard. "But really, I'm glad you're following your dreams and doing what you want."

"Thanks, Gordy. It's all I've ever wanted to do. And now, it's all I can do," I say, tipping the brown bagged bottle to my mouth for another gulp.

A few hours later we stumble through a one-drink-over-the-limit to a packed house of LA fans. The show is nearly disastrous; we took long breaks between songs to stabilize, smoke cigarettes, and chatter with friends and audience members. Every band is entitled to an occasional bad night, but most band members would agree that when they do, it's not in front of a hometown audience.

***

We're between a bunch of shows here in the states, Canada, and Europe, where we've played some of our best shows, and Interscope wants a video to promote our single, "Watch the Girl Destroy Me." A couple of years earlier, we made a video for that song with an old friend of the band on his groovy Super 8 camera that we like just fine, but Interscope is insisting on a new one. It feels like a lot of pressure; every week, new "Alternative" bands are coming out with singles accompanied by colorful videos in hopes of becoming MTV sensations. We don't want to make a video that'll determine our rock fate, but the label is insisting we do things their way on this one.

I've always thought that any group on the verge of major success that makes a bad music video is vulnerable to permanent damage. A crummy song with an okay video is tolerable, but an okay song with a crap video has the power to make fans turn on a band. I remember my first time seeing the Police video for "Wrapped Around Your Finger." There's Sting, doing aerobics in slow motion in a room full of candles in an outfit that looks like it's stolen from my good mother's closet. I was embarrassed for him in a way that almost ruined those first two Police records. On the other hand, I thought Michael Jackson's "Billie Jean" video good enough that it made me fall in love with the song.

Interscope's sent us a list of current, sought-after directors in hopes of producing a MTV-friendly video that'll shoot us into the big time and sell some records. We've been unable to agree on a director, so we're proceeding without one. Our idea of shooting a performance-only video has been shot down, in favor of one that captures the band cavorting around Silverlake. The result is a compromised montage of footage I'm not crazy about, featuring me as the thing I've been fighting to avoid: a cutesy singer. Someone's over color-corrected the final cut to make my eyes this impossible shade of blue, and edited a boring and formulaic video that's, to me, unwatchable. The label, however, loves it and is reassuring us that in little time, Possum Dixon will be a worldwide headlining act.

Despite my disdain for how the video looks, it's started receiving MTV airplay around the world. The weeks that follow are like purgatory—we know the video is being played and everyone's waiting for record sales to jump. We head back on tour, playing some of the same venues we've been at, noticing more kids wearing our T-shirts and singing along with our songs at shows. We leave directly from some shows to play crowded record shop in-stores to meet and greet new fans. My job's getting easier. All I have to do is show up and play.

At the request of the label's radio department, we've been stopping by radio stations all over the US for live acoustic sets and on-air interviews. We're doing most everything the label wants us to do to promote our record, and anytime I'm in need of a break, I remind myself how badly I wanted all this in the first place. Amid the grind of playing and promoting our record, some of these shining moments of getting what I want were met with tiring feelings of *"Is this what I wanted?"*

During the months that follow, we stay busy by joining one of our favorite bands, the Violent Femmes, on a US tour. Like the Dead Milkmen, they're gracious and encouraging to us as newcomers. We're playing a cover of the Modern Lover's "Pablo Picasso," in which the Femmes' bassist, Brian Ritchie, joins us during our set, making it the highlight of our set. Additionally, Celso's been joining them on trumpet for noisy horn parts of "Black Girls." No matter how burned out I get, watching Celso perform with them night after night never fails to produce incredible joy.

Our video's in MTV rotation, we're playing with bands we admire, buckets of fan mail are overflowing at the post office, and our record can be found in nearly every record store we visit, but sales are yet to make a huge jump. The answer to increase sales, they say, is stay on the road, play more shows, play on live radio, and do more interviews. We're starting to get burned out — I'm getting sick of us and wouldn't blame anyone for being sick of us, too. In the back of my mind, I'm beginning to suspect our video might not translate into the record sales everyone's hoping for.

***

The following months reveal that "Watch the Girl Destroy Me" isn't going to be the next "Louie Louie." We accept our fate and hop on a tour, opening a few weeks for rockabilly revivalists, the Reverend Horton Heat. We learned quickly that the fans of the Reverend Horton Heat are there for one reason: to see sweaty psychobilly, not angular power-pop by a band that sounds like they're from the South, but are among the furthest things from it. People who don't know our band but hear the name Possum Dixon probably expect some kind of roots/country/Southern-influenced group, and are disappointed by our new-wavisms.

Our first show on the tour was in Boston, and it should've been our last. As the stage lights dim, we walk on before the excitement of an oversold house. We're greeted with an unwelcoming barrage of flying bottles of beer exploding on the stage. It's nearly silent until we start our set. Every few minutes, whirling bottles of beer are spinning at full force at my head from the balcony, and I'm clenching every muscle, wondering what one of those things is going to feel like when it explodes on my skull.

I've never felt this kind of fear onstage. There's no way I'm saying anything after the Omaha Ranch Bowl gun-scare incident. It's a shut-the-fuck-up-and-play-your-songs kind of night.

We muscle through a short set, dodging the glass beer bombs, only to have a similar experience a couple nights later.

Things went from bad to worse as we walk on stage at Lupo's Heartbreak Hotel in Providence, Rhode Island. These two rough and tough-looking rockabilly guys are standing directly in front of my mic stand with hateful expressions that say they wish I was dead. I do all I can to ignore them, and step before the mic to start our set. I'm looking in the lights and feel a massive loogie hurled in my face. I look down and they have middle fingers pointing at me.

"Get the fuck off the stage you pussies!"

"Reverend Rules!"

I wipe the gooey spit off my face with my shirt, undecided as how to proceed. There's no time to think. Then I just cave in.

"I can't take these guys, I'm leaving," I say to Sully off mic after the first song. Much to my surprise, he fires back like an older brother, "Fuck those fools. Don't be a pussy, Zabrecky! Just keep playing—fuck them!"

My embarrassment turns to frustration, but I know Sully's right, so I continue playing, and they keep spitting and saying stuff between songs. I'm intimidated by these knuckleheaded rock-a-bullies who are putting a big dent in my performance, and it's all my fault. We forge on autopilot as that twenty-minute set feels like a lifetime. Inside I'm cracking up. By the end of the show I'd been spit on more times than I can count.

Burned out and in serious need of a break, we do the last thing we should by jumping on another supporting tour, opening for the Lemonheads in the Southwest. They too are at the end of a tour cycle, promoting their widely successful LP, *Come on Feel the Lemonheads*. On the tour things go from bad to worse. Everyone is tired and grouchy while sharing close quarters and we do all we can just to get through each show.

After returning to LA, we go our separate ways for a few weeks. Sully goes into hibernation with his girlfriend, Jean, Celso's embedded into the tomb a windowless Hollywood apartment with a girl called Shawna, and Rich is out hitting every bar and club in LA.

***

While we've got our thing going, Beck's star is on the rise. He's finished his Geffen album, and is doing some local releases on vinyl. One is a ten-inch disc called *A Western Harvest Field*, for a new label called Fingerpaint Records. He invited me over to his house in Highland Park for a listening party, and to finger-paint record jackets so that each record could have its own original artwork.

Excited to hear the record and help make some artwork, as my life is starting to feel like one big vacation, I decide to get high before joining the party. It was after I entered his Highland Park living room, that I realized the drugs I took were stronger than usual. Everything started going in slow motion, and I could barely keep myself upright. I walk into a crowded room to find myself painfully aware everyone notices just how high I am. I

avoid eye contact with everyone like I always do when I'm loaded, knowing the pupils of my eyes must've been reduced to pin
dots. I'm embarrassed, but do my best to stay awake and paint a
few covers, and meet some members of another LA band on the
rise called that dog. My words are coming out in a gravelly slur
that I wish they aren't, and my body is operating at half speed.
I sink into a nearby couch and nod out for what seems like an
eternity.

I wake up to experience two things at once: the feeling of a
wet spot on my shirt—this mortifying puddle of drool on my
chest—and a handful of people staring at me. My single goal in
life is to keep my eyes open while smearing paint across record
jackets, before getting sucked under a narcotic tidal wave and
nodding off again.

I make a quiet exit and drive to one of my go-to places to
disappear: a nearby hill in Echo Park at the top of Baxter Street.
Up there I'm free from anyone's judgement to get even higher,
listening to oldies in my car. As the band's reputation is becoming known nationally, I'm becoming known as a confirmed drug-
gie, and feel trapped.

***

Little do we know that the zenith of radio airplay for Possum Dixon has passed. Too stupid and preoccupied with getting high to gain control over the band that means everything to me, my world is slowly slipping through the cracks. Sully is tiring of my drug use, it's difficult to get a read on Celso, and Rich seems to be perpetually neutral about any band matters other than gigging.

After what feels like an eternity of touring and life experiences, we have a couple of unfruitful meetings with J and Interscope, and are informed that regrouping and making another record is our only option. Although we'd gotten off to a good start, selling around 75,000 records, we're nowhere near close to the sales the label projected. It's time to figure out the future of the band. As we struggle making any sort of decisions with the label, more creative and personal issues are appearing on the horizon.

That's when I became addicted to heroin. I broke my "weekends only" rule and started using daily. After getting loaded with some needle-addicted friends in LA, I learned the ropes on how to cook up and shoot the stuff. In a matter of a few days I went from smoking and snorting, to shooting. I spend most of my time, which I had a lot of, buying drugs off the street and retreating to Ellis Island to get high. If, for any reason, I couldn't cop, I'd become an irritable wreck with a runny nose.

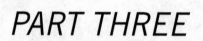

PART THREE

THIS IS THE PART WHERE I TELL YOU ABOUT JENNIFER

I T'S 9PM and I can hear John leaving his third message on my answering machine.

"Rob, you gotta come down to the Viper Room and meet the night manager. She won't stop bugging me about meeting you. Please, for me, just get down here and meet her. I'll leave your name on the guest list. Her name is Shannon, and trust me, she's super-hot. How many times you gonna make me do this?"

John's the soundman for X, whom I met last year on tour. Although I dig him and his X road stories, driving across town to meet up with a stranger—especially a hot one —sounds interesting but shoots down my plan of staying in. My second-floor outdoor balcony at Ellis Island has become my sanctuary from the club shows I've just finished, so driving to West Hollywood, to a nightclub of all places, is a hard sell. As of now, my plans consist of staying in, getting high, listening to music, and watching giant maple leaves cover the deck like a bed of giant Corn Flakes. Maybe later I'll roll around the USC campus on my trusty old junker bike *if* I get the urge to leave the house.

As if by witchcraft, a gush of warm October winds blows through the patio, sending the layer of leaves to sail above the deck. Something tells me to head out for an adventure. The next thing I know I've got my keys in my hand and my jacket on and I'm heading out the door. I climb into my old Ford Bronco, which is surrounded by big dry leaves and head west, as Ellis Island dissolves in my rear-view mirror. Trekking up Sunset Boulevard, I reflect that my former selves—the little wart kid and the one with the bullet wound—would've appreciated my path in music, having my own band, and living at a place like Ellis Island. My old boring Burbank life doesn't have a role in this new world, I think while driving over. And as long as I'm high, my new life protects me from my old one.

I park behind the club and go inside. After finding my name on the guest list, I head up some dark stairs and enter an even darker noisy room, which is nearly empty. Some band, whoever they are, have finished their set and are packing, and the few people left are filing out. Then a song that always makes me feel good, Bowie's "Heroes," starts playing at this nearly excruciating level.

In the distance, the form of a statuesque beauty catches every bit of my attention. An uncontrollable attraction is drawing me to this stranger, who's wearing nothing more than a fitted black slip and holding an armful of empty cocktail glasses above her head. A new feeling washes over me. The rest of the world melts away as she comes into full view—she's an amalgamation of every beautiful woman I'd ever dreamed about. She's practically glowing in the dark and her presence fills the place. Her straight dark hair is long and pulled back on one side, revealing her smooth rounded forehead, long neck, and slender figure. With little makeup, I can see her perfectly shaped, deep, blue eyes, a long straight nose ending in a perfect point, and a nicely shaped mouth with full lips. If you saw her, you'd probably fall in love with her. But there's more than just her beauty. There's something familiar about her, although I'm certain we've never met. I sense that her life, like mine, is hanging from a thread.

On the edge of some new sublime adventure, I thank myself for making the drive over. The strangest part about these dizzying seconds is that she isn't the girl I'm here to meet.

***

Sometimes I do bold things I have no control over. Sure, I showed up for John to meet the club's manager, but the moment I catch this female's eyes, I fall into a trance that prevents me from even saying hello to someone named Shannon. After delivering a drink to the last customer in the place, she locks eyes with me and starts walking in my direction. I look into those pretty eyes as some words pour out.

"You're not Shannon, are you?"

"No. But I know who you are," she says without skipping a beat and heading off to clear more empty glasses.

If she'd just said, "No," I could've taken the hint she wanted nothing to do with me and probably found this Shannon, but the way she looked at me when she said it gives me hope. While she's clearing more empty glasses, I approach her again.

"I don't know what time you're done here, but I'll be outside waiting for you."

She replies with the most powerful of gestures: she smiles and walks off.

Left hanging, I abort the idea of meeting Shannon, bail back down those dark stairs, and hold out in the parking lot. I smoke a couple of cigs, wondering if she might possibly be feeling the same way as I do, or if the whole thing's just a bad idea. After what feels like an eternity, she's emerging toward me with her purse over her shoulder, indicating she's off work.

"I'm Rob," I manage to squeak out.

"I know. Somehow every waitress knew you were coming in tonight," she replies nonchalantly. I intuit she wishes she could care less, but we're both a little blinded by the fireworks exploding between us.

"Feel like getting some coffee?" I ask, with a pretty good idea she's going to say yes. She looks at me for the longest time, like she knows something I don't, and replies.

"Sure."

Everything is right in the world, and I still don't know her name. We meet at my late-night go-to spot, the twenty-four-hour Astro Family Restaurant in Silverlake. Sitting across from each other, over coffee and cigarettes, she tells me her name is Jennifer. We pack our life stories into the span of the next couple of hours. She's even more pretty and clever under this terrible coffee shop lighting than she was in that dark club, telling me she comes from a good family in Orange County. She's taken the job at the Viper Room to make ends meet while trying to make it in showbiz. Then she throws a zinger at me.

"I'm sober. Have been for six years," she says, out of nowhere.

My heart sinks. My toes curl. My palms get wet. There's no way she's going to want anything to do with me after she finds out I'm a little strung out.

"Oh yeah? That's, great. I'm getting there," I say, lying as casually sounding as I can, feeling the drugs I took a few hours wearing off.

She's got visions of becoming a working singer and actress. One look at her and you just know that at some point soon, you'll be sharing her with the world. It's easy imagining her face on record covers and billboards, which she seems to be made for, but it's her perspective on the shallowness of Hollywood and slinging drinks in a nightclub that reels me in deeper.

"I know all the vampires who run this town. They show up at the Viper Room night after night, trying to get me to go home with them. They aren't interested in the music I want to make or the films I dream of being in. They just want to grind me into submission and check me off their to-do lists."

If I wasn't in love with her already, I am now for sure.

"I want to make records, go on tours, and be in movies. But I'm gonna let it happen on its own terms. Besides, being around all these characters gives me something to write about, and you might be one them."

I walk her to her car and we exchange numbers. I head back to Ellis Island as the sun's coming up, knowing I made the right decision to leave the house.

***

When you fall in love, everything moves fast. Life's moving at rocket speed with Jennifer and I. Since meeting, we've spent every possible minute with each other. Even though I'm freezing my ass off at a pay phone in the middle of the US, opening for the Violent Femmes, when I hear her voice everything's okay.

"Last night I had my first drink since I was a teenager," she tells me through the telephone in a relaxed, gravelly tone.

"You did? Really? What prompted that?"

"Well... I've been thinking about how life is short, and that I was never *truly* convinced I had a real drinking problem in the first place. I had two drinks with some girlfriends and I'm still here now."

"Congratulations, I suppose?" I say guessing, in no position to offer advice on sobriety. I'm still concealing my using around her best as I can.

"Thank you. We'll celebrate when you're back. In the meantime, stay out of trouble out there. I know you've got your little demons," she says in a silvery tone, without getting into the weeds of my drug struggles. "See you soon."

The tour ends and I get back to LA, where I spend every night off visiting Jennifer at the Viper Room. Elbowing past the club's famous patrons to get to the bar where Jennifer's stationed always feels like some weird dream. In that small, smoky, dimly lit room, I'll find myself sandwiched between the likes of Robert DeNiro and Iggy Pop, Gene Simmons and Harry Dean Stanton — each stealing glances at my new girlfriend's ass, who's busy slinging cocktails. Although I'm among this bustling Hollywood nightlife, the world of celebrity and fame makes me uneasy. At times amidst the hustle and bustle among celebrated and recognizable faces, I get squashed by waves of that 2nd grade isolation, wanting to run and hide in some dark alley in Burbank where I can be nobody again.

Tonight is Jennifer's night off, and Mike Keys is meeting us for drinks at the Viper Room. He's been working for various Hollywood studios, driving large trucks filled with lighting and sound gear, but still loves his Hollywood nightlife. As if it were rehearsed, the DJ just dropped the needle on the opening drum beat of "Lust for Life," and Mike Keys strolls into the club like Fonzie. Even though he's not famous, people look at him like he is. Everything's perfect, as he finds us at a booth in the corner and dives right in.

"I love what you've done with the place," he says, pouring his charm all over Jennifer.

"Oh thank you. Please, make yourself at home. Kick your shoes off and stay a while," she shoots back. I'm pleased, and unsurprised they have an instant rapport.

He gives me a long look. "Man, you look like shit. What the fuck have you been doing, Mr. Rock Star?" One of Mike Keys' most admirable attributes, one he's had since the day I met him, is his unadulterated way of being blunt, and that hasn't changed a bit.

"I've been on the road for the past year or so. What do you expect?"

"Okay. Whatever."

Mike Keys has changed, too. He's still getting by on his good looks, charm, and trademark deep olive tan. However, his nose is enlarged from being broken a few times from BPO brawls and bar fights over the years. But tonight he isn't out to fight anyone. I can see he's excited to meet Jennifer and Jennifer's excited to meet him. And as I'd guessed, they've hit it off instantly. They're looking at each other with a confident "Oh, you're attractive and have to deal with it" understanding. We're having an epic Hollywood night—gulping free drinks, watching a probably famous but forgettable band, and dancing to hits by the DJ. At the end of the night, Jennifer's off talking with co-worker friends and Mike Keys and I are back at the booth.

"Dude, you're lucky. She's special." His words reflect a tone that says that not only does he approve, but that also suggest that if I'm hit by a bus or something anytime soon, he'll be calling her. I understand wholeheartedly, and as I always did, admire his honesty. But that was the problem with Jennifer: everyone was always falling in love with her.

***

The following months have been a jumbled mess of passionate nights like the one we had with Mike Keys. We're engaging in every whim we can — late-night walks near USC, and exploring downtown LA and contemplating our pasts and futures. Our worlds have meshed and we've found what's been missing in our lives: each other.

My life is the closest it ever has been to being perfect, so two weeks ago we threw caution to the wind and surprised everyone by getting married. A handful of friends joined us for a small wedding in this small storefront turned Hispanic church in east Hollywood. We broke the news to each other's parents and started our new lives as husband and wife. I said goodbye to my friends at Ellis Island, as she did to her roommate, and we dragged our joint belongings to a 1950s Silverlake apartment near the reservoir. We're as happy and content as we've ever been, though some personal problems have started to surface.

Jennifer's been struggling with depression her whole life. It's a difficult and totally abstract subject for me to grasp. Depression isn't amongst my troubles, and I've never been so close to anyone who's fought it. She avoids talking about it, and I don't have any real understanding of it. It's my first encounter with someone who fights, sometimes daily, between wanting to live and not wanting to live. When I see her struggle, I don't know how to help her. At the most unexpected times, she bursts into these crying fits, contemplating the infinite injustices of the world and how stupid, trivial, and pointless everything is. All I can do is tell her I love her.

She's been experimenting with depression medication dosages and her moods swing wildly — sometimes several times a day. Her medication and why she takes it when it makes her unhinged are a touchy topic and mostly off limits for discussion. Anytime I ask her about how they're making her *feel* she shuts me down by changing the subject and rails me about how much and why I'm using. She's been going on drinking binges and I can see her reaching levels where she's out of control. I don't know how to stabilize her while trying to keep my own using under control.

***

Jennifer and I are just getting started as a married couple. We're laying around our Silverlake apartment when I get a call from my pal Dallas Don —the songwriting dynamo behind one of my favorite LA groups, 3D Picnic. Recently he formed a new band called Lutefisk, who've been making waves in the LA music community.

"Hey man. So, the bad news is that our rehearsal room was broken into and everything inside is gone," he tells me.

"Man, that's terrible."

"The better news is, we're doing a benefit show to raise some funds to get some new gear, and the good news will be if you'll be on the bill with us."

"Of course. Lemme check with the guys and I'll let you know, cool?"

"Yeah, totally. Thanks, Rob. Oh, Beck's agreed to play, too. It'll be fun, I mean, as fun as a show to recover all your lost, cherished gear can be. This new promoter named Mitchell is organizing the show. I'll have him reach out to you. Thanks again. Later." Ten minutes later I call Dallas back and confirm we're on.

On show night, Jennifer's in the kitchen laying out an assortment of colored pills in the shape of a happy face with its tongue sticking out. She's got an adorable way of doing things. They're usually tucked in the bottom of her space-age silver purse she carries with her everywhere. The few times I've asked about her meds, and what they do, she's changed the subject to something lighthearted. It's one of those off limits for now kinda things, which I can respect. But today is different.

"I don't even know what they do anymore. Some days they lift the shadows, and some days, they don't. It's no big deal," she says, swallowing the ones that make up the eyes and nose, washing them down with Trader Joe's cranberry juice. She's struggling to be present. Some dark force is casting a heavy shadow over her, burying her alive, and there isn't a thing I can do to help.

"When they do work, they bring out the incredible, talented, smart, funny, and pretty human being that I am. When they don't work, I feel like I can't be here."

She swallows the rest of them in one gulp, puts her glass in the sink, and lights a fresh cigarette for us to share. One of her super powers is jumping from one topic to the next so fast that you go along with whatever she's saying because you're under her spell.

"You've got a show to play. Is that what you're wearing? It looks cute," she says, looking over my go-to outfit: a button down black shirt and threadbare 50s trousers.

***

A dedicated line of local music fans wraps around the block of this new venue, seven doors down from our apartment on Silverlake Blvd. called Spaceland, and it's pouring rain. While heavy showers pound the club, 250 or so soaked and excited showgoers are packed inside, including a couple of under-aged Possum Dixon fans I snuck in by passing them off as roadies. Whenever I can sneak kids in to shows who are unable to get in for one reason or another, I do. It's part of the job.

Inside, a small but ample P.A. is tucked in the corner of the club, which is set up with lo-tech accommodations, producing a DIY atmosphere everyone's familiar with. At the last minute, we're informed a new band featuring the drummer from Nirvana, calling themselves the Foo Fighters, will also appear, playing their debut show. Just before showtime, I blow it by getting a little too high, which makes it hard to get through our set. I'm trying to keep it together and play as best as I can, but I know I'm messing up. I get how awful we are because I'm too far gone to put on a good show. By the crowd's response to our set, we are having what I'm calling an off night.

After our crummy set, inside the jammed club, Jennifer meets some of my friends from the Silverlake music community as well as Mike Keys and some old Burbank friends who showed up. Although I'm too high to embrace all the love and support around me, I can't deny the intensity of my past and present meeting right here on Silverlake Boulevard.

Lutefisk and Foo Fighters played loud sets that were so guitar heavy it was impossible to hear anything but distorted electric guitars. Beck seems like the only one who has a real handle on the night and deservedly stole the show. For his finale, he places a walkie-talkie right next to a microphone and starts wandering around with another walkie-talkie, ending up in the bathroom talking with someone in the toilet stall.

***

I'm picking at a guitar riff, trying to find the outro for a song I'm finishing called "Emergency," or "Emergency's About to End," I can't seem to settle on the title yet, when J calls.

"Zabrecky! Here's the deal: Interscope's enthusiastic about our next record and eager for us to return to the studio. I'm gonna book you guys a month at Hully Gully, so go in and write a great record, and start thinking about who you'd like to produce. No pressure. Later dude."

By now I've accepted the fact that our debut album isn't the international smash success it was said to be, and immersed myself in writing music for our next record. I'm doing all I can to focus on writing new songs, while trying to avoid the pressure of writing some stupid hit song for the label. But at least the label's letting us move forward with making another record.

While touring, I've written a few songs in hotel rooms and backstage areas. I've also been stockpiling ideas that didn't make it onto our first record on my old cassette recorder. I keep a cassette tape, appropriately titled "EYE-DEE-UHS," containing a random collection of melodies, chord structures, stories, and free-association word ramblings—all of which seem like viable notions for our next release. The band's goal is simple: to continue musically where we'd left off. But there are two obvious factors that we can't ignore: the first is that we've become a better band from touring, and the second being that I can't write songs anymore about a survival job I loathe.

Trying to make sense of my new life, I've captured a few glimpses of my road adventures and stuff that happened in LA between tours. These have become fodder for songs I'm calling "Go West," "Radio Comets," and "Crashing Your Planet." With our '70s influences still pinned tightly to our sleeves, we like the idea of a concept for a record that if it's good enough, could be our ode to our LA. In our own way, we want our "Los Angeles" by X, "Waiting for the Sun" by the Doors, or "Hotel California" by the Eagles. The album deserves a name that conjures the spirit of our beloved city, so the band agrees it ought to be called *Star Maps,* as an ode to the shady guys seated on turned-over buckets in low rent areas of Hollywood, peddling road maps to the homes of the rich and famous in the Hollywood Hills.

***

We just met with Interscope to discuss the way forward. They reminded us that we were given creative control and freedom to do things our way on the first record, but this time they want to do things a little differently. They want Possum Dixon to achieve the level of success of the likes of No Doubt, Weezer, and the Wallflowers. According to them, those groups achieved massive popularity by playing by their rules. This presents a problem: We're uncomfortable taking creative advice from them. To us, they're the company that presses and promotes our records, and that's it. We aren't interested in their creative input.

We want to work with Earle Mankey again, but the label's been urging us to go with a trendy producer who's cranking out hits for FM radio. So far, we've argued and balked and had long discussions that've been going nowhere. We like the sound of Wall of Voodoo's records and suggest hiring the band's seminal front man, Stan Ridgeway, who's been turned to producing records. The label's against the idea, not because Stan isn't brilliant, but because he hasn't made any records that are getting played on KROQ or the like.

Despite what they think, we invited Stan to our studio, and were pleased to learn that he isn't too different in person than he appears on his records. He's the truest of characters—a come-to-life shady character from a lost crime noir paperback. We're playing him some of our new songs, while he's sitting in the darkest corner of our rehearsal room, smoking cigarettes, fixing his gaze at the gum and beer-stained carpet like it's a valuable work of art. We finish our set and the room goes quiet.

"Well, guys, here's what I think. It's very important...to scare your record company," he says, cryptically.

We're not sure exactly what he means, but at the same time we know exactly what he means. It's the best advice we could ask for at a time when the label is pushing us to create a commercially viable record. We chat with him about his Wall of Voodoo days and he bails, knowing he isn't going to helm our record.

After negotiating over a list of potential producers with the label, we agree on Boston native Tim O'Heir. Tim's been recording bands in the Boston music community at the Cambridge-based studio, Fort Apache, working with Sebadoh, the Folk Implosion, Come, and some other interesting East Coast indie rock groups. The label isn't immediately sold on Tim because, like Earle Mankey or Stan Ridgeway, he doesn't have the glossy commercial credits they desire for us, but they like his work and agree to let us work with him.

Tim's a smart and charming guy who speaks our musical language and makes cool sounding records. He just flew in from Boston and we've established an immediate rapport with him. We can't be more excited to start recording. He's enthusiastic about our new songs and, unlike the label, advocates whatever artistic choices or directions we want to explore — especially one dedicated to our hometown. He understands that we're up against making a record that the label might not promote. The past few days we've been forging ahead and started pre-production with our new producing friend, feeling much of the same excitement we had while making our first record. It's all systems go for Possum Dixon.

***

Nothing could have prepared me for the news on Sunday evening. The phone rings during a band meeting at the Oakwood Apartments at the bottom of the Hollywood Hills, where Tim is staying. The band, J, and I are spread out across the room going over album stuff, and we see Tim hang up the phone and stand there with this stunned look on his face. Something's wrong.

The room becomes still, and Tim's collecting his thoughts while we are waiting for him to speak. "C'mon man, spit it out. What's up?" J inquires.

"Jennifer took her life. She's gone. I'm so sorry," he squeezes out before bursting into tears.

The explosive blow of those words stops my breathing. I can't believe it. As I slowly begin comprehending their meaning my body became numb. My peripheral vision fades, my consciousness jarred, the world unglued.

It doesn't seem real.

"They need you over there right away. The police and ambulance are waiting for you," says Tim.

"Let's go, Rob, I'll get you there," says J, with stoic strength.

I'm lost in a million thoughts, riding shotgun as J's driving like a motherfucker to Silverlake, completely stunned. It still doesn't seem real. My heart keeps dropping, deeper and deeper into this cold pit of anguish. Then it starts thumping really fast, and all I feel is horror and panic.

Night is falling as we're pulling up to our Silverlake apartment. The outside of our building — and the apartment where Jennifer and I slept less than 24 hours ago — is glowing like a carnival of turmoil. The blinding lights of the paramedic and police cars are flashing and walkie-talkies are buzzing with incomprehensible chatter. In slow motion, I exit the car and am met by a lady cop holding a notepad.

"Are you Robert Zabrecky?"

"Yes," I say, while shaking and trying to pull myself together and face reality.

"You need to come upstairs with me now."

I step inside our living room where police are rummaging through our apartment. I'm slowly comprehending that the girl of my dreams who I just married is gone, and I've got to be accountable for every bit of surrounding madness. The weight of a room is crushing. It makes it hard to breathe. I return to terra firma when someone puts something in my hand.

It's a goodbye note from her to me.

My guts are vibrating as I'm reading her words. They describe her reasons for leaving and leave no questions. The world's too painful a place for her to be alive in, so she's seen herself off while she's young and in love. The pressure of the weight of the moment almost crushes me. Holding her note between my fingers, there's law enforcement in my living room — one of them is asking me something, but I can't, or don't want to respond. Instead I stand frozen, not knowing what to do.

Her parents and family showed up an hour later. There's an insurmountable exchange of hysteria and confusion. Jennifer's gone and I'm faced with the worst day of my life.

***

I'm drifting in and out of one big self-induced blackout. I've been shut in our apartment for the past few days, upping drug doses to numb the constant, devastating pain. I don't want to see anyone. I don't want to talk about it. I just want to be alone, here in our apartment with every memory of her I can grasp.

I spent half of today hallucinating. If I get high enough, I can find myself in this zone where I enter this alternate reality — another portal of consciousness that separates my body from the physical world. It's cool, dark, and weightless room, and once I get inside, my body and mind transform into a spherical body that can feel and communicate with her ghost in its own spiritual language. The aura of her smiling spirit drifts in and out of the room and recalls our happiest days, the one's we will never live again. She stays just long enough to deliver a short peaceful message, and it's the same ever time: she wants me to move on.

In other half-lucid moments, I see flashes of glowing, orb-like ghosts huddling around each other, whispering to each other in the corners of the apartment. They seem as real as the furniture, the walls, or the ceiling and they freak me out. I don't think they're here to harm me, though.

Sometimes the drug hallucinations backfire. I'll wake up from a blackout to find myself in this alarming, panic-induced state, where horrifying black stains that look like feces are smeared all over the walls. When I do need to go out, I've become skillful at shooting up drugs in restaurant restrooms or inside my car to ensure that I don't have to face one real, sober minute.

It's been dreadful facing my family, the band, J, friends, the label, and the Viper Room crew, who are all by my side, and worried sick about me. Staying at our apartment is become intolerable. Today I just left. I packed my Bronco with my belongings and schlepped them a few blocks over to where J and Sully live. They've been renting this large 1920s Craftsman with a large empty attic. Up there it's quiet and dark, and has these long, unfinished, wood beams zigzagging everywhere. It's not much, but it's a place to sleep and get my head together. Some good friends from the Silverlake music community just helped me get settled and installed a plywood floor. I somehow dragged up a bed and an old record player and, for now, am calling it home.

I've spent all day staring at the exposed wood beams in triple-digit heat, chain-smoking my way in and out of consciousness. When I'm able to pee, which mostly I can't because of painful drug constipation, it's into one of those large Folger's coffee cans, which I keep right next to my bed. As the summer heat escalates, I remain still and quiet up here, contemplating this reality and distancing myself from everyone who cares about me, and it's beginning to drive me crazy.

To mix things up, I started splitting my time in the attic by crashing at a nearby drug dealer's dirty house—a dismal, east-side apartment where drug addicted rock stars are rotting away—or in the least comfortable option of them all, my Bronco.

Everyone close to me is doing all they can to look after me, and I feel like I'm failing them all. I've become closer with my old friend from our Al's Bar days, Naomi, who's been a great supporter and true friend. Without asking too many questions, she's been allowing me crash with her and her cat, Mookie, in her Silverlake hills apartment whenever I show up. Pleasant's also been keeping her back door open to her Beachwood Dr. abode if I need a place to escape, and a cast of druggies in Silverlake will always welcome a chance to hang and get loaded with a fellow addict. At least I'm getting out, I think.

***

I'm a haunted man. Everywhere I am so is some part of Jennifer — a barrage of wistful sounds and visions recalling her presence — reminding me to never forget her. Tormented by black waves of shame and guilt, I truly believed we were meant to fix each other. No matter how hard I try, I can't grasp she's gone forever. Bits and pieces of our brief but turbulent past replay over and over, day and night. I'm grieving myself into a prolonged, drugged-out state of mourning, and there's nothing I can do. I'm stuck. There are no take backs, second tries, or re-dos. What's done is done. All I know is she's gone and I've become a prisoner in my skin and a slave to the drugs I'm starting to hate.

My mirrored reflection is my enemy. Anytime I catch a glimpse of myself I'm reminded how bad I look, and how I hate my life. I'm barely eating and dropping weight, resorting to a bowl or two of sugar-sweetened cereal per day. I've nearly given up on hygiene. The feeling of running water on my body while I'm high makes me uncomfortable, and I'm lucky if I can pee or get my bowels to operate every other day. This extreme using is exhausting, and taking its toll. Doing all I can to avoid myself, every time I look in the mirror I can see how bad I'm fucking up. J arranged visits with two psychologists, but after they realized I was high, said they couldn't help.

The fact that she's gone remains unthinkable, but there's no way of avoiding it. My father's golden life lesson number one, about life not being fair, is echoing more than ever.

STAR MAPS

S OMEHOW WE'RE BACK in the studio to record *Star Maps*. I'm sure of little right now, and don't always know what day it is, but going in the studio takes my mind off everything and gives me something to do. During these foggy sessions, we made a difficult personnel change within the group and part ways with our drummer, Rich. Tim brought in this fiery eyed super-drummer for our upbeat tracks called Josh Freese, who's been making a name for himself by playing with Paul Westerberg and Frank Black. Josh has this uplifting spirit and would fit in our group perfectly, but is mostly a studio and tour only guy. Lucky for us, 'Byron Reynolds, who drummed with us for a short stint during our formative years, has rejoined as a permanent member. He's got to be the most soft-spoken musician I've ever known, and has the timing of a metronome.

Like our first record, *Star Maps* is shaping up with our usual array of musical inspiration: '60s surf and spy-movie riffs, power-pop song structures, and a little no-wave chaos. It also has a few slow tracks that mirror the mood of our band's current state. J and Tim have been champions, supporting any creative choices we're making along the way. While layering the basic tracks with overdubs, the band has been glued to the project, connecting with one another with a brotherly love. There's nothing anyone wants more than for me to recover and make a good record.

During what feels like impossible times, we wrap up the final mixes and put the songs in an order that sounds like an album and turn it over to Interscope for review. A few days go by. We don't hear a word. A week later we're confronted with the cliché that no band wants to hear from their record label: "We don't hear a single." I suppose we didn't give the label what they asked for, and in return they aren't going to give us what we want: tour support and money to make music videos.

Despite the label's lack of enthusiasm, they've agreed to release *Star Maps*, in hopes of radio stations picking a single on their own. We don't know what to expect from fans of the band—we're just relieved it's done. As of now, college radio stations across the nation have been embracing it and it's currently at the number-one spot on the fickle *College Music Journal* (*CMJ*) charts. With the support of nearly every college station across the U.S., we've got just enough steam to play some live shows, even without a major push from our record company. Uncertain how any of this is might go with my physical state and the way I feel inside, being around the band and trying to keep my mind off of Jennifer's passing is the best thing for me.

***

Without much promotion, *Star Maps* is met by a series of favorable reviews and critical acclaim in the alternative music press. *Spin* magazine wrote:

"Possum Dixon hit rock bottom before reaching new wave heights. The group's second record twitches and throbs with a chewed-fingernails sense of worry that often spills into panic. Zabrecky's new-wave noir vignettes are littered with overheard conversations, chattering radios, lucky numbers, and visitors from other planets—the markings of one man's attempt to make some sense out of postmodern chaos...'I listen to this record,' O'Sullivan says with understandable pride, 'and love it more than the first one, because it reminds me how we made it through this fucked up year. We'll never forget that.'"

As expected, there were mixed reviews. Music critic Marc Hirsh wrote:

"Should the mood to be made extremely nervous strike, Star Maps *should suffice. Possum Dixon leader Rob Zabrecky's hyper-paranoid lyrics and reedy voice entrench themselves in an eclectic mix of sharply angled guitar pop and keyboard-drenched sci-fi horror tunes. This split purpose works to both the benefit and detriment of the group. It seems like Possum Dixon are trying to be two bands, since their two key styles never really intersect to any degree. On the other hand, they master both so fully that it's hard to complain that the fast and loud 'Crashing Your Planet' and the equally excellent but slow and moody 'Party Tonight' sound like the work of unrelated bands. There's an underlying weirdness and musical incongruity throughout* Star Maps, *an album that credits the band's psychic as if she were in the group. It's in the opening 'Go West,' which comes across like the mutated offspring of T. Rex and the Cars, unabashed cool meeting post-modern paranoia. The spook keyboards and tremolo guitar of 'Radio Comets' and the vibraphone of the final 'Apartment Song' make Angelo Badalamenti's* Twin Peaks *music sound like easy listening."*

Regardless of who's saying what about *Star Maps,* we were just thankful that it's out. Shortly after its release, we joined the Lollapalooza summer tour to play a stretch of shows. The lineup is overall great; on the main stage Sonic Youth, Hole, Cypress Hill, Pavement, Beck, Elastica, the Jesus Lizard, and the Mighty Mighty Bosstones are performing. On the second stage, we're sharing the bill with Poster Children, Yo La Tengo, Coolio, Doo Rag, and occasionally Beck, when he feels like playing acoustic sets.

Emotionally and physically, I'm in no shape to be in public, let alone on tour, but have opted to keep moving. Anything's better than staying in Silverlake and reliving what'd happened. A few days before we left to join this tour, things went from worse to awful when I fell during rehearsal and twisted my foot badly. It's badly discolored and constantly throbs in pain. It looks broken and probably is, but I don't feel like going to a doctor who'd probably apply a cast and order me to stay home. So on this tour, I'm limping around in a painful cycle from van to stage to hotel room, feeling more broken and isolated than I ever did.

Somehow we've been making it through these hot, late, afternoon performances from Seattle to the Midwest. I've tried to conceal my using but it isn't much of a secret. Every chance I get, I hobble inside these hot and smelly plastic Porta-Potties, tie-off my arm with an old leather belt, shoot-up, and erase consciousness. I have little regard for what's going on around me. I don't give two cares if I'm gaunt, unwashed, and strung out. I do all that I can to score and smuggle dope from one city to the next, discarding dirty syringes out the back of the van before entering security barricades or the Canadian border. At best, being away from LA, playing shows, and obsessing on getting drugs distracts attention from how fucked I feel inside.

***

We return to LA in the dog days of summer. I'm still checked out. While taking a break from the sultry attic heat, me and my still-aching ankle were hobbling down Sunset Boulevard in Silverlake, looking for something to help fill the void of losing Jennifer, and heard a commotion from a nearby storefront. Live music came pouring out the doors of a nearby, storefront window, jammed between two junk stores. As I got closer I see it's a Hispanic church service in full swing. I stuck my head in, thought, "what the fuck — this'll pass some time," and took a seat in the back.

In a small commercial space with low ceilings and fluorescent lighting, the band emanated this uplifting mystic energy, before a captive, all-Mexican audience of all ages, which somehow recalled my early days of seeing bands for the first time. Although I couldn't understand more than a few words, being there stuffed in with these Mexican families offered a temporary cure for my broken heart while wandering around LA somewhere between this world and the next.

That visit led to a string of church-crashing at Hispanic services in the neighborhood. It's hardly the kind of place a non-Spanish speaking white guy from Burbank could expect to find spiritual bliss, but trust me, it is. Although I don't understand 99 percent of the services or song lyrics, I know I'm in the right company. The band assembles each evening to perform for joyous attendees who don't mind me occupying one of their folding chairs and nodding out. Not once have they asked for money, what my faith is, or for me to leave. I feel their unspoken love for me — they can sense I'm not well. It's here in these low rent churches that I can sense myself slowly starting to mend emotionally. Though in some unexplainable cruel way, every time I start to feel better, I despise myself for trying to get over her death.

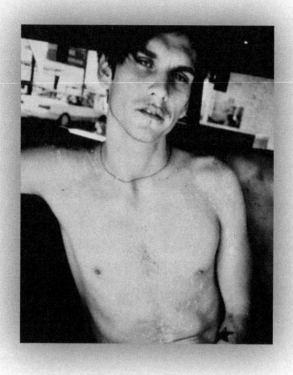

***

Possum Dixon ventured out on a string of unmemorable shows in the Midwest, returning to LA once again to regroup and strategize the way forward. The whole experience has been joyless for me and the band, and at this point it's my fault. My using has brought out the worst in me, and them. Although drugs have been helping my grieving, they've begun to backfire and brought out short-tempered, nasty sides that I hate about myself.

I've tried quitting but the withdrawals cause more pain than they're worth. When I do try and stop, it's not long before I get achy bone pain, unshakeable chills, annoying itching, and violent dry-heaving and vomiting. The physical pain is one thing, but the mental pain is another. Every time I try to quit, I find at least one good reason to use one more time. Getting high has become nothing more than an annoying necessity, and I can't see a way out. I've felt so much emotional and mental discomfort this past week I'm wondering if I still want to live. I've resorted to hiding myself from everyone, visiting fleabag crack hotels and hanging around drug-dealer apartments to stay on my drug-shooting spree.

With some nudging from J, Interscope provided us a budget to create a music video for "Radio Comets." Sully, his girlfriend Jean — who's still totally obsessed with Talking Heads — and our friend from the Silverlake music community, Jonathan Stearns, created a concept featuring live performance and alien abduction. We made most of it right here at J's in the saddest of times, where for much of it, I was in my bathrobe just trying to keep my eyes open.

***

The days drag on. I can't take the numbed agony anymore. With the aid of some friends, I start attending recovery meetings. Even though I've been showing up high, I have a true desire to quit. The stories I'm hearing inside community centers and church basements across LA are just what I need. Hearing bits and pieces of my story of addiction from the mouths of middle-aged women and ex-convicts alike are comforting, even though they fail to provide an immediate cure, I'm forcing myself to be around sober people, wishing there were some magic pill I could take to be like them. The band, the label, and J are constantly confronting my issues, urging me to get medical attention.

Today at what I thought was a band meeting was an intervention.

"Dude, none of us can imagine what you're going through, but if you don't mellow out with the using, you're gonna be gone, too. We've looked in to a rehab that'll take you tonight if you're willing to go," says J on behalf of the band who are huddled nearby. I don't like the sound or look of any of this. Yes I want to quit. Today is not the day.

"I know. I know. I know. I'm fucking up, but I'm working on it. I just need a little more time to sort things out," I plead, wondering if there's a running van outside ready to ship me off to some recovery place in Pasadena or something. The immediate reality of this drug free concept frightens the hell out me and I'm starting to get real nervous.

"Look man, we want to help, but you can't keep going like this, Rob," Sully adds, looking as drained and fed up as I've ever seen him. Rich nods in agreement.

I can see the pain in their eyes, especially Celso's. I'm pretty sure he's as high as I am, but I'm not in any position to rat him out.

"Through hell and high water, we're gonna get you through this," he adds in a raspy voice, itching his nose, and sparking a cig.

I'm trapped. I'm ashamed. I need cigarettes. I need more drugs.

"You're right. Okay. I'll go," I say, lying right to their faces.

A sense of relief breaks in the room.

"You'll be glad you did this," J says picking up the phone to make the next arrangement. I'm getting out of here, now.

"I'll be right back. Gonna hit the liquor store for cigs," I tell them, trying not to raise suspicion. They all look at each other, trying to get a consensus if I'm bullshitting or not.

"Mind if I go with you?" Sully says, half calling my bluff.

"Okay, head over in 10?" I say.

"Cool," he says. The phone rings and he slides into his room to take the call.

Meeting adjourned. As the tension in the living room disbands, I feel more trapped than I ever did. I slip out the back door, slide inside my Bronco and start driving up Sunset. I hated seeing the pain I caused them and putting them on like that, but today's not the day to kick. The only thing that makes immediate sense is to avoid the reality that my life needs to change.

Through this stoned contemplative darkness of a reality—where my life keeps flashing before me—came the smallest beam of light. I started hearing my little kid voice-of-reason, reminding me of my childhood promise. I don't want to die like Uncle Ed, yet it's never been so clear I'm following his trail. This time, more than ever, I need to sort things out before losing my mind for good. That's when I thought I'd pay a visit to Arthur.

ARTHUR'S HIDEAWAY

I WAKE UP IN A FOG and realize I'm flat on my back, looking up at a mirrored ceiling of square panels, many of which
are cracked or missing. The ones that are missing expose
ugly moldy plaster coated in a thick layer of dust. The walls were
just as I remembered them before nodding out: paneled with a
thin veneer of fake wood that's splintering everywhere. It reeks
of a combination of bleach, bug killer, and death.

As I pull myself up, my body makes a crunching sound
against the sheets, which have been bleached so many times
they're like me, frail and paper thin. This scuzz deluxe room and I
have something in common: we're both damn-near condemned.
Years of layered filth cake the low-grade threadbare carpets. The
bathroom walls are coated with a thick mud-like mold and the
shower curtain looks like it's been witness to a murder scene or
two.

The day and approximate time? No idea.

The presence of someone or something was with just me,
and for a moment, I welcomed the idea that I might be sharing
the room with Jennifer's ghost. Or maybe it was the drugs. It
doesn't matter — no one, living or dead, could stay here too long.

All I know for sure is that it's sometime after dark, and that I
must have checked myself in here, into my go-to fleabag motel,
Arthur's Hideaway. Arthur's is a place where people go to disappear. From my window on the ground floor, skanky hookers,
revved-up crack heads, and meth zombies are roaming the parking lot, talking to themselves and anyone who remotely looks
their direction. Besides being its own source of entertainment,
the Arthur's goon squad makes me feel better about myself.

***

I first encountered Arthur's as a teenager in the mid '80s. There it was, on a sketchy strip of Ventura Boulevard right in the arm-pit of Studio City, not far from Hollywood. It was among the last few standing, pay-by-the-hour, motor lodges that used to be common along that gateway to Tinsel Town. I romanticized the hell out of it, envisioning it during Route 66's heyday as a place for clean-cut Midwestern families visiting Hollywood.

I saw it while passing by in my old VW, long after it had de-volved into Studio City's seediest crash pad — a flophouse that thrived on pay-by-the-hour customers, prostitution, and people on rampant drug benders. The parking lot was a real-life freak show. Sometimes I'd go out of my way just to drive by and gawk at the cast of perverts and weirdos who were coming, going, or lurking. There was always plenty of activity outside—shady peo-ple bringing video cameras in and out of the rooms, whacked-out transvestites running around in a parallel universe like it was the end of the world, and lost souls who stood around like extras from a zombie flick. I never thought I'd be one of them, but with what I know as God and the Devil as my witnesses, I, who haven't eaten or washed myself in days, am there with them both this evening. "How'd I end up here? I must be seriously fucking up," I think to myself while sparking a cigarette.

Staring into a dirty ashtray trying to collect my thoughts, my mind races to a hundred things that I could have done differently over the past several years that would have put me anywhere but here. It was one thing tripping out on all the subversive activity as a spectator, watching the weird theatrics at Arthur's from the sidelines, but it's a totally different feeling being in the game.

One person I remember who I'm certain won't judge me for being here is my old girlfriend Melanie, the peculiar, though beautiful, drug-addicted Jewish girl from the Valley who introduced me to heroin a few years earlier. She's been committed to more rehab centers than anyone I've ever met. I remember how unbelievable it was to see her burn through so much of her parent's money on dope and to witness the emotional damage she caused herself and her family. I watched her sink into the hell of addiction as she sold nearly a closet's worth of her mother's high-end designer clothing to the shady second-hand Claudia's Boutique in Studio City, not far from here, and crashed her dad's Jaguar after nodding off at the wheel. Her God-given movie-star looks provided leverage to pull all kinds of shit and her impossibly long and beautiful hair, which resembles Veronica Lake's, makes her a real head-turner. But there's always been something "off" about her that I could never place, something behind her eyes which also makes her intensely magnetic. I've always hated her as much as I liked her. She's, by far, the worst junkie I'll ever know, and I know if I invite her to join me, I'll feel better about myself.

Outside my room, three lowlifes are huddled by the pay-phone. Reaching for my front pocket to find a quarter to call Melanie, one of them starts barking at me.

"No! No! No! You can't use this phone. We're waiting for a call."

I nod with an empathetic gesture, knowing they were deep into some life-or-death drug deal, so go across the street to the gas station, where I call Melanie and invite her to join me. It's my lucky night because she picked up, and she's heading over.

I must have been nodding out when she arrived because her knock on the door sent a jolt though my body. I jump to my feet to greet her, opening the flimsy door to see a twinkle in her drugged-out eyes. I'm reminded of my attraction to her in the first place. "You feel like dying tonight, Mr. Zabrecky?" she says with a devilish chuckle.

"Right this way, madam," I reply with a welcoming arm gesture. She walks into the doom pit and places her purse, which I know contains more dope, down onto a scratched-up side table. I watch as she sits down on the bed. She personifies the definition of a drug addict and I'd always used my calculation of her addiction as a measuring stick. In the harsh light of the bedside lamp which she sat near, her beauty was waning— she's totally strung out, and isn't half as hot as she once was.

"Quite a place you've got here," she says, looking around the room in disapproval. I sensed she's spooked out, which comes as a bit of a surprise. Her disregard and detachment from the world always made me feel she's fearless, but when her eyes caught mine, it's clear she's freaked. She takes a long look at me. Her silence is concerning. She finally says, "My God, you're light green. You look like *death*. I can't be here." She grabs her purse and stands up. "I've got to go," she says, shutting the door behind her.

Her leaving in a hurry like this has driven me to new revelatory realization. If *she* thinks I'm in bad shape, I must be truly fucked. On the few short steps into the bathroom for a little physical examination, the worn-out, sandpaper-like carpet irritates my naked feet. I flick the switch and am nearly blinded by an instant flood of fluorescent light.

In the cracked mirror above the dirty leaking sink, I take a long look at my disappointing reflection. Drugs have become for me what alcohol was for Uncle Ed. I'm well down the trail of deterioration — the one I swore to myself as a kid I'd never step foot on — and for the first time it's scaring the hell out of me.

For the thousandth time, I was angry with myself for the stupid and selfish choices over the past few years that brought me here.

I finish the miserable stay at Arthur's, shooting up small wads of gooey black tar dope and drifting in and out of depressing consciousness. Empty stomach pain and constipation are combating my battle to stay high. Every hour or so I pop-up in a startling panic from dreamy nods to see Rorschach-style ink spots splattered on the walls before recognizing them for what they were—just more ugly hallucinations. I sulk around the premises and head back over to the 7-Eleven, where there's some sort of hint of normality, but I'm numb to the activity around me and head back to my room. I must get out of here, but don't know where to go or what to do. I sneak back up to my Silverlake attic where things aren't much better. I'm running from myself and right on my tail all at once, caught in a repetitive circle of confusion.

***

The world's a different place when you're a drug addict. In some ways, it's simpler than regular life. The single goal of living is to get and stay high. I'd do whatever it takes to get loaded again and again — living and breathing like a selfish prick around the clock. I feel guilty about being so selfish, but not guilty enough to quit. Becoming an addict is an unplanned study into the unbound depths of selfish desires and self-pity. My life has become this hedonistic warfare against myself, nearly eliminating my existence from the present state of the world. My single pursuit is finding that elusive, faraway warm and fuzzy place.

A place that's becoming nearly impossible to find.

I've painted myself into a corner and can't get out. Emotionally destitute and spiritually broke, I have little regard for life, and any moments of clarity are spent being mad, angry, and frustrated with myself. I'm tired and bored by the junkies I know, and the drama that comes along with knowing them. Someone is always getting arrested for buying dope or stealing something to get it, going to rehab, contracting disease, or overdosing. I've always been a clean freak with my needles, fearful of contracting HIV or other debilitating diseases that some of my drug acquaintances caught after sharing syringes. Any romantic notion of the junkie life is dead to me.

I want to change more than anything, but am painfully aware that once the effects of the drugs wear off I'll be left with those uncomfortable withdrawals and its ensuing emotional chaos. Sick of being sick, I hate myself for who I've become. But quitting, and all the changes I need to make to live clean, are just too hard.

***

An earthquake went off under my skin shortly after shooting up one afternoon in J's attic. It began with a violent attack of uncontrollable chills, followed by an explosive headache. The little bits of light that leaking in were blinding. My brain was piercing from all sides with sharp unrelenting pain that made me think I'd shot up poison and was dying.

"This is it. Someone's going to find my dead body up here," I think, as my mind and body throb with intense steady pain. Then came a wave of nausea. Dry-heaving in the coffee can where I'd been peeing, I realize I might have contracted the IV drug user's nightmare: Cotton Fever. At one point or another, every junkie I'd known had gotten it while accidentally shooting up microscopic cotton fibers, which run amok in the bloodstream and induce a nasty 24-hour fever. I hope that's all it is, anyway.

Fearing the notion of getting myself to a hospital and kicking drugs in some stuffy hospital or rehab facility, I stick it out alone and fight my pathetic way through it. Going on record to talk with doctors or whoever about what kind of drugs I'm addicted to, and why I'm addicted to them, seems like a fate worse than death. Instead, I lie on my bed like a curled-up roach that's been sprayed with bug killer and stare at the aged wood beams holding up the roof of the house until I eventually passed out.

I wake up with the second-worst headache I've ever felt. I had so much trouble breathing that I took the day off from smoking. Sick, and mad because once again the drugs are backfiring, I feel both ripped off and broken all over. I seriously contemplate driving myself to the hospital, but instead, stick it out and sleep another day — one that felt like an eternity.

By a major stroke of what some might call good luck, after that terrible episode, I start feeling a little better. The single upshot is that while being that sick and out of it, I couldn't use. I stop for a day. Then two. Then three.

SPELLBOUND

I'D LIKE TO SAY I had the big spiritual awakening—like the ones I'd read and heard so much about in the recovery rooms—but I didn't. It wasn't even close. It wasn't even spiritual. My escape from drugs was just another random shot at getting clean after that ugly drug fever. After a handful of days without using, it became abundantly clear that no drugs meant no blackouts, no degradation, and no self-loathing shame. But, somewhere within my skin and organs, I could sense what I'd known as my spirit giving me permission to move on.

Fighting off the ongoing desire to get high was an arduous daily practice, but I did it. Without drugs, I became a prickly prick, constantly feeling an agitation and torment that drove me up the walls. That's when I started finding comfort in recovery. During this round of meetings, I started to engage in the fellowship. Instead of feeling like a coffee sipping alien inside stuffy church basement recovery rooms, I slipped through a crack in the wall of resistance I'd kept up for all those years and began to enjoy the brotherhood and community of it. That's when it became a something I needed to explore.

Attending recovery meetings all over LA, I once again identified as an addict and started sharing bits of my story. Sobriety brought the idea of letting go of every idea that'd been wearing me down. Slowly, I started to release the psychic and physical pollution brought on by drugs. It felt like the biggest breath of fresh air while releasing the need to get high before facing the day. Life isn't over, I kept telling myself.

One of the biggest surprises recovery has brought has been releasing an ideology that's impacted me more than I knew, and that I've been unaware has been eating at me: the concept of cool. Here's what I learned: the desire to be cool isn't cool at all. It's stupid. For years, I've experienced people subscribing to the unwritten, pretentious preoccupation of being cool as a style choice, whether they were or not. A new idea of what's cool has started to coalesce. It's my way of saying goodbye to the dark shadows cast by the Lou Reed academy of cool: that drugs and subversive lifestyles are some way of life. Now, focusing on a desire to live in a drug-free world, where I still embrace creativity, is my new cool.

These newly sober moments are beginning to neatly stack on each other, and on good days, provide glimpses into the future. During my most sober moments, I've stumbled onto a few enlightening roads that have helped realize new concepts of self, engaging in simple theories for thinking and living, and examining what's truly important. Music. Friendship. Honesty. By realizing that I'm letting go of aspects of my identity, I get this weird sense I'm abandoning a piece of myself. Part of me feels like a traitor to the drug world. Some of the addicts I used with think I've betrayed them by getting clean. So many of the things that have defined me for so long are in flux, but with this burning desire for transformation, reinvention is beginning to surface.

By challenging the mental patterns that for so long preoccupied my selfish desires, I'm presented with a refreshing perspective on life. By abandoning using, self-destruction, and the life that had been defining me for so long, it's nearly impossible to envision how I'll cultivate a new way of living. Once again, there are many questions and few answers. But for now, I'm over the hump of withdrawal, and trying.

***

A buzzing electric charge ignites my heart anytime this one young woman comes to mind. Her beauty first caught me off guard when I saw her at a Hollywood party Jennifer and I ended up at last year. In a modestly cut vintage dress, she was dancing alone on somebody's hardwood living room floor in the middle of the night. Bopping around like a teenager in her room with the door locked to loud to '80s new-wave hits, she moved to the music with an unconcerned freedom, the kind that said she couldn't care less if she was being watched or not. An undeniable fox, her classic cropped bob hairstyle swayed above her willowy body and soft, nicely rounded face, while her spellbinding blue eyes shot lasers in whatever direction she looked. Jennifer and I watched in awe as she performed this flawless magic dance — the kind of dance that gives music its meaning. Something about her evoked the spirit of my fondest teen memoires.

This radiant free spirit was a girl with a boy's name, Tommi. She worked with Jennifer at the Viper Room, and after that night I'd occasionally see her while visiting Jennifer at work. While co-workers on the Viper Room staff regarded Jennifer's beauty as threatening and competitive, Tommi couldn't have cared less. The two admired and fawned over each other.

In my post-Jennifer, post-narcotic, post-forget-cool world, I can't deny these feelings I have for her. My stomach tingles and I get a little nervous when she comes to mind — two things that give me hope that I can have these kind of emotions for another person. I mustered up the courage and asked her out, as friends of course, and she agreed. Although I'm cautious and reticent about my feelings for her, I can't fight wanting to know more about her.

With no idea how she felt about me, my emotions took over and I confessed my attraction to her. I caught her off guard, realizing that to her, I'm the guy from that band who'd recently lost Jennifer, and was probably on drugs. I know I'm not the best contestant for a dating candidate, but there was an undeniable spark between us. After spending a little time with her, we started dating. With a newfound sobriety and romantic interest, my personal life is starting to change.

Tommi's world is just how she wants it, but it wasn't always that way. To say her upbringing was unconventional is an understatement: her father a tattoo artist and biker, her mother the freest of spirits who danced in topless nightclubs and ate LSD like it were See's candy. She discovered music and fashion at a young age, went through punk as a teen, burned through a cast of crazy boyfriends, and somehow turned out unscathed.

She sees value in stability and living in a non-destructive reality. She's got this innate sense of cool. You can just tell by seeing her it's not a crutch she's preoccupied with, instead it's her sound and desirable moral compass that turns me on. It's like she possesses some secret understanding about how the world works. She's got a rare grace for a girl in her early 20s that's enchanting, but it's her eyes, which when I look inside, see signs of my good mother.

***

We kicked off our *Star Maps* tour by playing two live shows in LA, one at the Whisky a Go Go and the other during the afternoon in the parking lot of Aron's Records. Just before launching into our set at Aron's, I feel a smile forming around my mouth when I see Mike Keys, whom I hadn't seen since the night he met Jennifer at the Viper Room.

"Out of my way, I've known the singer since third grade," I hear him saying, pushing his way through the crowd and planting himself among some hipster fans before the stage. It's a whole different experience playing sober, and another playing rock music in outside under sunlight. For years I'd been on one thing or another before starting our sets, but a few songs in, I feel really good, and in more control than before. After the show, Mike Keys wastes no time in offering his take on things.

"Dude, great show. Waaaaay better than that night at—what's it called?—Spaceballs, in Silverlake or whatever. Anyhow, you look better, almost normal again. Sorry about Jennifer," he says, giving me the straight report.

The next month, we invite our friends and label mates Lifter and Red 5, who both have debut albums coming out, to join us on a US tour. Outside of LA, both bands are relatively unknown, so drawing crowds is up to us. Two things can be disheartening while being in a band trying to support a new record: playing to empty houses and finding your new record, the one that felt like life-or-death to make, in cutout bins at record stores. On this tour we're having our share of both. Labeled as "sell outs" by many of our original fans after the commercial radio success of "Watch the Girl Destroy Me," we've been, in a sense, alienated from the burgeoning Indie Rock community. We've also earned a reputation for being an erratic and inconsistent live act, based on the shows where I'd been a strung-out loser. So as a live act, we're almost starting over.

The tour is an emotional roller coaster. In smaller cities, we've been fighting disheartening moments playing to smaller crowds, sometimes to nearly empty clubs that we'd once filled. Every empty seat brings on waves of depressing self-doubt. For the last five years of my twenty-something life, I've poured everything into this group. We don't know from one night to the next how our audiences will react, or if they'll be there at all. Things haven't been all bad; in bigger cities like Chicago and Minneapolis we've played sold-out shows to enthusiastic Midwest fans.

Meanwhile, other bands we've known and met along the way are becoming mainstays on Alternative radio, and the Indie rock is thriving on college radio. We can't help but feel left behind, with an album that's just as worthy as theirs. Looking out the van window from one highway to the next, I'm starting to wonder if my music dream is dead.

***

It's late afternoon and we just loaded our equipment into a Baltimore nightclub. My cohorts and I decide we'll distract ourselves for a couple of hours before sound check by doing a little sightseeing in downtown Baltimore, rather than kill time inside our stuffy hotel rooms. I'm fanatical about the early work of Baltimore bizarro filmmaker John Waters and feel like paying tribute to him by trying to see the downtown area as he might have during his heyday there in the early '70s.

Downtown Baltimore looks like some faded version of its '50s self. I recognize some of the locations he used to film scenes from *Pink Flamingos* and *Female Trouble*, but the heat today is becoming unbearable. We're meandering through downtown and find ourselves on a main street with rows of mostly deserted small businesses. Storefront awnings provide a mild refuge from the sun but it's apparent why the streets are empty: it's simply too hot for anyone to be outside. The shops are the types you might find in any city—a hardware store, a bakery, a post office.

And a magic shop.

A dripping air conditioner is vibrating outside the magic shop. The very word "magic" evokes images of Siegfried & Roy, white tigers, purple jumpsuits, girls with big hair and bronzed bikini bodies stuffed in spandex, and mustached men with mullets. It also recalls my embarrassing grade-school experience, when Ronald McDonald forcefully poured "evaporated" milk into my head and mortified me in front of my schoolmates. The whole idea of whatever might be inside makes me a little uncomfortable, but I figure I can kill twenty minutes and cool off, so break away from the group and head toward the shop.

The storefront window reads "Ken Zo's Yogi Magic Mart." I push through the door and notice two things: a major drop in temperature, and a wiry man with a push-broom moustache standing alone behind a large glass counter. Everywhere I look are things you could expect to see in a magic shop: brightly colored feather-flower bouquets, small tables with stenciled rabbits, top hats, straitjackets, and posters featuring images of

Houdini—all of which I couldn't care less about. I might as well be in the hardware store or the bakery. After cooling off, I'm feeling a little guilty about loitering and not making some sort of nominal purchase. An idea pops into my head, and I approach the man who just might be Ken Zo himself.

"Do you have something I might be able to perform at a nightclub, by chance? I'm not a magician or anything," I ask, realizing how stupid I sound. I'm pretty sure he knows I'm not a wizard, like he is.

There's a long pause. "Well...what about this?"

He rolls up his sleeves, slowly removes a small, colored, silk handkerchief from his pocket, displays both sides, then gradually pushes it into his closed fist and makes it vanish. It's fantastic. And beautiful. And unbelievable. My newly sober brain is temporarily warped. For the life of me, I can't fathom where that handkerchief I'd seen a moment earlier could have possibly gone.

I'm nearly as astonished this incredible miracle I just witnessed can actually be purchased. "I'll take it," I say, pouring out the words as quickly as I can. I pay him, he reveals how the trick is done, and I try to replicate his instructions a handful of times. I shove the vanishing gimmick into my pocket and exit what feels like a *Twilight Zone* episode, with me in the leading role. My new trick and I head back out into the heat, and back to the nightclub where I fumble with it a little more.

It's about midnight, and we're a few songs into our set when Celso breaks a string. Ugh, another uncomfortable sober encounter with a drunk late-night audience. Then I remember the small piece of magic apparatus in my pocket. In some whimsical instant, it occurs to me that what I'd bought at Ken Zo's was a method for vanishing a small object — and it doesn't need to be that little, colored, silk handkerchief.

"Anyone have a rubber — a wrapped one, preferably?" I ask on a whim.

A guy in the audience holds up a wrapped condom.

"Throw it up here."

He tosses it my direction. I catch it, unwrap it, and wiggle it high above my head for our modest, late-night audience of Indie Rockers and hipsters to see.

"Hey, look at this. Watch. See this?" I say in some disaffected, non-magical tone.

And then I make it disappear, kind of like the way Mr. Ken Zo showed me, but with much less skill.

"Gone!"

The condom vanishes from my hand and the crowd bursts into an unexpected applause. I'm as amazed as they are. From the sound of their response, vanishing that condom engaged them as much as one of our songs. Almost accidentally, I entertained them, and certainly myself. For them, it's just some peculiar little moment of our show, but for me, it's an epiphany — and a revelation. Celso finishes re-stringing his guitar and we finish our set.

The next night we're performing in New York City, and I arrange with the band that after the third song I'll perform the trick again. I did, and it was no fluke—the audience responded the same way they did in Baltimore. After our last show in New York we start the 3,000-mile drive home. In each town we stop in, I scour the Yellow Pages for magic shops, and visit every one possible to see what other tricks might be suitable for nightclub audiences during song breaks. After that night in Baltimore, every addictive part of my personality is focused on magic.

***

I arrive back in LA nearly a week later with a handful of new tricks I've been fumbling with in the back of the van, while dreaming of seeing Tommi again. We've remained in touch through daily phone calls and letters I've sent from the tour, and are falling for each other.

She mentions she received an invitation to visit a private magic club in the foothills of Hollywood. It's called the Magic Castle, and is located inside a large Victorian mansion and has a strict upscale dress code — which could be a welcomed, hipster-free break from the Spaceland sect. Thrilled by the prospect of seeing magic performed live, I cobble together a mismatched suit, while Tommi appears like a beauty from a silent movie, and we head in.

We enter its dimly lit Victorian parlour-style lobby, where there are no visible doors leading into the club's interior, feeling like we're in some living game of Clue. Our names were checked off a guest list, and we're given some magic words and instructions to get in. A little shy about the protocol, I mutter the words to a small carved wooden golden owl set in an antiquated bookcase to gain admittance. After I do, the bookcase unexpectedly slides open, and we enter a portal—one completely different from the rock nightclubs we both know so well. The interior is magnificent. It features wood-paneled walls with long hallways and staircases that exude the grandeur of the Masonic Temple in Pasadena where my grandfather lived and worked. It seems familiar, shrouded in the Mason-like secrecy in which you could look but couldn't touch or be too nosy about.

Wandering around and admiring the decor, something astonishes us everywhere we look. Beautifully designed turn-of-the-century lithographs advertising stage spectacles from magic's Golden Age are nicely framed and artfully placed on the walls. Advertising posters for Houdini, Thurston, Herrmann, Carter, and Chung Ling Soo appear around each corner, while posters and caricatures of performers with fancy names such as The Professor, Senator Crandall, and Richiardi are neatly displayed throughout the dark and slightly musty interior inside this incredible old mansion. We caught a couple of white-haired magicians who performed baffling sleight-of-hand in spotless tuxedos, being amazed by one trick after the next. But the most stunning thing here is Tommi, and I can't take my eyes off her.

It's late and we're in the main bar, the Grand Salon, as it's known to people around here, and something important occurs to me. Magic, like music, or painting, or any other creative thing you can express yourself through, is an art form. Magic just got a lot more interesting and the Magic Castle is our new favorite place. Being here is as new and exciting as it was seeing bands in the early '80s. I've been "bitten by the bug" and struck with some conceit that I can be a magician.

***

As our *Star Maps* tour is coming to a slow and uneventful finish, we're back in LA taking a needed break from racing from one city to the next, promoting a record that's loved by few and disregarded by most. While regrouping, Sully's been expressing discontentment with being in the band. He's tired of playing big brother to Celso and me. Since joining the group, he's been the only truly responsible one among us; always asking the right questions in band meetings, and chiming in to address important issues relative to the group's success and future. He's also unsatisfied with his creative voice in the group. He's fallen in love with classic country music, and wants to incorporate some of his country influence into our next batch of songs. As narrow-minded and rigid as I've become, especially since getting clean, I'm still not sharp enough to get my head around how any kind of country influence could work into the band's sound. By this point, Possum Dixon's direction is for better or worse established, and we haven't evolved enough to explore new ground. After a difficult discussion, he decided to pursue music of his own and quit the band.

Knowing he's irreplaceable makes any forward motion band matters nearly impossible. His ability to write counter-riffs around my vocals, ideas for song arrangements, and his voice of reason are gone, and I can't blame him for leaving. Half the time, I don't want to be in a band with myself, and know I haven't been the most agreeable person to make music with. The emotional aspects of him leaving are hitting me hard — we've grown up beside each other and are like brothers.

***

For the past seven years, living out my music dreams in this group served as a salvation tool, but it's being shared with my newest passion. Music is my profession, but magic's playing a larger role in my everyday creative life. The odd chain of events that led me to magic is still baffling, leaving me wondering what strange treasure map I'm following. A love of music has guided me through childhood and led to being in a band; my affection for John Waters movies drew me to Ken Zo's magic shop and seeing that first trick; and Tommi's invite to the Magic Castle took us to a place where I fell in love with magic. Who could have predicted that the AM radio, a chance visit to a magic shop, a broken guitar string, a condom, and a visit to private magic club in Hollywood would have led to this mad obsession?

After a few more visits to the Magic Castle, I learned about becoming a member. With the help of Tommi, I've cobbled together an audition from of a few magic effects I've been learning. The idea of performing magic inside this creaky Victorian mansion in Hollywood one day has inspired all kinds of dreams, endless rehearsal sessions, and helped me tap in to some courage I didn't know I had.

I auditioned, and must've brought enough of my performing mojo with me, because even though I was more nervous than I was when taking my driver's exam, I passed and now I'm a magician member. I've found new purpose and my new home away from home, a place I can go seven nights a week to practice magic, watch magicians perform.

Something I've found attractive about magicians is that they aren't focused on the idea of cool — they're a different breed altogether, motivated by entertaining audiences by presenting skilled artistry without musician cool pretense. From what I can tell, most of them discovered magic at a young age and had favored playing with magic kits rather than blasting Cheap Trick, KISS, and Blondie records and simulating electric guitars with tennis rackets, and that was a breath of fresh air.

I get the same kick from practicing magic as I did learning how to play music. Learning about magic and becoming a practitioner of this art that I know so little about has become a major source of motivation for being alive. Unlike music, its history is shrouded in secrecy. Learning about Houdini, Chung Ling Soo, and Thurston turns me on the same way listening to records, reading music magazines, and studying record covers once did. But the idea of ultimately finding a voice in magic through creation and performance — something I can't seem to live without — is leading the way to becoming my own version of a magical entertainer.

Performing magic is harder than it looks. Anytime I attempt even the simplest card effects for Celso or Tommi, my butt shakes, my heart beats like crazy, and I can barely hear the words, "pick a card," coming out of my mouth. My nerves get the best of me because I want to get it right and share the wonder I felt at back at Ken Zo's in Baltimore after seeing the silk handkerchief vanish into that man's hand.

After performing a dozen or so botched tricks for them, I'm learning I have no interest in performing magic as the newly sober Rob Zabrecky of Possum Dixon, and nobody wants to see the newly sober Rob Zabrecky of Possum Dixon trying his hand magic, especially aging hipsters in Silverlake nightclubs.

"Can you *really* care what those people think? So what if it's not their thing? It's yours. That's what's important. You've never seemed to care too much if people like your music or not, so why should you care if they like your magic?" Boom. Her punk philosophy is one of the million things I love about her. Everything makes sense, except what she sees in me. A smart and pretty girl like her could have anyone she wanted, and here she is telling me it's okay to be a magician. It's probably a good idea I don't try and talk her out of being with me.

Once a week I've been trying my hand at presenting some of the pocket tricks I picked up on the road in the Magic Castle's dimly lit, intimate basement. The basement is the go-to place for magician members and working pros to rehearse and practice their sets, and it's the right place for me to figure things out.

The bigger picture, one that's not quite in focus yet, is one that'll employ a Frankenstein type of character built from an array of influential sources — ones that have nothing to do with magic, but are magical — then I might actually have something worthwhile. But first I have to become a competent magician.

After absorbing more magic effects through books, videotapes, and demonstrations seen at Hollywood's one and only magic shop, Hollywood Magic, the practicing is up to me. A kind and talented employee there named Woody has generously offered informal magic lessons. Once a week or so, I head from Silverlake to his second-story Hollywood apartment — a two story multi-unit 50s complex on Franklin Ave. that houses a cast of working and unemployed magicians — to show him what I've been practicing, and he gives me pointers, constructive feedback, and a million things to think about.

The time and isolation spent practicing between those sessions with Woody remind me of the similar secrecy, fuss, and ritual I know so well from the private world of drug addiction — it's something that can't be done with others. But the outcome of sharing a magic effect with someone, first Tommi and Celso, and then kind and forgiving friends, and then for small groups in the basement of the Magic Castle, is far more satisfying than trying to hide ugly pin-pricked arms, droopy eyes, and a gravelly voice from the world. Although I'm terrible at magic I have a burning desire to turn the practice into a craft, and the craft into art. And Tommi is rooting me on every step of the way.

Tommi embodies the few things that are worthy in this current world of mine. And in this part of her life, she repels bad energy like Kryptonite. With loving arms, she's embraces this whimsical chapter that others are dismissing. Her unrelenting encouragement reminds me to spend time on these things I love, rather than engaging with unimportant nonsense. At a time when mentally and physically I feel like damaged goods, she makes me feel good about myself.

With a head half stuck in the past, I'm becoming more comfortable with who I am. Scared of failing again in a serious relationship, we're taking our time, and finding ourselves in this beautiful new world together. From the wreckage of where I've been is the beginning of a new relationship, with new ideas about the way forward. I'm becoming what I've feared for years: an adult who cares about living, and I'm falling in love again.

RUN RABBIT RUN

THE RUMBLING BACKSTAGE ATMOSPHERE at the Roxy is familiar to everyone; a sound collage of twangy electric guitar strings being tuned, beer bottles clanking in good spirits, and overlapping chatter from performers and backstage crashers. As that noise buzzes outside our cold and still dressing room, I realize it's just another day in the office for them, but for Tommi and me it's a pretty big night, one of unexplored creative terrain in front of a live audience. This year's Ringling Sister's *Fun Raiser* includes an added twist: a magic show! And Tommi and I are the magic show.

"You guys are on in five minutes," Pleasant says, popping her head inside and checking us out. She shoots us one of her up-and-down looks — the kind that's impossible to distinguish if she loves you or wishes you're somewhere else. "You look amazing. Have a great show. Mwah!" Then all in one swoop, she takes the last drag from her cigarette, stabs it right into the dark brown faux-wood wall paneling, and disappears. Tommi and I turn to one another with raised eyebrows, wondering what we've gotten ourselves into. Five minutes and counting.

Like me, Pleasant burned out on music and discovered other creative outlets to express herself. Besides publishing some salacious poetry books like *Escape from Houdini Mountain, Senorita Sin,* and *Princess of Hollywood*, she's also managed to reinvent herself as a belly dancer under the alias Princess Farhana, and formed her own belly dancing troupe, Raks Majnoun. On this LA winter night, she's doing it all: reading poetry, belly dancing, emceeing, and producing the annual *Fun Raiser* to benefit orphaned kids at Christmas, like the one Possum Dixon played with Jim Carroll at the Palace five or so years ago. This year's benefit includes sets by X's John Doe & Exene, Concrete Blonde's Johnette

Napolitano, poetry by LA underground faves S.A. Griffin and Exene's husband; local poet and yet to be famous actor named Viggo Mortensen; an acoustic set from the Dream Syndicate's Steve Wynn; and performances from other stalwarts from LA's nascent punk world.

***

A few months earlier Pleasant phoned, requesting Possum Dixon perform a short set as part of the benefit. As we were chatting I told her I'd been getting into magic and had been working on an act with Tommi. I'd told her how we'd become inspired to have our version of a magic act after several visits to the Magic Castle and binging on silent movies. She must have assumed we'd be competent enough in time for the show, and invited us to join the bill in place of a Possum Dixon set.

At first, the idea of performing magic instead of music for LA music fans, especially with an act that hadn't been audience tested, seemed like a bad idea. I could barely get through a trick without messing it up or making it look at least slightly fishy, while Tommi had as much training in magic as I did, but hadn't performed a day in her life. After we discussed the prospect, we conceded the *Fun Raiser* was an exceptional opportunity and accepted Plez's gracious offer. Melding our new passions for magic and silent film into an act, and performing it for a rock crowd, couldn't be too difficult, could it?

After agreeing to the gig, we've been tirelessly rehearsing the show after Tommi returns from long days managing Viper Room chaos and I fulfill my band duties, which involve band rehearsals and meetings with J and the record label. In many ways, constructing the act with her and dreaming up something from nothing evokes the spirit of writing music. The difference is with music, I've become bored with the outcome; write song or riff, collaborate on song or riff with band, rehearse song or turn riff into song with band, record song with band, and perform song with band. Over the past decade this equation's lost its luster, whereas a magic act has infinite possibilities. The more we riff on the act, the more Tommi's brilliance emerges. Her ideas to transition seamlessly from one idea to the next, or throw a left turn or twist to an existing idea, are as good as anyone I've worked with on music.

We refined our brainstorming sessions to a 10-minute performance. It's a combination of a handful of visual stage-style magic effects, choreographed to Italian film music. We've been fussing over the show's style and tone, nitpicking our aesthetic and music selections as much as we have been rehearsing the act. Garbed in fancy vintage '20s costumes and caked-on make-up, we look like a ghoulish throwback duo from a lost Chaplin movie.

Our act incorporates a classic, simple plot that goes like this: boy sees girl, boy desires girl, boy uses mystical powers to place girl in hypnotic trance, boy performs spooky magic on girl to win her affection, boy revives girl from hypnotic trance, girl falls for boy. And throughout the storyline, I perform some classics of magic. The first trick is an instantaneous appearance of a flower bouquet, produced to capture her attention, blow her mind, and win her affection. When that doesn't faze her, I quickly produce a second bouquet, then a third. Unimpressed, I up the stakes by swallowing a handful of razor blades along with a long piece of thread and regurgitate them as one, neatly strung together, razor necklace, all from my bloody mouth, to prove I'm unquestionably the Romeo to her Juliet. Still not impressed, I do what any aspiring wizard with a few months of experience under his belt would do: present her a metallic silver ball the size of large grapefruit, and float it around on a silky black scarf, commanding it to come alive and move around on its own whimsical accord. Unaffected by the flowers, bloody razors, and the weird floating silver ball, I resort to placing her in a trance, laying her on a plank, and suspending her from her chair, parading around her to the music, more like The Damned's Dave Vanian than David Copperfield. At the conclusion, I place her back in her chair, break her trance, and reel her mind and body back to Terra Firma, where, in her bewitched state of mind, she's mine and I'm hers.

This would, without fail, be a provocative magic act to see, wouldn't it?

Regardless of whether it will or won't be, we're standing costumed in the dressing room with our props pre-set onstage, moments away from being introduced to the LA alt rock crowd as "Griffith & Clementine."

The pre-show tension is getting more intense than I imagined. There's nothing we can do but accept we're about as good as anyone performing their first magic show. The difference between us and any other magician starting out is that we're debuting to a crowded house on the Sunset Strip for the cool kids in Hollywood, not some kid's 10th birthday party.

***

It's almost show time. There's no fighting it. My body's nearly paralyzed with sober nervousness. Without needing to ask, I can sense that Tommi — soon to be known as Clementine — feels the same. Performing rock music behind a barricade of guitar riffs, loud drums, and intoxication with my best friends had become a simple task, but trying to pull off a magic show, totally sober with my girlfriend, is a whole different thing. And this time, there's no intoxication to take the edge off—just this overwhelming sober desire to do something new and uncharted.

This five minutes seems like five years. I'm looking in the dressing room mirror, applying another layer of eyeliner I don't need, when I catch Tommi's perfectly poised reflection. She's a brave, sexy, and fierce vision, costumed in her vintage 1920s black and white lace dress. Her hair and make-up are applied perfectly, evoking the swirled essences of silent cutie Louise Brooks and first-wave screen vamp, Theda Bara. She sure as hell looks ready to do something. "Okay, let's see how this goes," I say, taking the last deep drag from my cig and flicking it out the window. The embered tip twirls like a cheap Mexican firework, exploding on a closed dumpster down by the famous Rainbow Room Bar & Grill, where a group of unaffected rockers are passing around a joint. "Let's go have a look at the audience," she says, starting her way to have a peek at the crowd. Before exiting, we look into each other's made-up eyes and give each other a crazy smile— like a couple of school kids who are about to ditch class and have sex in an empty janitor closet. Her bravery to go through with this is a total turn on and I'm falling more in love with her by the minute.

"C'mon, I'll introduce you two freaks now," Pleasant says jokingly, snapping us out of our crowd-spying trance. As we're following her down the same beer-stained, carpeted stairs I'd been down five years earlier when Possum Dixon played our glorious record release party with Beck and Glue, I feel this warming emotional shift, stepping into the unknown. As we're waiting at the bottom of stairs, the stage lights go dark and the house music, "Los Angeles" by X, fades. The stage lights come up to reveal Plez as Princess Farhana, attired in an Arabic sparkly costume, adorned with hundreds of little shiny bells and chimes. As she moves, her costume makes these small waves of peaceful sounds. Those sweet little noises amidst that raucous setting are comforting. They symbolize Plez's reinvention at this exact moment when I need to be reminded of reinvention. A few random cat calls are heard from around the room as the crowd settles, focusing their attention on her as she takes the mic and addresses them like a probation officer reprimanding a bunch of juvenile delinquents.

"Okay, you guys, these *Fun Raisers* are about bringing you great entertainment for an amazing cause, and nothing is more fun and entertaining than magic! Especially when it's performed by Griffith & Clementine. Let's hear it for them!"

As she jingles offstage, the stage lights dim and we find our marks, waiting for the music to start. My heart pounding against my chest is distracting. I hope we remember everything.

As the applause quiets down, the room goes near silent.

WHAM! I'm blindsided by a couple of things that instantly throw me off; our show music kicks in ten times louder out of the Roxy's house speakers than it did from the boom box we rehearsed with in our living room, and the lights are up at a nearly blinding intensity. These abrasive audio and visual blasts, along with the pre-show nerves I already have, send my mind and body into a near blackout mode. It's like I'm back at BeBop Records, performing the first Possum Dixon show, but I'm totally sober and painfully aware of every little thing.

There's nothing more we can do than thrust ourselves into the motions of what we rehearsed so many times back in our Silverlake bungalow. Once my nerves settle and I regain control of my consciousness, I realize we're on track, performing the show as we rehearsed it. The effects and choreography we labored over are being executed without any major hitches. The production of the flower bouquets receives a few patches of obligatory applause, but it's a far cry from hearing a room full of excited fans rooting us on and singing along with our songs.

As I acclimate to the stage a little more, I can sense that those who know me from Possum Dixon are watching me like I have two heads, wondering if the act is some big joke. While my head is busy calculating what the audience is thinking, my body is relying on muscle memory, getting from one trick to the next. As I'm struggling with these mind-versus-body dilemmas, Tommi's not missing a beat. She's brought her beauty and smarts to the stage, following the story and choreography impeccably.

Then, for some unknown reason, I can't hang on any longer and lose control. I can sense the audience knows I'm in my head, and don't have the magic experience or technical skill to pull it off. There's nothing soulful to my performance, just a rapid succession of artless, shaky, and clumsy self-conscious motions, dying to finish. With the lights in my face and nearly deafening music coming at me from the monitors, I have this revelation that magic is harder to perform than it looks, especially in front of an unapologetic crowd of jaded music fans. It isn't like I'm expecting them to cheer us on as if we're Penn & Teller—I'm painfully aware it's our first gig, but somehow I thought it'd be easier than this. As the audience comes to understand we aren't going to make an elephant appear or blow their minds with dexterous sleight-of-hand, I realize we lost them, even though we didn't have them in the first place.

By the end of it, sweat infused make-up is dripping down my face and the crowd seems mildly amused, at best. As we bow and exit, I can feel the audience consensus of "What'd we just see?" and certainly don't blame them. It's over, and as the lights dim and the house music fades back up, we grab our props and quickly leave the stage. Walking back up the stairs we descended less than 15 minutes earlier, I don't try and fool myself into thinking what we did was great. I know it wasn't.

It's over, and we hung in. One thing we did do right was stay true to our vision, which provided a small and satisfying triumph.

We retreat to the dressing room to decompress. "We got through it," she says with a huge sense of relief. "Yes, and we'll never have to do our first magic show again," I say under my breath, removing what's left of my make-up with a big wad of toilet paper, trying to find some humor in the whole thing. She steps outside to greet some friends while I change back to my regular clothes and start organizing our stuff into an old suitcase. While packing up, I overhear part of a conversation outside our room I wish I hadn't.

"Did you just see Zabrecky's little magic thing?" one guy says to another.

"Yeah. It was horrible. Heard he's a magician now. So lame," the other responds.

Fighting the urge to stomp over and remind them that performing your first magic show, with your girlfriend, for a gaggle of affected hipsters isn't as fucking easy you'd think, I wad up the make-up and fake-blood-drenched bathroom tissue into a tight ball and throw it across the room, where it banks off the wall and makes a perfect landing inside a wastebasket. The 10-year-old benchwarmer in me is proud of the shot.

As the sting of their criticism shoots up my spine and fades, my father's golden rule that "Not everyone is gonna like you" resonates louder and clearer than ever. Over the years my skin has certainly thickened from being in a band, but hearing this noise, while my heart's still racing and my body's still sweating, hurt.

Realizing there's probably plenty of truth in what they were saying, I spark a victory smoke in honor of following through with the show we dreamed up. Looking down on a new group of young rockers loitering near that Rainbow Room dumpster, I come to this great realization: I'm glad we weren't well received. Tommi and I are off on our own path and no one can touch it, and if snobbish music critics or anyone else scoffs at us, it's their problem, not ours.

As the night moved along, the other performers delivered soulful sets. The Roxy isn't the worst place for a first gig, I think, as John Doe and Exene perform a stripped-down version of "White Girl." In its own way, per some intergalactic cosmic law, we needed to be bad, and needed to be bad in front of lots of critical people. Our show served its purpose as a rough sketch of some better picture to be filled in, and I can hardly wait for the next chance to do it again and make it a little better. If I want to perform magic, and do it well, it's going to take time, energy, and devotion, and I can't afford to be concerned about what anyone else thinks or says about it.

One thing's evident: spending my waking hours trying to art-fully master the next sleight, learn the next trick, or obsess on the next magic show, instead of writing new songs, informs me that my music dream is more dead than alive. Since starting Possum Dixon, it's the first time I've felt uncertain about the direction of my life. The idea of having a career like singer/songwriter jour-neyman like John Doe, Johnette, or on a grander scale, Debby Harry or Tom Petty, is feeling more elusive, and less desirable.

This curiosity to discover all I can about magic and find a place in it is keeping me alive. If I stay with it, I might eventu-ally have something I can call my own. Here I am with this un-controllable desire to put my creative efforts into something I'm naturally gifted at, just to see where it might lead. I'm taking plea-sure in shrugging off goons from the music community, who've been giving concerning looks and asking patronizing questions, like the one from this Indie rocker I encountered at Rockaway Records. While flipping through old movie soundtracks, looking for some instrumental tracks to perform magic tricks to, he asks:

"I heard you're into magic now. Really, or is it a joke?"

"The joke is on anyone who thinks keeping a band together for more than a few years is a good idea. You try it," I respond. I'm getting tired of musicians and how great some of them think they are.

Whether magic is some passing phase to help pull me through this rut I'm in with music will be determined by the way ahead. Reinventing myself from musician to magician is the most punk rock thing I've ever done.

NEW SHEETS

I T'S SOME WEEKDAY MORNING, and side two of John Cage's "Music of Changes" is playing while I'm practicing my zombie ball routine in the living room of my Silver Lake bungalow while Tommi's shuffling papers at the Viper Room. I should be listening to Cheap Trick for inspiration or finishing the second half of the song I'm stuck writing but this is way more fun. The front door knocks and it's J.

"One sec," I say, taking the needle off the record and resting my shiny zombie ball and the piece of silky black fabric it floats on onto the creaky Victorian sofa we aquired from Sully's girl-friend Jean, who just moved to New York. I open the door and in comes J, who's in a good mood.

"Yo! Z! Hey, what's that?" he asks, nodding to the zombie ball.

"Uh, it's nothing," I say, uninterested in showing him some new moves I've been working on for my routine. I read in the zombie ball instruction booklet to practice for a long time before you show anyone new material and to never tell how a trick is done. Magicians' rules.

"Well, here's something: you've been invited to attend a songwriter's retreat," he says, like I just sold a million records or something.

"Uh huh. Go ahead."

"So, it's actually this pretty cool thing. Every summer Miles Copeland—you know, the former I.R.S. Records head-honcho and brother of Stuart Copeland from the Police? That guy. Anyhow, every summer he hosts these week-long songwriting retreats at his medieval castle, somewhere in the south of France. He invites a small group of notable songwriters and they write new material for each other's upcoming albums. He wants to know if you'll come."

I don't like the way these words sound together. I feel like I've done something wrong and I'm getting shipped off to fat camp, like Brian Willis did in fourth grade.

"What do you mean, 'notable songwriters'? Like who?" I ask, taking a creaky old chair by the bed.

"Well, over the past few years he's had Cher, Carole King, Olivia Newton-John, Ted Nugent, Difford & Tillbrook of Squeeze, and a whole bunch of others."

"Why me?" I say, knowing my place in the world as a recovering addict from a marginally successful band that none of these people had ever heard of. I'm pretty sure I look a little stunned, too.

"Miles was talking with Jimmy Iovine and Chuck, and they thought you'd be a nice new face to this year's lineup. They like to mix up the talent. Oh, and the Go-Go's are going, too." Suddenly my interest level piques. I've always dreamed of meeting the Go-Go's.

"Look man, no one's making you go, but it'll encourage the label to get behind the band again. Who knows? Could be amazing. Think of it as a free trip to France," says J in a tone that suggests go.

I get it. Interscope, who's just about had it with me, wants me to go and come back with some hit singles for our next record. They've given us a couple of tries at making records our way, and if we're gonna make another record for them, it's time to negotiate a little. They feel like we owe them one. The thing is, we do want to sell records — but on our terms, not as mindless morons willing to do anything to make it. We're at a standstill with them, like when a relationship starts to go awry and both people discover they might not be with the person they thought they were in the first place.

Aside from what Interscope wants, we're entering an uncertain band phase. When we started eight years earlier, our ideas were niche, but idyllic. Nobody expected anything from us. We're not the same guys we were then, pissing on the Hollywood hills from the ruins of Errol Flynn's crumbled mansion while out of our minds on crack. These days, I'm preoccupied with my girl-friend, studying magic, and trying to feel less uptight about being sober. And for the life of me, I can't get a grip on where Celso's head is. I just know we both want to see this record through.

"Okay, I'm in," I say, thinking about the prospective French adventure to meet some teen idols.

"Cool, I'm calling 'em right now and letting 'em know. Zabrecky in France! Love it! Au Revoir, Z!"

***

It's taken me two planes, a train, and a few taxis to get here, but I made it. I'm standing with an old suitcase and guitar in front of the closest thing I've ever seen to a real fairytale castle — the kind of place stoners would call paradise. Set deep in the woods, it's a real deal castle, complete with its own curtain wall, corner towers, and gatehouse, plus it's surrounded by these massive trees that look like they've been here since the beginning of time. For the next week, this fourteen-bedroom Château Marouatte in the Dordogne Region of Perigord Vert will be home. I'm greeted by a friendly staff who insist on taking my bags and usher me in.

I'm being shown to my room and taking the whole thing in. The interior is appropriately decorated with the kinds of tapes-tries, medieval furniture, and oil paintings you'd expect to see in any medieval castle. "We hope this is suitable for you, Mr. Zabrecky," says a middle-aged French woman as she turns the key to my room. There's a perfectly made king-sized bed with an antique bedspread, oil paintings of French patriarchs placed in all the right places, an impossibly high ceiling, and a corner fireplace with a raging fire. It's a far cry from the cheap roadside hotel rooms I'm accustomed to. I've never experienced this type of hospitality and as impressed with this place as I am, I'm un-comfortable. I get settled and head to dinner to meet the others, feeling like I've found myself in some surreal cinematic drama—somewhere between *Mad Monster Party* and a lost episode of *Fantasy Island*.

I'm seated at the longest dinner table I've ever sat at across from the Go-Go's. I'm nervous, and avoid any sort of eye-contact, telling myself to keep cool and not say anything I'll regret later. The last time I got excited about meeting someone I admired so much was with Jim Carroll, and that went awful. But this time I'm not out of my mind on meth and have a shot at making a decent impression. I'm in mid-thought, telling myself to sit back and not be an idiot, and hear a naturally high-pitched friendly feminine voice.

"Hi, I'm Jane. What's your name?" she asks, like some kid from third grade on the first day of school. Suddenly I'm the kid with the warts again. I wonder what might happen if I just get up and run.

"Oh, I'm Rob. Hi," I say, thinking she's cute like a Keane painting is cute.

"Hi, Rob. This is Belinda, and this is Charlotte. We're the Go-Go's." Boom. I've just met the band I've dreamed about meeting since 1980. Pretty soon I tell them I'm from LA and they're trading off stories about their early days living at the Canterbury Apartments amid the early punk world of the late 70s, and I'm loving every second of it. They're telling me about their ascension from playing Hollywood clubs into the mainstream, while the other songwriters, whom I don't recognize, look like they're having a great time. They're as cute, witty, and interesting as I'd hoped they'd be. Without knowing it, they're helping me ground, though I still feel like an unwanted guest at a dinner party.

At the end of dinner, Miles Copeland rises from his seat and the room goes quiet. "Welcome to Printemps des Troubadours. I'm pleased you're all here and hope you're getting a chance to meet each other. Tomorrow morning you'll break into small groups and start writing. I encourage our newer, emerging artists to write with those of you who have been here before. We've got workstations with recording gear and tech engineers set up in various rooms around the castle to record demos, so anytime you've got a song, see an engineer and get it on tape. I hope by the end of the week you'll all leave here with some incredible new material."

Nearly 6,000 miles away from home and my new life that I'm barely grounded in, the pressure's on to crank out songs with people who know what they're doing. I'm sure this model for writing songs works fine for anyone who can write music on command with strangers, but I can barely write songs when I'm writing them. My songwriting process remains a mystery — songs fall out of some part of my unconsciousness whenever they feel like it, and that's that. From there I adjust and tweak basic structures for weeks, sometimes months, working from those initial flashes of inspiration. The uncomfortable mounting pressure makes me wonder if I should pack my suitcase and bail before Copeland and company realize I'm not qualified for this endeavor and send me home.

The next morning my instincts are confirmed. I quickly learn how uneasy I become writing music with people I don't know. I'm sitting on a velvet settee in room lit by stained glass with two songwriters who are probably famous but I don't catch, or really care to catch their names. They're picking at piano and guitar riffs, and playing chords I never bothered to learn. I pick around at a counter riff, but am bankrupt, idealess, and cold. This is my best shot, I think, begrudgingly trying to keep up in the ensuing writing session with these musicians. Being here, and doted over by the castle's staff, isn't worth the price of being thrust into forced, inorganic, songwriting sessions.

The next couple of days are the same. They begin mid-morning and go way into the night, with meals prepared around the clock by a chain-smoking Cordon Bleu chef called Jacques. While I'm nearly useless, self-doubting myself to death, the castle staff fusses over us around the clock. I take long breaks, hiding out in the kitchen and chain smoking with Jacques and petting his little dog with no teeth, Scraps, and wanting to crawl from my skin.

Halfway through the week, I find respite riffing with Charlotte and Jane, who made me feel at ease. After riffing with them a little, some ideas start coming and I'm able to work out some chord structures and melodies that seem right. I connect with three other musicians I felt at ease around: Pat MacDonald, of the '80s underground sensation Timbuk 3, Don Was of Was Not Was fame, and Mark Hudson of the Hudson Brothers, who'd produced musical giants Harry Nilsson, Ringo Starr, and Aerosmith. If it weren't for them, I would have bailed. After a few long sessions, I have foundations for new songs called "Faultlines and "Always Engines," which are co-penned by Charlotte, Jane, and Pat MacDonald. By the end of the week I'm more than ready to return home where my new life is waiting.

***

I'm gripping the café bars of the '73 Honda 550 Super Sport motorcycle I bought last week, weaving through the deserted streets of downtown LA. There's a full moon and streets jammed with weathered buildings and closed theaters. I've got the whole place to myself, except for the drug zombies I occasionally dodge. Every few thoughts, my mind goes back to the struggle we're having with Interscope to find a producer. Like before, they want us to pair with one of the current alternative hitmakers, and once again we don't want that. These motorcycle rides help reduce the noise of record company drama and replace the adrenaline I still crave.

The next morning I check my messages and there's one from J. "Z, it's J, call me, man. Just heard from the label. I think we've got a producer."

Here's the news: Former Cars front man, Ric Ocasek, is interested in producing our record. He'd achieved massive success after making incredible sounding hit records during rock's '70s heyday, and has moved on to produce. Over the past couple of years, he produced two big ones for Bad Religion and Weezer. The label thinks he's a great choice, and he's impartial to our rocky history. He seems like the right guy to produce our record and can start soon, but wants to meet us first to ensure our personalities are compatible.

The next day Celso and I are on a plane to New York City to meet him in person.

Ric Ocasek has one of the most recognizable faces from the '80s. No one on Earth looks like him, or so we thought. We meet him at a coffee shop in bustling Union Square and immediately hit it off. He's this artful and lanky, gentle man, and exudes a calm and caring temperament. You can just tell from listening to him that art is the focus of his life. With his jet-black bowl cut, tight black jeans, and big, black, trench coat and sunglasses, he's certainly someone famous. While he's riffing on ideas to record our songs, people crane their necks to catch a glimpse of him. As we walk from Union Station to the West Village to check out the famous Electric Lady Studios as a potential studio, I'm surprised people are constantly mistaking him for two other New York celeb giants: Joey Ramone and Howard Stern. It must be strange for him to be famous, and constantly mistaken for not one, but two other famous people.

We like the atmosphere of Electric Lady and agree it'll be a wonderful place to make our record. Before heading back to LA, I can't stop myself from making a pit stop at New York's oldest magic shop, the Flosso-Hornmann Magic Shop. It's right across the street from the Empire State Building and exactly what you'd hope an old magic shop to be: a jumbled mess of vintage magic apparatus and dusty posters everywhere, and run by an elderly man, who's the son of the original owner, named Jackie Flosso. He's shuffling around and mumbling to himself, carrying on like W.C. Fields. I'm looking around, overridden with my enthusiasm for all things magic, torn between making another record and working on new routines. I'm falling in love with every type of magic; the close-up tricks done right in front of the spectators' eyes, the parlor magic performed for groups of forty or fifty, and stage magic for larger audiences in theaters and nightclubs. Before Celso and I know it, we're back on a plane to LA, where some awful unfinished business awaits.

***

It's a smoggy messed-up afternoon near downtown LA. I'm heading towards a ginormous cement fortress known as the Los Angeles Men's Correctional Facility. Somewhere inside, Celso's starting a sentence for a drug conviction. It's his second one, and the court didn't let him off easy this time — he's here for six weeks. The idea of Celso, of all people, being locked up like a caged animal is one crushing ugly reality.

I'm here on the first hour of the first day he's allowed visitors. It's the only and, if I have any say in it, last time I'll ever be in a congested line like this; one of sad and defeated-looking people, mostly women, children, and crying babies, waiting their turn to visit. I sign in, and take a seat in this large overly lit room that features all the unpleasantries of the DMV, free clinic, and animal shelter, combined. A big TV is mounted just below the ceiling, like they are in hospitals, and a commercial for Bad Boys Bail Bonds is playing on repeat. I just want to see his face and know in some way he's okay.

"Robert Zoobrookie. Zoobrookie? Enter at window four," a guard mutters my name, saying my last name twice, exactly wrong the same way both times, but like she got it right the second time.

I'm admitted into another big cold room, like the kind you've seen a million times in movies; bare cement walls with thick window panes equipped with phone receivers on both sides, two chairs facing each other on either side of the glass, lit by ugly, overhead, bright fluorescent light. On the other side of the glass are a dozen or so inmates, awaiting their visitors. I scan each window in this odd state of disbelief, until I see the smallest, most handsome guy — the bright-eyed one with the contagious smile who changed my life when it needed changing most — the one who doesn't belong with the others. From the neck down he looks just like the other guys in the jump suits, but from the neck up, there's my best friend.

I'm unprepared for how awkward and painful this'll be until we lock eyes between the thick plate of glass. The worst kind of sad pain thrusts into my gut. I take a big breath and choke back tears, knowing the pain I have can only be a fraction of his. We mirror each other in disbelief and take a moment to settle in. He looks ashamed and defeated. I better say something.

"Worse than it looks?" I squeeze out, knowing what stupid questions these are. I'm holding back a dam of tears, reminding myself I'm here to be a friend, not break down in weakness.

"Hard to say. First day. I'm surviving. Less than six weeks as of now." Celso says in this scared and uncertain way.

We look at each other and shrug, waiting for the uncomfortable moment to pass. "Some of these guys don't seem so bad. The food is awful and sleeping situation looks fucked." As he goes on, I start seeing random flashbacks of our hi-jinx from the years before, wondering for the first time why we were so pre-occupied with getting high as often as we did. None of those reasons matters now, I think, because it's too late to redo them.

Each dreadful second evokes the pain from losing Jennifer. He's only a few feet away but it's like he's gone, too. This time I'm sober, and as idiotic as it is, I can't help but think how much easier this visit would be if I were high. How it easily it could have been me on the other side.

"I've stayed clean. Hasn't been easy," I confess.

"Well, go out and see if you can get arrested. I could use the company."

We laugh and settled back in silence.

"I fucked up bad this time, but it's given me time to think. I'm glad I know you, Rob."

"There's nobody else I'd rather visit here. Well, maybe that guy over there. He looks friendly," I say, gesturing to an inmate who looks like John Wayne Gacy.

Jokes aren't funny in this kind of situation. After a minute of quiet time, I'm escorted out.

I get on my motorcycle and take the side streets to nearby downtown. At some red light on Broadway I burst into tears. Aimlessly riding through the smogged-out streets I don't know what to do with myself. I'm looking for some fast-forward button that doesn't exist.

The reality of where he is versus where I am is unfair. We'd copped drugs on the streets together for years. Through what I know as good luck, I never got busted. During the past few years of fiendish using, nearly everyone I used with had been busted, overdosed, and on occasion, died from using. Somehow I'm here on the other side, generally unscathed, with a clean record and decent bill of health. All it would have taken was two dope busts and I would have been serving time, too.

An hour later, I'm in Glendale, and decide to pull into Forest Lawn Cemetery to visit my grandmother's grave. Although I only have a couple fragmented memories of her when I was a young boy, like when she bounced me on her knee and fed me these awful tasting Polish dumplings called pierogis, I'm certain that if she were here, she could've done or said something to put matters into some digestible perspective. I stretch out on the grass below the tree that hovers over her grave, hoping for a comforting message from beyond, but all I feel is regret. Nothing can take my mind off Celso and what it must be like for him right now. I'd share his sentence if they let me.

In the middle of this cloudless weekday afternoon I'd like to erase myself from, I start piecing together my puzzle of a life. I'm transfixed by the different types of the pain I'd gotten to know so well over the years: the daily agony caused from my awful warts, the mind-stinging realization learning my hero of an uncle was an F.B.I. impersonator, the devastation of losing

Jennifer, the hell of my own addiction, and now Celso. I remove a barely working pen from my pocket, and on the back of the cemetery map, scribble:

You've gone way, way too far
All stretched out behind bars
They don't know you, cause they don't want you
And new sheets won't drag you down

Cameras shoot off like shooting stars,
In each and every one of us you will be found
Bright lights go round on a disco ball,
You're in each and every one of us

You've burned all your bridges, walked out of doors,
But you still look suspicious as you wander off the dance floor

Stare at the sun as we're jumping trains,
We laugh together we've got love and it's in vain

***

Six weeks and a couple more uncomfortable visits with Celso later, he's released. We meet up for Mexican food, like we always do, and I can tell he doesn't feel like talking about any of it. He looks exhausted. All he says about it is, "Stay clean, Rob. You don't ever want to be there." And that's that.

We dive back into band business, and discuss who might be able to replace Sully. We agree to ask our close friend and guitarist, Matt Devine. Matt's been a part of our band's world since the get go, back to our late teen years at Valley College before we formed. It was Matt who gifted me some of the important records that helped shape the band's sound nearly a decade earlier, and his musical taste and songwriter talents could be a nice asset to the group, we thought. He'd also helped out with earliest recording days at Ellis Island, playing electric guitar on our first

7-inch. We'd been supporters and former members of his bands, Lazytown and Ventilator, and performed with his band that we admired, Permanent Green Light. Yeah, Matt for sure, we agree.

To prepare for recording, we begin a rigorous rehearsal schedule. The label is footing the bill for this spacious rehearsal room located in a sturdy brick building on the outskirts of downtown LA, not far from Skid Row. Wild dogs and hobos roam the surrounding desolate area where we can come and go as we please and rehearse as often as we wish. An old-timey service elevator slowly lifts us to the fifth floor, where we have a big room with a nice P.A. and a killer view of East LA. The location is in its own way ideal — it's away from the Silverlake music world that's becoming toxic and claustrophobic. Band morale is beginning to build up again. Celso's embracing a newfound sobriety, Byron couldn't be more enthusiastic about making a new record, and Matt's rolling with all things Possum Dixon.

The label's pressuring us for one more co-written song with an established songwriter, so before I know it, I'm on a plane to New York City for a week to write with my co-writer of choice, the singer of the B-52's, Fred Schneider. He's as interesting and colorful in person as he is on record. We brainstorm in his Chelsea apartment over a few writing sessions that result in a seed idea for a song we call "Firecracker!" and before I know it, I'm back in LA.

For the next couple of months, I ride to and from our sacred studio from Silverlake on my motorcycle, weaving through the city streets, coming up with new lyrics, contemplating the latest song arrangements, and adjusting to my new life. Everyone's contributing long hours, working hard on the new material. Along the way, some of our jittery, art-rock edges are smoothing out for easier-sounding songs. It's like we're starting over as new, less fucked-up people.

Tommi and I moved in together. We found a peaceful 1920s Spanish-style bungalow just above the Silverlake reservoir. We're beginning new lives together and, for the first time, I'm feeling

moments of stability in what's developing into a solid relationship. Attending recovery meetings and gaining insight to the sober world has helped, and I'm understanding that if I was going
to make it sober, I have a long way to go. I'm still experiencing
moments — sometimes daily, sometimes hourly — of agonizing
frustration where I want to run off and get loaded. On a whim,
I can become an irritable prick if things aren't going my way. I
fight the urges as they come and hold my ground, fighting for a
new life.

That winter, Celso, Byron, Matt, and I pack our bags and
head to New York City to record. Band morale is up high and
we were jazzed to be in New York. The label and J set us up
with a comfortable, sixteenth-story, furnished apartment near
Wall Street, walking distance from the World Trade Center. By
day, the area bustles with the Wall Street working class and thriving local businesses. By night it's a ghost town. We refer to the
area after dark as the "murder district," because every corner
looks like a potential homicide scene. We waste little time before
jumping into rehearsals. It's now up to Ocasek to find clarity in
the batch of songs we imported from LA. It's also time to prove
to myself that I can rise above the adversity of our past, and in
a perfect world, sell enough records to justify our existence on
the label.

I'm walking around the East Village one night, reminding
myself how much I've changed. Gone are the reckless days and
nights, buzzing around the Lower East Side searching for inebri-
ating black-outs and sex.

No more dizzying sexual encounters in bathroom stalls with
near-strangers before passing out.

No more waking up and vomiting, sitting with my head in
my hands, wondering what happened the previous night.

No more pulling myself together to get on stage the next
night.

No more ending up in small apartments with musicians and
scenesters to score dope and get high. Those opportunities are

all still there if I want them, and I know it—and it keeps me a little scared, all the time.

To keep my mind off the idea that my life is hanging by a thread, I borrow a rusted three-speed from Sully's ex-girlfriend, Jean, my imagined kid sister who relocated to New York. Every off hour away from the band is spent pedaling around the nearly frozen city that's quieting down for the winter. For super thrills, before heading to the studio, I ride as fast as I can through mad Broadway traffic while listening to classical music at full volume on my Walkman. Riding in the middle of street, weaving between swarms of cabs and delivery trucks, provides a bit of the rush drugs once did.

After rehearsals, I ride around the East Village like I'd been doing on my motorcycle in downtown LA. I'm searching for some new thing, but don't know what it is, or if I'll even recognize it once I find it. It's like I'm on a kind of life hunt, searching for this new undetermined thing.

During these aimless efforts to find the way ahead, I keep getting caught looking back.

I find myself riding around the East Village, romanticizing the pasts of punk icons like Debbie Harry, Richard Hell, Tom Verlaine, David Byrne, and Alan Vega. I drift into a deep fog, wondering what their lives were like during those haywire times in the mid-'70s at CBGB, as the first wave of punk revealed itself in lower Manhattan. What an exciting time it must have been to be alive, I imagine while zigzagging the streets, pretending to be them. My idea of their pasts is more exciting than the present I'm experiencing, even though I'm living the life I dreamed up in Burbank a decade earlier.

We started recording, and the band and I are riding this wave of momentum and hope. We're getting on like school friends, routinely bundling up and taking the subway from our downtown Manhattan apartment to the famed Electric Lady Studios in the West Village. We're putting in long hours, trying to get the right sounds and make the right record. The

Go-Go's guitarist, Jane, came out from LA for a couple of days to provide dreamy backup vocals on "Faultlines," the song we co-penned at Miles Copeland's song-making castle, and Fred Schneider rolled in to lay down some vocals on "Firecracker." These sessions are moving along at a swift pace, and even with the help of these new wave giants helping us, I can't help but wonder if there's too much hand-holding going on. There's a voice telling me we're overdoing it, but we've come this far and it's too late to turn back.

***

Tommi's here on her first visit to New York. Between recording sessions, we walk around the cold city like tourists in love. I'm with the girl I'd fallen for and can't imagine being with anyone else. Watching her observe the city is like being here for the first time. My marriage with Jennifer, as short-lived as it was, is a black hole and something I can't say much about, but being here now and sharing these new adventures with Tommi inspire new and unexplored life. Here I am with this burning desire to prove to

Tommi that I want to be with her as long as we live, and proposing seems like the only way to do that. Although we've never discussed marriage, asking her to marry me seems like the only thing to do.

During a solo visit at my go-to magic shop the other day, Flosso-Hornmann Magic, I'm telling Jackie Flosso about asking Tommi to marry me and he makes a suggestion.

"I worked with Woody Allen on an idea for one of his movies where the lead character proposes to his girlfriend on top of the Empire State Building. They're up there on this perfectly clear day, and he shows her an empty box, then a piece of silk ribbon. He places the box and string into a small velvet bag. He removes the string and it's attached to the box. When the box is opened, it's tied to an engagement ring. I mean, who's gonna say no with that kind of lead in. Besides, Woody hasn't used the idea, so it's all yours, kid."

Sounds like a fine idea, and doable. I purchase a modest 1920s diamond ring in the West Village and rehearse the trick with the ring, the string, the box, and the bag in the studio between takes.

It's Saturday, our day off, and I carefully load the ring and magic props in my jacket before Tommi and I head out to explore the city. It's was one of those days where everything seemed to be going right. We're sharing a bag of honey roasted peanuts in Union Square, and an older couple politely interrupts us.

"Please don't take this the wrong way, but you two look like characters from a French New Wave film. Have a nice afternoon."

"They do," says an older lady photographer who looks like Diane Arbus' sister, snapping photos of us.

"Interesting." Snap. "Looking." Snap. "Couple." Snap.

Then she's gone, but for that moment in the city, we were an attraction in and of ourselves.

These encounters are green lights. The time is right but I'm more nervous than I ever remember being. When we arrive at the top of the Empire State Building, the conditions are less than ideal. I fail to calculate that on Saturday afternoons, the roof is a tourist destination with large crowds blocking every possible view and talking so loud you can't hear your thoughts. Unaware of my dilemma, Tommi says something that changes the course of my plan.

"Doesn't this remind you of one of those awful movies where the guy proposes to the girl in front of a bunch of tourists?"

"Yeah, it sure does. Let's get out of here," I reply, escorting us to the elevator and scheming a quick plan B.

We take a long walk down Broadway into downtown, agreeing to end the day at Windows on the World restaurant in the

World Trade Center. We might be entering a similar situation as the Empire State Building, I think, but I'm determined to ask her before this night is over, and we can't get any higher than the Windows on the World.

By the time we arrive I'm a wreck. One-hundred-and-seven floors above the cold city, we get a table, order a couple of Cokes, and rest our tired legs. A twelve-piece band plays for swing-dancing couples and an enthusiastic but small audience. Between sets, I look out over the city, and I know it's now or never.

You never know how nervous you are until you ask your girlfriend to marry you. All the things I thought about saying, and half the moves of the magic trick, are escaping me.

"I'll be right back," I say, as I hit the bathroom to double check my magic props and figure out how I'm going to pull this off.

I tell myself it's okay if she's not into it. After all, who could blame her if she says no. I take a breath and wait a beat before heading back to our table. She's sitting there looking as incredible as she ever has, watching the band. I crouch down next to her and get on both knees and remove the small box. Then the ribbon.

"What's that?" she says, seeing I'm up to something.

"Well, this goes in here, and this goes in here…" I say, partially guiding myself through the procedure of the effect, placing the box and ribbon in the velvet bag. My hands are about to shake off my wrists.

"They go in here, and now there's this," I tell her, holding the ring in my fingertips.

"I want you to be my wife," I say, barely getting the words out.

She looks a little stunned and needs clarification.

"Wait, are you asking me to marry you?"

"Yes. Will you?"

"Yes." She replies with biggest smile I'd ever seen.

Up there above Manhattan, the world is just right. I'm engaged to the prettiest girl with the biggest heart in the world's greatest city — and I can't remember ever feeling this relieved.

***

We add finishing touches to our record at New York's Chung King "House of Metal" studios. Tommi, Celso, Byron, and Matt head back for LA while I stay for a week to complete some additional tracking at Ric's New York apartment. During the sessions, Ric and I form a solid bond as we're coming up with some last bits and pieces to add to the record. Seeing him work at home reveals how music is only part of his identity; he's a husband, father, and his interest in art and poetry rivals his interest in music.

"Here you go, I think you'll enjoy these," he says, handing me two books of poetry by E.E. Cummings. "I hope you'll see there's similarities in your writing styles."

Poring over Cummings's work before I crash for the night, I drift to sleep, excited to have a new favorite poet and a new friend in Ric.

It's my last day in New York, and Ric hands me an advance cassette of our record. We say our goodbyes and I pop the cassette into my faithful Walkman for one last brisk walk through Greenwich Village. Listening to the tape as loud as my Walkman would play it, it's all there, and as far as I'm concerned we hit the target we were aiming for. After side two is done playing and the hiss of the tape fades, I hit stop on my Walkman and take a seat on a cold bench in Washington Square Park, recapping the last couple years and feeling relieved for a change.

I'm looking around with my headphones still on and my ears ringing, wondering if the park's famous monument arch could shatter at any second from the near freezing temperature. I hate being cold more than almost anything, but force myself to sit there for a moment to try and get my thoughts together. Out of nowhere I start hearing the imagined voice of Holden Caulfield from *Catcher in the Rye*, which I just finished reading for the fifth time. Then I picture him as he's described in the book, in his goofy red hunting cap, blazer, and overcoat, sitting right there next me. Our imagined conversation went like this:

"I listened to your record," he says in a tone that tells me he's not exactly a fan.

"Yeah, what'd you think?" I say, feeling my cold skin thinning, knowing I'm in for a beating. That's the thing I appreciate about Holden — I can trust him.

"It's not great, that's for sure. I mean, it's okay for your third record, but you guys were better back in your PikMe-Up days, before you tried to make it big and had a record deal and all that stuff. I mean, there's a couple of good parts in some of the songs, but mostly it's boring. And it doesn't sound like you guys. There are so many bands that are way better than yours."

His indie rock cynicism is little overwhelming. Now he's on a roll, but I guess you could say I asked for it.

"Besides, what was the point of making a record with a bunch of hot-shots who've already made it? Couldn't you have just done it on your own? All the kowtowing you've been doing with your record label has only made your band worse than you already were. You could've taken a hint when that label guy said he wanted to 'dress you' and all that jazz," he says, hitting an exposed nerve.

"This hasn't been the easiest last couple of years."

"Well, you asked. If I were you — and I'm pretty god-dammed glad I'm not — I'd quit music and do something else."

Either he's got me cornered or I've had it with this conversation. I can't tell, so I snap.

"If you're so great, start your own band. Go to hell, Caulfield."

"I wouldn't be in a band if you paid me. Your band is your problem. You go to hell, Zabrecky."

He rises from the icy park bench and dematerializes through the park's arch. I head back to my apartment, pack my suitcase, and hop on a plane back to LA.

THE WIT OF THE STAIRCASE

I T'S SUNDAY NIGHT and I'm driving home from seeing a friend's band. For old time's sake I tune in to KROQ for old Rodney's radio show, Rodney on the Roq. After back announcing a few songs from bands I've never heard of, he announces, "Here's something from the LA band, Possum Dixon. They have a new album coming out soon called *New Sheets,* on Interscope. This one's called 'Firecracker!' Here it is."

The bass riff kicks in. Then the drums. Then the guitar.

The song sounds good on the car radio, I think, feeling my musical history come full circle. I wouldn't have believed you if you told my 12-year-old self that one day I'd co-write a song with Fred Schneider of the B-52s and it'd be played on Rodney on the Roq. For the next few minutes, I'm overwhelmed with a sense of vindication through my car stereo. Who cares what Holden Caulfield thinks.

From brushes with stardom, I know by now how fleeting success can be. I know being played on Rodney won't make or break us—the days of one DJ breaking a band are a thing of the past. As the song ends and his next selection starts, I can't help but feeling that the rock-and-roll universe owes us a radio hit after the ride we've been on the past few years.

The next day I head over to Tower Records on Sunset Blvd. to check out a massive painting of the cover of our third album, *New Sheets,* mounted in the parking lot. I'm standing here just marveling at the way it looks. It's even better than I'd imagined. It was designed to look like a vintage magic poster, and created by graphic designer Rachel Gutek — a dear friend of the band who helped create some of the earliest Possum Dixon artwork. But no matter how much I dig it, it's going to take a lot more than a cool record cover to sell records.

The music industry, like life, isn't fair — and album reviews are reminding us of that. Ric Ocasek encouraged and engaged every idea we had, but along the way we changed and our sound became a little muddled. Crunchy guitars and keyboard-driven melodies panned out for us in the studio, but critics are saying the tension that originally set us apart from other bands is lost, and replaced by tones reminiscent of Ocasek's former group. After reading a handful of reviews, the consensus is that critics think we generated an overproduced album that sounds more like the Cars than Possum Dixon, and I can't argue with them.

While working up a live set, Celso, Byron, and I decide to simplify the band's lineup. We made a hard call of relieving Matt of touring duties and move forward as a trio. While re-learning the songs for a live set, Celso's become unreachable. I've spent the past four days worrying about him. In the process, I'm painfully reminded of the burden I must've caused everyone when I was unreachable all those times before. After a week of trying to find his whereabouts, he finally calls.

"Listen, I can't do the band right now," he says from what sounds like a payphone.

"You picked a hell of a time to bail. Can we get together and talk?" I plead, trying to sound like I'm not pleading.

"No man, not right now. I just need a break. I gotta go." Click.

My heart sunk. I could tell from the tone of his voice that his mind's made up. He's not the kind of guy who reasons the way most people do, nor is he the kind of guy who just comes out and says exactly what he means. You have to intuit him, read him like a cat. That's always been part of the magic of being his friend. And now more than ever, I intuit he doesn't want anything to do with me, my new life, and stab at sobriety. Different things are making his life work now, and I'm not part of them. All I can do is be defeated. I don't want to let go because I care too much, but there's nothing I can do. It's time to say goodbye to the idea he's not coming back.

Letting go of the most important person to me for all those defining years — the guy who taught me how to live like tomorrow doesn't exist, throw every bit of caution to the wind, and let it all ride and fuck off — hurts badly. Our 20s: the decade when our lives were so intertwined that we'd rarely gone a day without knowing what the each other had for lunch or dinner, is over. We exited each other's lives as fast we entered them back in our late teens.

***

I'm facing a picture of the future I don't want to see: one without Celso. There's more at stake now than there ever was. J, Byron, the label, and my lifeline are all depending on the band to support the record. There's a new sense of desperation I've never felt being in the band, and it makes me cringe. Possum Dixon is all I have — it's my only future. If our band were a building, the ceiling's falling and the walls are caving in. But with a finished album and pressure from the label to promote it, Byron and I begin circling a bathroom drain, down the corroding pipe of disillusionment. But still, we've got to see this record through.

For most bands, half the excitement and challenge of making a record in the first place is playing it live and finding ways to perform live versions of the recordings. But now my desire to play live is at an all-time low. The band, and the idea of being in a band doesn't seem right anymore.

We enlist help from some longtime friends from the Silverlake music community to join us. Carey Fosse, the whiz guitarist for the Abe Lincoln Story, has jumped in for guitar duties, and Stan Fairbank, formerly of My Sin, has offered to join on keyboards. Suddenly we're back to being a quartet again, with half the original members.

We book our record release party at the Roxy. To weave the record's magic theme to the night, we hire a comedy magician Tommi and I met at the Magic Castle who calls himself Handsome Jack, to perform during a pre-show party at On the Roxx. Part of me wants to forget the show altogether and watch Mr. Handsome do fancy card tricks, rather than face our hometown audience without Celso and Sully. Carey and Stan are doing a fine job of bringing a new spin to our songs, and as much as I admire their unique musical nuances and performing with them, the band isn't the Possum Dixon I know, nor the one I remember during our heyday the night we nearly exploded on stage a few years before.

***

The new Possum Dixon lineup is out on a month-long US tour. The glory of exploring cities for the first time, playing for new audiences, and reading reviews in local papers has lost its luster. Byron and I are committed to trying to make things work, but with Celso gone, the spirit of the band is lost in some sad void.

Overridden by defeat, I'm feeling less pressure about everything. For the first time I don't know, or care, what the band is about. With no sense of band morale, we're slugging through the tour and fulfilling our obligations. During the twenty-three hours I'm not onstage, I write letters to Tommi and daydream about some new life, coming to grips that the band is downshifting to a slow halt.

To amuse myself and liven up our show, I'm performing a string of magic tricks while the band plays an improvised instrumental in the middle of our set. Audiences are dumbfounded as to why I'm doing fire and rope tricks instead of playing "Watch the Girl Destroy Me," or "Emergency's About to End." Performing magic during our set is the only artistically challenging moment I feel under the spotlights. They're keeping me from losing my mind.

"I've seen lots of bands do lots of things onstage, but I've never seen anyone do that," R.E.M.'s Peter Buck says to me after a show in Seattle. From the cool and neutral tone of his voice, I'm certain he's less than impressed with my feats of legerdemain during our set. That's okay, because I agree. We weren't any good and I know it. There's this part of me that feels like I did when I was 15, waiting to get canned from one job or another.

The label's started promoting the first track of *New Sheets*, "Lenny's Song." The radio department at Interscope tells us it's making small waves on various college and FM charts and alt-rock stations in a few big cities. The prospect of a hit college or FM charting record is sparking these small moments of hope. If things start going well again, maybe Celso and his lost smile will resurface, Sully will rejoin, and we can pick up where we left off. But these flashing moments are fleeting daydreams and I know it.

Celso isn't coming back.

Neither is Sully.

A month later the final Possum Dixon lineup is out playing a handful of radio shows around the US to support the airplay for "Lenny's Song." For the first time, playing live music is more trouble than it's worth. Instead of feeling the rush from playing live, I'm finding myself joylessly going through the motions and counting the songs on the set list until we can leave the stage. While inching through spiritless performances, I'm certain I don't want to be in a band anymore.

During the painful realization that the band is through, the label helps put our fate to rest. The "Lenny's Song" airplay isn't translating to a jump in record sales. Somewhere in the Midwest, J informs us that our tour support is cut off and after this last string of shows we need to head home. After a show in Lawrence,

Kansas, the trusty Possum Dixon tour van drives back to LA for the last time. What should have felt like a blow is a relief.

***

Some bands break up over creative differences, others from mutual love interests, and others because of greed or money. Others disband when a disdain of one another becomes irreconcilable—some from a toxic combination of the four. With Possum Dixon, there wasn't one big blowout or definitive final moment. Our demise happened after our star burning brightly those first few years, before crashing into bits over days and slowly disintegrated over weeks, months, and years.

A few months after the release of *New Sheets,* I let go of the band I'd spent a third of my life pursuing. On one hand, I'm grateful we sustained as long as we did. On the other, I feel like I've done it all wrong.

Our experience with a major label was everything that could be expected. My Gemini mind is overridden with conflict, reminding me we probably wouldn't have reached as many ears without their support, and might've done just fine putting out our music on smaller labels on our terms. That critical voice likes to remind me how many times I'd screwed up when I should've been paying attention to the details of the single endeavor that meant everything to me, disappointed in the way I handled band business—or how I failed to cope with anything at all when I was out of my mind.

I torment myself with every "what if" and "why" when I know I should be pulling up my boot straps and moving on. The only way I can deal with the reality of not having the band anymore is by consoling myself with that old corny adage that "everything happens for a reason," which makes me even more annoyed than I already am with myself.

***

I'm on a long walk through Silverlake and I can't stop thinking about the past 10 years. Passing under a hundred palm trees, I ought to be treasuring the millions of details in this neighborhood that can only be seen on foot, but instead my mind's going in circles thinking about how I'd messed things up, and how it was too late to fix my failures.

Heading east on Sunset Blvd., I'm trying to clear my head. Looking around I'm reminded how the neighborhood is changing; new boutiques and pricey restaurants are popping up for young Urbanites, looking for the next new and cool place to live. It's a far cry from the place I remembered from the late '80s when the area flourished between the copacetic mash-up of Mexican and queer cultures, living in harmony amidst low rent apartment buildings, perfectly manicured mid-century houses, and Mediterranean and Craftsman homes. Although I'm as guilty as this influx of upwardly mobile hipsters who thought it'd be cool to live here, the idea gentrifying an area that doesn't need it, makes me resent myself for coming here in the first place and sneering at the others, who like me, call Silverlake home.

I stop in my favorite little liquor store to grab a Dr. Pepper and rest my feet a second. I pick up an LA Weekly and flip through it. I stumble onto some article about "the Silverlake sound" citing Beck, Possum Dixon, Ethyl Meatplow, and Lutefisk as the early Silverlake bands and musicians, hailing an influx of new groups to check out. My era had come and gone as quickly as it happened and is already being romanticized. The joke's on me for picking up the paper in the first place, I think, setting it back where I found it and continue walking.

Up Sunset Blvd, I spot a small new café a couple blocks north of Millie's Diner. Passing by I sense the Euro vibe it's going for: a few outdoor tables with large umbrellas and a cute girl in fitted black and white clothes taking orders. It's equally chic and misplaced, sticking out between the junk shop and Mexican Botanica it's sandwiched between. As I get closer, I see the waitress taking orders from Beck, who's in a big straw cowboy hat and big cheap woman's sunglasses seated next to a couple of members of the Beastie Boys. At the next table is Courtney Love in conversation with what looks like the team of Jacoby & Meyers.

It's a little overwhelming seeing these two who I'd kicked around with a few years earlier, when nobody had a record deal or was headlining tours in faraway places. Part of me wants to stop, say hi, and congratulate them on their successes. The other part of me resorts to the shy and introverted kid who's resenting himself for mismanaging and blowing his music career. It'd be awkward to interrupt, I think, and perhaps explain I've fallen into magic of all things, so keep my head down and walk on by. Catching that glimpse of them was a reminder that my former Silverlake life, when life revolved around being in a band and engaging in Jabberjaw's music world has evaporated into bits of memory. Now, the whole idea of what cool is, or is supposed to be, is a bummer. After my warts disappeared and I was welcomed by the cool kids, I never thought I'd want out of the cool club. But here I am, wondering where I can cancel my subscription.

Sauntering on, I stumble upon a worn-out cement staircase in the foothills of the Silverlake hills. It's supposed to famous from being in some Laurel & Hardy movie from the '30s, but nobody I know seems to know for sure. Climbing the stairs triggers a Rob Zabrecky retropective of sorts. With every few steps I climb, some milestone that's defined my creative life through the ages comes to mind; hearing music on the AM radio, standing alone on the Masonic Lodge stage, playing air guitar, failing at ventriloquism, running with the PPA and shedding those god-awful warts, discovering Rodney, bands and artists that impacted me in one way or another, starting a band with a guy I love and a name I hate, and falling into magic.

I'm doing all I can to let go and force myself into feeling gratitude. I've experienced success that most guys only wish for. It's my fault for being nearly brainwashed into thinking I'd be the next Mick Jagger or something. Sure, I wanted more, but can accept the truth, sometimes through these hurt, bitter, and self-loathing moments. The upshot is that for a brief but thrilling time, I performed my life's soundtrack with my best friends, among an interesting and unique music community.

I think back in quick succession about that 10 years of being in a band. We accomplished much more than what we originally set out to do, play that first gig at Al's Bar on a Saturday night. Those first four band years are the fiercest ones I've lived, when I felt like I had some other purpose after high school, and when, in my eyes, we were the most special band in the world. They're the most cathartic and invigorating experiences I've had. From my bedroom on California Street, I dreamed of something that became a reality, and embraced it with all I could.

Over those ten years we grew up from being those wide-eyed kids fresh out of high school, biding time at community college, looking for some bigger adventure. We built our band from a beautiful friendship and wrote about the experiences that stemmed from our adventures, which built a bond some bands only dream about. Our love for each other conquered life's annoying pains that came between those early gigs — when we still lived under our parents' roofs and music was our gateway to freedom — looking for something more than going to college and ending up handcuffed to a desk, devolving under dimmed fluorescent office light. Inventing a dream and going for it the way we did, hitting our own jackpot by playing our hearts out to legions of kids who sang along with our songs, and later, feeling the sounds from our instruments evaporating into empty clubs. Those unforgettable memories of being young, carefree, and reckless aren't going anywhere—they're mine to keep. If nothing else, the memories of the band's salad days are my consolation prize.

But the real prize is walking away from something that felt like your life's purpose and knowing there's something ahead.

From the top of the staircase, I'm looking down on the street from which I came and see these three young teenage boys zip by on the sidewalk. Two are on BMX bikes and one's trailing behind on a skateboard. From one glance, you just know they're putting around, sharing their last days of innocence like Mike Keys, Richard, and I did in Burbank's Magnolia Park. I start thinking about Mike Keys and Richard, how we've gone our own ways, and how people grow up and change. Mike Keys and I stay in touch every few months and get together to see bands and riff on the Burbank years. He's driving trucks for the film studios, with dreams of modeling and acting. I saw Richard on my last stop in Seattle and was relieved to see how he'd turned his world around, living clean and sober and doing fine. Meanwhile, my brother and sister married high school and college sweethearts and are starting families. They're busy raising my two nieces and nephew, leading respectable lives, while my parents are retired in nearby Palmdale.

I'm taking all this in when I realize it's the first time I've stopped to catch my breath since I started the band. It's like I'd been playing a continuous 10-year game of Pac Man, and am finally done chasing blinking prizes and pulsating ghosts to stay in the game.

Stopping to think long and hard meant coming to the one thing I can't let go of — the heartshattering realization that I've lost Celso. In some ways, letting go of him is harder than losing Jennifer. Her exit was an unexpected hurricane and now she's physically gone. Celso's heart is still beating. For all I know he's a block from here. I have this dream of finding him, steering him off his collision course, and moving on to find our next adventure. If there's one thing I've learned from cleaning up my act, it's that I can't change him. I'm barely in control of my own thoughts and actions.

Instead, I start resenting myself for insisting my life is so important. I get a massive urge to say fuck it to everything and get high. I'm walking, trying to get away from myself, and I've got this devil on my shoulder telling me to erase myself from all of it. Heading back down the stairs, I think about how my biggest and only real commitment is to Tommi, and she'd have no problem finding some great guy to go with if I bail.

I'm in a bit of a freak out mode, walking by the Tropical Bakery, where there's about a dozen people I know and recognize outside ready to start a 12-step recovery meeting. One of my recovery friends spots me and calls me out.

"Hey Rob! Meeting starts in five minutes. You coming?

Of two minds, I duck in and join them, taking a seat in the back to rest my feet and remind myself that timing is everything.

I can't tell you too much about what everyone's saying — it's against the rules. All I'll say is people here want to live better lives than the ones they had, understand, empathize, and help each other.

Someone's sharing a story about being on the fence about using, and all I can think is that five minutes ago I was ready to make a bee line for my motorcycle, find drugs, and get high. But now if the urge is still bad I'll go on a long motorcycle ride or treat myself to a roller-coaster binge at Magic Mountain, where I'd ridden coasters as a kid. Plunging nearly straight down at eighty miles per hour always creates an adrenaline buzz that recalls shooting dope those first bunch of times.

The thing about today is I'm reminded that the thrill of the drop is the very thing that makes me feel alive. Although I'm older, that sense of unexpected exhilaration never gets old. Some of the best things that happened in my life happened fast — with an intensity and force which blinded me to the outcome. *Don't be afraid to take risks. Do everything you can while you can. Trust yourself. Don't get too caught up in the past —it's over and you don't get to do it again.* These short truths have become my modus operandi for the way forward.

And when I can't help but looking back, if I had one wish I could make come true it would be knowing that Jennifer found peace. Daily, sometimes hourly, shadows of remorse and guilt pass through me when I least expect them and remind me of her. No matter how hard I try, in some deep part of myself, I still hate myself for getting over her death.

I trek back to our bungalow, kick off my shoes, and throw myself on our hand-me-down Victorian sofa. It'd be nice to know what this day has been about, but now that my thoughts are settling, I'm more lost now than when I was out wandering around.

An hour later Tommi returns from a full day at the Viper Room with an armful of groceries and some fresh cut flowers. She's a sight for sore eyes.

"You look like you've seen a ghost," she says, arranging half a dozen Stargazers in a vase.

"Got the number for Ghostbusters handy?" I kid with her, propping up my achy legs on sofa pillows.

I know she knows just what I mean, and doesn't pry. Instead, she grabs a blanket, dims the lights, and slides a VHS in the VCR. It's a compilation tape of 1920s silent films, some of which were shot in our neighborhood some 70 years earlier. Together, we crash out harmoniously to black and white cinematic bliss.

***

It's mid-afternoon and I'm almost home from a downtown motorcycle ride. I pull off the steep incline of Duane Street into our garage, just below our bungalow, and kill the engine of my motorcycle. I grab the sunglasses off my face like I always do, pop off my helmet, and look around. Something isn't right. The spot where I'd been storing my upright bass is now a gaping and empty space, revealing a concrete wall.

"Ahh. Forgot to shut the garage door before leaving," I groan, knowing the bass bandit is on his or her way to some pawn shop for quick cash. I get this short riled wave of anger and kick a cardboard box marked "Old Stuff" about as hard as I can — not because I'm mad about the bass being gone, but because someone ripped me off. Then I feel this wave of stupidity, followed by one of ecstatic relief. Yes, big relief. I calmly exit, close the garage door, and look down on the still Silverlake Reservoir. There it is, another nice day in Southern California, and I'm glad to be alive. "Less stuff, less headache," I tell myself. I'd been had, and the stolen bass is a sign to get on with things, whatever they're going to be.

I sit on the curb and try collecting my thoughts. I'm fed up questioning where my life is going, and just sit there and feel okay with where it is for a change. I welcome this era of personal reinvention, rethinking who I can be, versus who I was, or who people think I was. Another transformation is taking place. The scars on my arms—where a bullet or needle went in, or where the warts were burned off—are little souvenirs to remind me not where I'm going but where I'd been. I'm entering something I didn't expect would come so soon: the beginnings of mid-life.

Realizing I'm entering some new realm, one I didn't know existed, releases the need to struggle with who I am and how the world sees me—the awkward wart kid, the homecoming king, the rock singer, the drug addict, and the magician. By sitting on this curb, doing nothing, I've turned a major corner, feeling a massive sense of relief they're all behind me. And inside me. I'm a new man, welcoming my former selves to join me in the way forward, a place where I won't let any one thing define me. You never know when you're going to have a revelation or find salvation.

EPILOGUE

If you're wondering what happened to some of the people from within these pages, here's what I know. A few years after shooting me, Uncle Ed disintegrated from cirrhosis of the liver and died at 42. Mike Keys continued driving trucks for Hollywood film studios, and unexpectedly passed from a freak bicycle accident in 2007. He was 39. After leaving Possum Dixon in 1998, Celso formed his own group, Pill Module (with Matt Devine) and gigged around LA for a few years. Like Mike Keys, he left us too soon, from pneumonia complications, in 2012. Sully and Richard are alive and well, residing in Southern California with their beautiful families. My father is gone, but my Good Mother is alive and good as ever. I married my true love, Tommi, in 1998. She continues to inspire and amaze me in new ways and plays a huge role in navigating my creative life. We're a great team. We live in Los Angeles with our three dogs. I've remained clean and sober since 1996. I continue to practice and study magic and work as an actor in TV and film. In 2013, 33 years after my shooting incident, I underwent surgery and finally had the bullet removed from my arm. On windy days, I bike ride through the streets of Burbank, listening to loud music on my headphones, reliving my strange cures.

PHOTO CREDITS:

Cover: Joshua Erkman
Uncle Ed, 1979. Photo: Ralph Zabrecky
The Good Mother, 1970. Photo: Ralph Zabrecky
Robbie Zabrecky, 1973. Photo: Renee Zabrecky
Zabrecky siblings, Laura, Gordon, & Robbie, 1974. Photo: Renee Zabrecky
1222 N. California Street, Burbank, California, 1980. Photo: Ralph Zabrecky
Members of the Panta Punk Army, 1980. Photo courtesy of author
Mike Keys & Robbie Zabrecky, 1981. Photo courtesy of author
Richard Williams, Mike Keys, Robbie Zabrecky, 1983. Photo: Beverly Keys
Robbie Zabrecky, 1983. Photo: Beverly Keys
Fake ID, 1984. Photo courtesy of author
First band, Castaways, 1984. Photo: Scott Leonard
Yearbook photo. Courtesy of John Burroughs High School
Peculiar Chris, 1985. Photo courtesy of author
Peculiar Chris & Zabrecky. Photo courtesy of author
Homecoming dance, 1986. Photo courtesy of author
High School graduation, 1986. Photo courtesy of author
Nights at Lhasa, 1987. Photo courtesy of author
Celso Chavez. Photo: Arlan Helm
Zabrecky & Jabberjaw proprietor Gary Dent. Photo courtesy of author
Zabrecky at Al's Bar, 1993. Photo: Arlan Helm
Possum Dixon at East Hollywood's Onyx/Sequel, 1993. Photo: Jeffoto
Ellis Island. Photo courtesy of Rush Riddle
Possum Dixon live at Ellis Island. Photo courtesy of author
Hully Gully Studios. Photo courtesy of author
Jim Carroll & Possum Dixon performing a speedy version of "People Who Died," 1994. Photo: Jeffoto
The heart and soul of Possum Dixon; Celso Chavez. Photo: Craig Cutright
Members of Possum Dixon & Beck, Boston, 1994. Photo courtesy of author
Zabrecky at the Chateau Marmont, Hollywood, CA, 1994. Photo courtesy of author
With Jennifer, 1995. Photo courtesy of author
Possum Dixon, 1995. Photo: Carol Sheridan
Zabrecky, 1995. Photo courtesy of author
Zabrecky, 1995. Photo courtesy of author
Arthur's Hideaway. Photo courtesy of author
Arthur's Presidential Suite. Photo courtesy of author
Tommi Jean Tucker-Ross, 1995. Photo courtesy of author
Possum Dixon, 1996. Photo courtesy of author
Sequence of Zabrecky in performance. Photo courtesy of author

Robert O'Sullivan, 1993. Photo: Arlan Helm
Griffith & Clementine, 1997. Photo: Storm Hale
Tommi & Exene. Photo courtesy of author
Possum Dixon & Ric Ocasek at Electric Lady Studios. Photo courtesy of
Interscope Records
Rob & Tommi, 1997. Photo courtesy of author
New Sheets Advertisement at Tower Records, Hollywood. Photo courtesy of author
Celso Chavez, 1995. Photo: Jean Railla
Zabrecky performing last leg of Possum Dixon shows, 1998. Photo: Craig Cutright
Zabrecky in Silverlake. Photo courtesy of author
Zabrecky photographed for BAM Magazine in Silverlake, 1998. Photo: Vicki Berndt